Cleaning Windows Vista For Dummies

MW00764652

Top Five Ways to Free Up Hard Drive Space

What to Do	How to Do It	Find More Information
Empty the Recycle Bin	Right-click the Recycle Bin and choose Empty Recycle Bin.	Chapter 6
Empty your Deleted Items and Junk E-Mail folders	In your e-mail client, choose the folder and choose File⇨Empty Folder. In some clients, you can right-click the folder and choose Empty Folder.	Chapter 9
Clear the temporary Internet files cache	In Internet Explorer, choose Tools⇨Internet Options⇨General tab⇨Delete.	Chapter 11
Delete files ending in the extension `.tmp`	Use the Windows Search function (Start⇨Search) to locate and delete the files.	Chapter 6
Delete or archive files ending in the extension `.bak` or `.old`	Use the Windows Search function (Start⇨Search) to locate the files.	Chapter 6

Top Five Ways to Make Your Programs Run Faster

What to Do	Why Do It?	Find More Information
Increase your RAM	Windows works best when you have plenty of RAM.	Chapter 17
Transfer your pagefile to a faster hard drive	The pagefile is used by Windows to store virtual memory when you don't have enough physical RAM. Moving the pagefile to a faster drive means Windows can access it faster.	Chapter 17
Don't access data over a network	Grabbing data from a network is inherently slower than grabbing it from your local hard drive.	Chapter 19
Place frequently accessed data on a faster hard drive	If you have multiple hard drives on your local system, place your data on the one that has the fastest rotational speed.	Chapter 17
Defragment your hard drive	Fragmentation slows down programs, data access, and Windows itself.	Chapter 14

For Dummies: Bestselling Book Series for Beginners

Cleaning Windows Vista™ For Dummies®

Cheat Sheet

Top Five Built-in Windows Cleaning Utilities

Utility	What It Does	How to Use It	Find More Information
Disk Cleanup	Allows you to identify and remove the most common forms of clutter on your hard drive.	Choose Start⇨All Programs⇨Accessories⇨ System Tools⇨Disk Cleanup.	Chapter 6
msconfig	Modifies how your system starts.	Choose Start⇨All Programs⇨Accessories⇨ Run, type `msconfig`, and click OK.	Chapter 13
Check Disk	Checks for hard-drive errors and corrects simple ones.	Choose Start⇨Computer, right-click a drive, and choose Properties; on the Tools tab, click Check Now.	Chapter 14
Defragmenter	Analyzes disk drives for fragmentation and removes as much as possible.	Choose Start⇨Computer, right-click a drive, and choose Properties; on the Tools tab, click Defragment Now.	Chapter 14
Registry Editor	Allows you to examine the contents of the Registry, back it up, and make changes, if necessary. *Use with extreme caution.*	Choose Start⇨All Programs⇨Accessories⇨ Run, type `regedit`, and click OK.	Chapter 20

Glossary at a Glance

adware: A program that delivers advertising directly to your computer, typically in the form of pop-ups.

cache: A storage area used as a repository of temporary files. Caches are typically implemented by programs because reading information from a cache is much quicker than retrieving it from the primary source.

cookie: A small data file, stored on your system, designed to save information about you and your preferences.

firewall: Software or hardware designed to prohibit unauthorized access to your system across a network.

orphan data: Data files left behind by a program long-since removed from a system.

pop-up: A form of advertisement that results in small browser windows "popping up" on your screen. Pop-ups can be displayed by visiting Web pages that include code that displays them or by the installation of adware on your system.

program inventory: A list of what programs should be installed on your system.

RAM: An acronym for random access memory. RAM is used as the working area for both programs and data being processed by the computer.

Registry: The central repository of all configuration information in a Windows system.

spam: Unsolicited e-mail received from people or companies that you have no prior relationship with or from people or companies that you previously severed your relationship with.

spyware: A program that reports information about you or your actions to someone else, all without your knowledge.

temporary files: Data files created by programs for temporary use. Sometimes, temporary files aren't deleted properly, and they end up cluttering a system with unnecessary data.

virus: A program designed to interrupt or change your computing efforts, or corrupt or destroy data.

Cleaning Windows Vista™

FOR

DUMMIES®

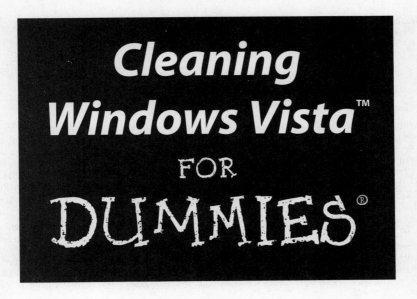

Cleaning Windows Vista™ FOR DUMMIES®

by Allen Wyatt

BICENTENNIAL
1807
WILEY
2007
BICENTENNIAL

Wiley Publishing, Inc.

Cleaning Windows Vista™ For Dummies®

Published by
Wiley Publishing, Inc.
111 River Street
Hoboken, NJ 07030-5774
www.wiley.com

Copyright © 2007 by Wiley Publishing, Inc., Indianapolis, Indiana

Published by Wiley Publishing, Inc., Indianapolis, Indiana

Published simultaneously in Canada

For general information on our other products and services, please contact our Customer Care Department within the U.S. at 800-762-2974, outside the U.S. at 317-572-3993, or fax 317-572-4002.

For technical support, please visit www.wiley.com/techsupport.

Wiley also publishes its books in a variety of electronic formats. Some content that appears in print may not be available in electronic books.

Library of Congress Control Number: 2006934838

ISBN-13: 978-0-471-78293-3

ISBN-10: 0-471-78293-9

Manufactured in the United States of America

10 9 8 7 6 5 4 3 2 1

1B/SY/RS/QW/IN

WILEY

About the Author

Allen Wyatt, an internationally recognized expert in small computer systems, is president of Discovery Computing, Inc., a computer and publishing services company located in Mesa, Arizona. He has worked in the computer and publishing industries for almost two decades, writing more than 50 books and numerous magazine articles. Allen's popular lectures and seminars have reached audiences throughout the United States, as well as throughout Mexico and Costa Rica.

Besides writing books and technical materials, Allen helps further the computer book industry by providing consulting, production, and project management services. He publishes two free weekly newsletters, WordTips and ExcelTips (www.VitalNews.com).

Allen can be reached by e-mail at awyatt@dcomp.com.

Author's Acknowledgments

I would like to thank the good folks at Wiley for their invaluable assistance in bringing this book to fruition. The people I worked with — Greg Croy, Nicole Sholly, and Laura Miller — were all very professional and helpful in creating what you now hold in your hands. I also extend a special thanks to Jim Kelly for his technical expertise, liberally provided as a technical reviewer.

Publisher's Acknowledgments

We're proud of this book; please send us your comments through our online registration form located at www.dummies.com/register/.

Some of the people who helped bring this book to market include the following:

Acquisitions, Editorial, and Media Development

Project Editor: Nicole Sholly

Executive Editor: Greg Croy

Copy Editor: Laura K. Miller

Technical Editor: Jim Kelly

Editorial Manager: Kevin Kirschner

Media Development Manager:
Laura VanWinkle

Editorial Assistant: Amanda Foxworth

Sr. Editorial Assistant: Cherie Case

Cartoons: Rich Tennant
(www.the5thwave.com)

Composition Services

Project Coordinator: Patrick Redmond

Layout and Graphics: Carl Byers,
Barbara Moore, Barry Offringa

Proofreaders: Rob Springer, Lisa Young Stiers

Indexer: Techbooks

Anniversary Logo Design: Richard Pacifico

Publishing and Editorial for Technology Dummies

    Richard Swadley, Vice President and Executive Group Publisher

    Andy Cummings, Vice President and Publisher

    Mary Bednarek, Executive Acquisitions Director

    Mary C. Corder, Editorial Director

Publishing for Consumer Dummies

    Diane Graves Steele, Vice President and Publisher

    Joyce Pepple, Acquisitions Director

Composition Services

    Gerry Fahey, Vice President of Production Services

    Debbie Stailey, Director of Composition Services

Contents at a Glance

Introduction 1

Part 1: The Basics of Cleaning Your System 7
Chapter 1: First Things First: Why You Should Clean 9
Chapter 2: Determining What to Clean and When 21

Part 11: Programs and Data 35
Chapter 3: Identifying What You Have 37
Chapter 4: Making Your Programs Run Faster 53
Chapter 5: Getting Rid of Old Programs 69
Chapter 6: Data, Data Everywhere 83
Chapter 7: Organizing and Archiving Data 97

Part 111: E-Mail and the Internet 111
Chapter 8: Tackling E-Mail Overload 113
Chapter 9: Organizing Your E-Mail 127
Chapter 10: Banishing Internet Villains 143
Chapter 11: Managing Internet Information 157

Part 1V: The Operating System 171
Chapter 12: Cleaning Up the User Interface 173
Chapter 13: Streamlining Windows 187
Chapter 14: Speeding Up the File System 211
Chapter 15: Managing Windows Updates 223
Chapter 16: Getting a New System 231

Part V: Advanced Cleaning for the Truly Brave 245
Chapter 17: Memory and Storage 247
Chapter 18: Becoming Security Conscious 257
Chapter 19: Cleaning House in a Networked Environment 271
Chapter 20: Jumping Into the Registry 283
Chapter 21: Wiping the Slate Clean 299

Part VI: The Part of Tens **309**

Chapter 22: Ten Troubleshooting Ideas 311

Chapter 23: Ten Online Resources to Help You Clean 315

Chapter 24: Ten Cool Things in Vista...319

Index **323**

Table of Contents

Introduction 1

How to Read This Book 1
Assumptions About You 2
How This Book Is Organized 2
    Part I: The Basics of Cleaning Your System 3
    Part II: Programs and Data 3
    Part III: E-Mail and the Internet 3
    Part IV: The Operating System 3
    Part V: Advanced Cleaning for the Truly Brave 4
    Part VI: The Part of Tens 4
Customs and Practices 4
Icons Used in This Book 5
Where to Go From Here 6

Part 1: The Basics of Cleaning Your System 7

Chapter 1: First Things First: Why You Should Clean 9

Telltale Signs of an Unclean Computer....................................10
    The view from the desktop isn't pretty 10
    Traversing the Start menu jungle is an adventure..............12
    Your PC is slower than molasses...13
    You have files older than your dog 13
    Your Notification area looks like a parking lot 14
Cleaning Up: The Pros and Cons 15
    The pros 15
    The cons 16
    Balancing pros and cons 17
Keeping Your House Tidy..18

Chapter 2: Determining What to Clean and When 21

How to Eat an Elephant 21
Precautions for Safety's Sake..23
Finding the Right Tools 25
    Finding Windows tools 25
    Finding third-party tools 27
Creating a Cleaning Schedule 28
    Now. Do it now — right now...29
    Once a week should do it 30

It's the end of the month already! 30

Time for the annual clean-a-fest 32

Time for an Overhaul? 33

Is New Hardware the Answer? 34

Part II: Programs and Data 35

Chapter 3: Identifying What You Have 37

Creating a Program Inventory 37

The think-tank approach 38

The laid-back approach 39

Finding Out What Programs Are Installed 40

Inspecting your desktop 40

Scrutinizing the Start menu 42

Checking the Control Panel 43

Peering in program folders 45

Discovering What Programs Run When 46

Starting up for all users 47

Starting up for just you 48

Figuring Out What's Running Right Now 49

Making a Game Plan 52

Chapter 4: Making Your Programs Run Faster 53

Common Sense for Programs 53

Turn off whiz-bang features 54

Watch out for networking "gotchas" 54

Never upgrade unless you have to 55

Speed up specific software 56

Speeding Up Access to Large Data Files 60

Change your hardware 60

Reconfigure your data 61

Reconfigure your program 62

Are We Compatible? 62

Playing Games 64

Pushing the Envelope: Multimedia Editing Programs 66

Chapter 5: Getting Rid of Old Programs 69

Identifying Candidates for Removal 69

Unused programs you installed 70

Preinstalled software 70

Stuff you find in the Program Files folder 70

Four Ways to Remove Unwanted Programs 72

An application's uninstall command 72

The Installed Programs area of the Control Panel 74

Third-party software 75

The brute-force method 75

Eliminating Remnants of Failed Programs 80

Chapter 6: Data, Data Everywhere 83

  Finding Temporary Files 84
    Locating and deleting files from temporary folders 85
    Finding and eliminating specific files 86
  Tracking Down Orphan Data 87
  Doing a Disk Cleanup 88
  Finding and Eliminating Duplicate Data 91
  What to Do with Multimedia Files 94
  Empty the Recycle Bin Often 96

Chapter 7: Organizing and Archiving Data 97

  Organizing Your Data 97
    Adding and partitioning hard drives 98
    Creating a folder structure 99
    Watch your depth 101
    Moving, renaming, and deleting folders 101
  Clearing Out Your Root Directory 103
  What About the Default Folders? 104
  Archiving and Backing Up Data 106
    Archiving what you don't need 106
    Backing up what you still need 108
    Storing backups and archives 109

Part III: E-Mail and the Internet *111*

Chapter 8: Tackling E-Mail Overload 113

  Using Different Accounts to Manage and Reduce E-Mail 114
    Managing incoming mail 114
    Reducing unwanted mail 115
  Psychology 101: Don't Answer That Phone . . . er, E-Mail 116
  Why You Get Spam 118
    Harvesting addresses 118
    Guessing addresses 119
    Purchasing addresses 120
  Tactics for Limiting Spam 121
  Implementing Spam Filters 122
    Types of filters 122
    Types of filter technology 124
  Combating Spam with a Challenge/Response System 125

Chapter 9: Organizing Your E-Mail 127

  Using Folders Effectively 128
  Smart Move: Using Mail Rules 129
    Creating a rule 129
    Rearranging the rules 133
    Deleting a rule 134

Deleting E-Mail Regularly 135
    Determine a cutoff point for e-mails 135
    Empty the deleted items folder 135
    Empty the junk mail folder 136
Watching Out for Attachments 138
Archiving Valuable E-Mail 139
    Enabling built-in archives 139
    Using the Mailbox Cleanup tool in Outlook 141
    Rolling your own archive process 142

Chapter 10: Banishing Internet Villains 143

Uh-Oh! Do I Have a Virus? 144
    Finding viruses on your computer 144
    Blocking viruses 145
Sizing Up Spyware 146
    Identifying spyware 147
    Getting to know spyware 148
    Eliminating spyware 150
Blocking Pop-ups 153
    Employing pop-up blockers 154
    Blocking Flash ads 156
Resisting the Lure of Trinkets 156

Chapter 11: Managing Internet Information 157

Are Cookies a Reason for Worry? 157
    Blocking cookies 158
    Managing your cookies 160
    Deleting all cookies 161
Negotiating Newsgroups 162
Organizing Web Favorites 163
Taming Web Cache Files 165
    Cleaning the cache 166
    Finding the cache 167
    Changing the cache size 169

Part IV: The Operating System 171

Chapter 12: Cleaning Up the User Interface 173

Master of the Desktop 173
    Displaying the traditional desktop icons 174
    Renaming and deleting icons 175
    A word on themes and screensavers 176
Ordering the Menu System 176
    Picking a Start menu layout 177
    Customizing the Start menu 178
    Moving items in the All Programs list 179
    Creating your own program groups 180

Effectively Using the Taskbar 180
   Birds of a feather 181
   Cleaning the Notification area 182
Cleaning Up the Control Panel 185

Chapter 13: Streamlining Windows 187

Installing Just What You Need 188
Setting Performance Options 189
   Understanding visual effects 191
   Advanced performance options 192
Using the Microsoft System Configuration Utility 193
   Modifying the startup process 195
   Modifying startup files 196
   Modifying what's started 197
Working with the Latest Drivers 198
   Checking a driver's signature 198
   Checking for updated device drivers..............................200
   Removing device drivers 200
Going on a .DLL Diet 201
Shut Down Unused Services 202
   Services in the Computer Manager.................................203
   Services in msconfig 205
Putting System Protection to Work..206
   Configuring System Protection......................................207
   Setting a restore point 208
   Reverting to history...208

Chapter 14: Speeding Up the File System 211

Which File System to Use?...212
   The FAT file system 212
   The NTFS file system 212
   Making your choice..213
Changing File Systems...214
   Seeing what file system you use.....................................214
   Converting to NTFS...215
   Converting to FAT...216
Defragmenting Your Drive..217
Checking for Errors...219
   Using Windows' disk tools 219
   Using chkdsk 221
To Compress or Not? 222

Chapter 15: Managing Windows Updates 223

Getting Updates the Way You Want 224
   Manual updates 224
   Automatic updates 225
   Picking an update method 227
Which Updates Do You Really Need? 228

Chapter 16: Getting a New System **231**

When Is a New System Justified? 232
What Should You Get? 233
    High-end systems 233
    Mid-range systems 234
    Low-end systems 235
    Portable systems 235
Preparing for the New System 236
    Collecting pieces and parts 236
    Collecting information 237
Reinstalling Programs 242
Transferring Data 242

Part V: Advanced Cleaning for the Truly Brave *245*

Chapter 17: Memory and Storage *247*

How Windows Uses Memory 248
Determining Whether You Need More Memory 249
Will Another Hard Drive Help? 250
    Faster speed 251
    Move your pagefile 252
Choosing Between Internal or External Hard Drives 254
    Easy backups 255
    Easy data transfer 255
Alternative Storage Solutions 256

Chapter 18: Becoming Security Conscious **257**

Battening Down the Hatches 258
    Physical security 258
    Data loss 259
    Data recovery 259
    Malicious programs..260
    Insecure passwords 261
Staying Secure on the Internet 261
    Using Internet zones 262
    Harnessing SSL 264
    Closing down security problems..265
Adding Firewalls 266
    The Windows firewall..267
    ZoneAlarm 268
    Hardware firewalls 269

Chapter 19: Cleaning House in a Networked Environment **271**

Getting Rid of Old User Accounts 272
    Deleting network user accounts 272
    Deleting local system user accounts 272

Moving Frequently Accessed Data..274
Removing Shared Printers 275
    Limiting shared printer hours 275
    Turning off shared printing 277
Removing Shared Folders 278
Cutting Your System Off the Network...280

Chapter 20: Jumping Into the Registry **283**
Groking the Registry Behemoth..284
    Seeing the trees in the Registry forest.................................284
    Buzzing through the Registry hives......................................285
    Unlocking Registry keys 286
    Appreciating Registry values 287
Editing the Registry 287
    Backing up the Registry...289
    Finding information 291
    Editing values...292
    Adding keys or values...293
    Deleting Registry items...294
Using Registry Cleaning Software 295
    Registry analyzers 295
    Registry cleaners 296
    Registry compactors 296
Restoring the Registry 297

Chapter 21: Wiping the Slate Clean **299**
Doing a Windows Reinstall..299
Using an OEM System Restore Disc 301
Wiping Out Your System 303
    Preparing for the wipeout 303
    Doing the deed...304
    Picking up the pieces 306

Part VI: The Part of Tens...*309*

Chapter 22: Ten Troubleshooting Ideas **311**
Check Your Startup Files..311
Install Windows Updates..311
Run a Spyware Removal Program 311
Remove Unused Programs 312
See What Processes Are Running...312
Run the Disk Cleanup Utility...312
Defragment Your Disk Drives...313
Check File Sizes 313
Check the Size of Your Registry 313
Start Your System in Safe Mode 313

Chapter 23: Ten Online Resources to Help You Clean **315**

Sysinternals..315
Google...315
Gibson Research Corporation 316
Symantec Security Response..316
SpywareGuide..316
SpywareInfo 316
Experts Exchange 317
Spam Arrest 317
Urban Legends Reference Pages 317
Vista Software Archive 317

Chapter 24: Ten Cool Things in Vista **319**

Windows Firewall 319
Sidebar and Gadgets 319
Greater System Protection 320
Parental Controls 320
Performance Information..320
Network Administration...320
Virtual Folders 321
Snipping Tool 321
Tabbed Browsing..321
Phishing Filter..321

Index...*323*

Introduction

· ·

A computer is nothing but a tool. It's bigger than a hammer (well, most hammers), heavier than a screwdriver, and generally less noisy than a chain saw — but it's nonetheless a tool. You can do more stuff with a computer than you can with a hammer and a screwdriver, but hammers and screwdrivers are simpler to use and easier to clean up. (Chain saws are another story; things can get messy really fast — although I've seen some really amazing things done with them.)

Your computer *does* get messy; have no doubt about it. Programs load and unload, files pop into existence and then slither off to unknown parts of your hard drive, and spyware tries to adhere itself to your operating system. Every day, your system changes as information is added and new demands are placed on old programs.

All these things add to the unique clutter that comes to define and weigh down your system. You can redefine your system and free your system, all by identifying and removing the clutter. *Cleaning Windows Vista For Dummies* shows you how.

How to Read This Book

I'm a firm believer that you should read this book out loud, while standing on the coffee table in your neighbor's living room. It surely will make an impression on the neighbor's kids and free up time you previously spent going to dinner parties.

Whether you decide to read this book out loud or not, you should read the first two chapters before reading any others. Dire consequences won't result if you decide not to, but those chapters lay a pretty good foundation for everything else you find in the book.

After that, read whatever strikes your fancy. You know your system better than I do. If your big problem is properly getting updates to Windows, skip to Chapter 15. If instead you want to focus on archiving your data, turn to Chapter 7.

You get the idea — this book can be as flexible as you are.

Assumptions About You

Being the amazingly gifted and highly skilled author that I am, I can report that I've achieved every author's ideal and made no assumptions about you in writing this book.

Well, I guess that's not entirely true. I do assume that you read English. And that you're using Windows Vista. And that you know how to turn your computer on. And that you know how to navigate through your system by using Computer (from the Start menu) or Windows Explorer. And that you think your system might be cluttered. And that you want it to be less cluttered.

Nope; I make no assumptions at all, other than those. Oh, and that you know how to use a Web browser. And an e-mail program. And that you aren't afraid to try new things once in a while. And that you want your system to run like it did when it was new. And that you're tired of menus longer than the want ads and file folders that go on forever.

That should be it. Except that I assume you're tired of being deluged with e-mail. And that you want to protect yourself from spyware and viruses. And that you aren't sure if cookies are a bad thing. And that you think you can do something to make your system cleaner.

Dang. I guess I do make some assumptions about you. But, being the somewhat gifted and nominally skilled author that I am, I know that these assumptions only identify you as a person who wants to use the computer better and recognizes that cleaning that computer can help toward that end.

Working together, we can make that happen. (That's why assumptions can be a good thing.)

How This Book Is Organized

My editor tells me that organizing a book into parts is a good thing. It helps keep the chapters from running into each other. (Apparently, having unrelated chapters freely associating with each other is unhealthy.) To keep with longstanding tradition, and to keep my editor from yelling at me, I've organized *Cleaning Windows Vista For Dummies* into the following parts.

Part 1: The Basics of Cleaning Your System

Get off on the right foot by discovering why you even need to clean your system (as if you didn't know). You find out what you should clean, when you should clean it, what tools to use, and whether you should consider getting a new system.

Part II: Programs and Data

Programs and data are the two great components of any computer system — including yours. Part II focuses on identifying what programs you have, how to make them run faster, and how to get rid of programs you no longer need.

You can also find out how to identify all the data on your hard drive, as well as targeting and deleting the data you no longer need. I've dedicated a full chapter to concepts about organizing and archiving your important data.

Part III: E-Mail and the Internet

E-mail and the Internet are, for better or worse, a part of most people's daily lives. This part zeroes in on how you can manage the glut of e-mail you get daily. You can discover how to deal with spam and organize the e-mail you keep.

You can also find out the tell-tale signs of virus and spyware infections, as well as how to get rid of these troublesome pests. Finally, you can discover how to deal with information (not related to e-mail) that you may receive when using the Internet.

Part IV: The Operating System

Windows Vista is nothing if not flexible and configurable. Part IV discusses how to clean up the user interface so using Windows is easier than ever before. You can discover how to streamline Windows so it runs faster, as well as how to speed up the file system.

Microsoft wants you to have the most up-to-date system possible, and Windows Vista makes it easy to stay updated with automatic downloads. You'll understand how to use the update system and find out when it makes sense to get a new system rather than clean up the old one.

Part V: Advanced Cleaning for the Truly Brave

This part focuses on things you can do to implement deep-cleaning strategies. You can determine whether you need more memory in your system or whether you need a larger hard drive. You can discover ways to make your system more secure and thereby minimize the chance of having others clutter your system. I also discuss the special needs of cleaning up in a networked environment.

An entire chapter covers the ins and outs of working with the Registry, your computer's central nervous system. You can find out how to edit the Registry and use special software to keep it in tip-top shape.

The final chapter in this part explains different ways to fix a corrupted Windows installation. You can even find out how to start all over by wiping out your computer system and installing Windows anew.

Part VI: The Part of Tens

Ahhh! The Part of Tens. Here's where you find small, bite-sized tidbits that can help get your system cleaned up and keep it that way. You can find troubleshooting ideas, a multitude of online resources to help you tidy up, and some of my personal favorite things in Vista.

Customs and Practices

I followed a few conventions that you might be interested in. Why? Because then you know why I chose to do something, and we can understand each other better.

First, if I talk about clicking the mouse, I mean clicking the left button. If I want you to click the right button, I specifically talk about right-clicking. (Quite a bit of right-clicking goes on in Windows.)

If a procedure takes more than a couple of discrete steps to complete, I try to detail those steps as much as I can. It's frustrating as heck to read "do this" in a book, and when you do it, the steps don't work for you. The steps should work if you're using Windows Vista; I've tried them out, as have my editor and my technical editor. (Three heads are better than one.)

Finally, if you must make a series of choices with the mouse, I separate the choices with an arrow. For example, if you see "Choose Start➪All Programs➪ Accessories➪Notepad," that means you should click the Start menu, then the All Programs option, then Accessories, and finally Notepad.

Icons Used in This Book

As part of agreeing to write this book, I insisted that Wiley break with tradition and include cute little icons that call your attention to things that I think need your attention. They tried to balk at my demand, but I held firm, with my only desire to put the needs of you, my reader, first. Finally, they got tired of my expert negotiating and gave in to my demand. (I hope the other *For Dummies* series authors appreciate all my hard work in this area.)

With that in mind, you see the following icons sprinkled liberally throughout this book. Pay attention to this; you have a test later!

If something is really short and really cool, I used this icon. Tips are bite-sized nuggets of information that can — hopefully — make your life easier and more fulfilling. (They should at least make you feel better about cleaning your Windows system.)

This icon alerts you to the gotchas of cleaning your Windows system. Ignore these tidbits at your own risk. (Ohh . . . that sounds ominous!) Warnings are given for a reason: primarily to help you avoid problems that can cause you grief and a whole lot of extra work.

This icon doesn't mean you can forget everything else in the book. Nope; I included it so you can make special note of something you need later. Or it could be a piece of information designed to jog your memory about something you should have picked up earlier in the book. Remember — the remember icon can help you remember what you need to remember.

A few of these icons are thrown into the mix so that the geeks among us feel comfortable. If geekiness scares the bejeebers out of you, ignore anything with this icon. If you really want a moment of technical clarity, you should find anything with this icon very illuminating.

Where to Go From Here

I think the best place to go is to the next page, but it doesn't matter what I think. You can use or abuse this book in any way you see fit. If something on page 153 strikes your fancy, then go for it! You can always return to page 152 (or any other page) at a later time, when the need arises.

You see, that's the really cool thing about cleaning your system and *For Dummies* books — they don't have to be done or read in any particular order. And the sky is the limit in *Cleaning Windows Vista For Dummies*. You can start reading anywhere you like, on any topic you like. When you tire of that topic, move to one that strikes your fancy.

As for me, I still think the best place to start is on the next page. . . .

Part I
The Basics of Cleaning Your System

The 5th Wave   By Rich Tennant

UBER-USER DWAYNE GRANTZ CHALKS UP BEFORE PUTTING WINDOWS VISTA THROUGH ITS PACES.

In this part . . .

Discover why you need to clean your system, what you should clean, when you should clean it, what tools to use, and whether you should consider getting a new system.

Chapter 1

First Things First: Why You Should Clean

In This Chapter
▶ Determining whether your system needs cleaning
▶ Balancing the pros and cons of cleaning
▶ Focusing your cleaning efforts

My system isn't messed up, is it? (What? Me worry?)

Yes, you should worry. Or, you should at least be aware that you may need to worry. Computer systems easily and quickly become untidy and messed up. If you don't clean yours, you run the risk of big problems down the road.

Do I really need to point out the benefits of a clean computer system? (Probably, so I do — a little later in this chapter.) Does someone need to come into your house and point out why you need to pick up your clothes, dust the furniture, wash the dishes, and tend to the dog? Probably not; you know that a clean house is healthful, inviting, and safe.

It's the same with computers. Over time, your computer can become cluttered with unused programs, unknown data, and unwanted visitors. With a little effort, you can clean your system so that it runs at top form, and you can breeze through your work faster and easier than you can on an unclean system. In addition, clean systems are more reliable, less prone to failure, and easier to protect from attack by malicious programs.

Before you can begin cleaning, however, you need to recognize the need to clean and why you should spend the time to do it.

Telltale Signs of an Unclean Computer

How can you know whether your system needs cleaning? I've compiled a list of several sure-fire signs that you need help. (Envision Jeff Foxworthy standing in front of your computer, speaking with his signature twang.)

You know you have a messed-up computer . . .

- ✔ If you have to leave a trail of breadcrumbs so you don't get lost finding your way through the options in your Start menu.
- ✔ If every pop-up on your computer inspects your computer, notices the mess, apologizes for bothering you, and quietly closes on its own.
- ✔ If you try to install a new program, and the installation program automatically reports your system to the Board of Health.
- ✔ If you think "Defragment" is the name of a new rap song by Busta Rhymes (Yo!).
- ✔ If the only way to add more icons to your desktop is to get a larger desktop.
- ✔ If you start the program to balance your checkbook, only to find that your son's illegal copy of *World of Warcraft* ate the last month's worth of transactions.
- ✔ If someone mentions "backup," and chills run up and down your spine.
- ✔ If virus software refuses to install itself on your system for fear of contamination.

Perhaps such observations aren't worthy of Jeff Foxworthy or the Blue Collar Comedy Tour, but this list highlights some good indicators that your computer needs cleaning. The next few sections detail some other obvious signs that you need help.

The view from the desktop isn't pretty

Does your desktop look like the one shown in Figure 1-1? If so, you have problems. Maybe you bought into the old adage that a clean desk is a sign of a sick mind, and in the process lost your ability to effectively use your system. Whatever got you to this point, you need your Windows cleaned. Badly.

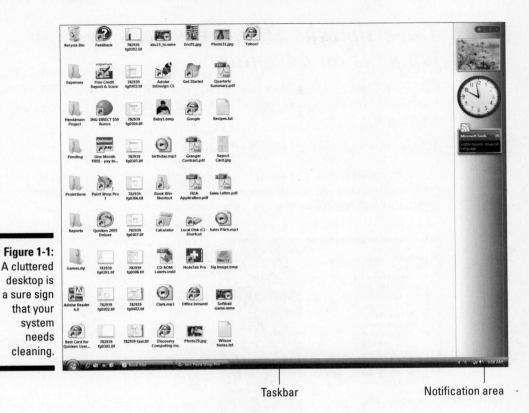

Figure 1-1:
A cluttered
desktop is
a sure sign
that your
system
needs
cleaning.

Taskbar   Notification area

Your computer desktop is supposed to be a clean, inviting place where you store only a few icons of your most commonly used programs. For too many people, the desktop becomes a catch-all repository of every stray icon that comes their way.

A cluttered desktop is a good sign that your entire PC is cluttered. The solution is to clean your system and rid yourself of all that mess.

If your desktop is as cluttered as the one shown in Figure 1-1 — and especially if it's even more cluttered — head to Chapter 12, where I give you some help regaining control.

Traversing the Start menu jungle is an adventure

Can you imagine running Windows without the Start menu? Neither can I. The Start menu is indispensable for quickly and easily finding the programs you want to run.

At least, that's the way it's supposed to be.

On many systems that I've seen, the Start menu gets cluttered with lots of programs the user seldom, if ever, uses. Figure 1-2 shows one such Start menu, just itching to be cleaned.

Figure 1-2: Long, deep, and cluttered Start menus can hinder your work.

The Start menu is supposed to provide a convenient path to all the programs installed on your system. Over time, some paths are used more than others, and some paths become completely unused. Even though the Windows Vista Start menu is a bit easier to traverse then in previous versions of Windows, you can still benefit by removing unused items from the Start menu and organizing what is left.

When you remove unused programs from your computer (which I show you how to do in Chapter 5), your Start menu will look better and better. When you really need to give your Start menu a makeover, Chapter 12 (where I discuss taking back control of the user interface) will be invaluable.

Your PC is slower than molasses

Shortly after microwave ovens first came out (yes, I'm that old), I remember watching my grandma use one to bake some potatoes. She anxiously looked through the oven's door and mumbled, "Hurry up, hurry up."

I chuckled about it then, but years later I find myself doing the same thing with my computer. When I got the computer, it seemed really, really fast. Now, after using it for a year or so, it seems to be slower than I remember it. Yes, it is still faster than doing things the old way (sort of like baking potatoes in a conventional oven), but I find myself talking to the computer, begging it to "hurry up."

If your PC seems slower than it should — particularly if it seems slower than when you first got it — your system is a prime candidate for cleaning. Over time, the detritus that your computer collects during everyday use can start to bog it down. If you don't periodically banish that junk, it can affect the work you do. The change is typically slow, ever so slow, until you notice one day that your computer just doesn't run like it used to.

If you want to make your programs run faster, you're in luck because I show you how to do that in Chapter 4. To make Windows itself hum right along, check out Chapters 13 and 14, which cover getting the cobwebs out of Windows and making your file system run faster, respectively.

You have files older than your dog

I've had my dog for just over 3 years, which makes him in his 20s in dog years, right? Does that mean he's been chewing up my son's shoes for 3 years or 20 years? Hmmm. Converting people years to dog years may be philosophically confusing, but there is nothing confusing about examining the age of the files on your computer. If you look at the files on your computer, I'll bet you could find some that are 3, 5, or even 10 years old.

I can hear you now: "Not on my system. I just got it a year ago, so I don't have anything as old as your dog." Wrong, bucko! Computer files tend to follow you around, over the years, without you even realizing it. For instance, computer files are commonly transferred from an old system to a new system. When transferred, the files retain their old file dates — they are old files.

You may also share files with other people in your office, family, or circle of friends. Place the files on your computer, and you may quickly forget about them. But they are there, aging like a not-so-fine wine, taking up space and adding to the general clutter of your system.

A large number of old, old files are a sure sign that you need to clean your system. You can archive your data or create backups that allow you to remove unneeded data from your hard drive, freeing up space for other data and tasks. Chapter 7 gives you the straight scoop on how to keep only the data that you need.

Your Notification area looks like a parking lot

You know what the Notification area is, don't you? (Come on; you can admit it — nobody's watching.) Well, come to think of it, you may not know what it is, but you may know what it was. You see, Microsoft decided to rename what used to be known as the system tray so it is now known as the *Notification area*.

In case that doesn't help you any, the Notification area is at the right side of your Task bar. Take a look at the bottom of your computer screen. Do you see the Start menu button? (If you don't, you may need to move your mouse pointer to the bottom of the screen to make the button appear.) See it? Good. Now shift your eyes all the way to the right. What do you see? You probably see the current time and maybe a few icons. Even if you don't realize it, you're looking right at the Notification area (refer to Figure 1-1).

In Windows Vista, the Notification area is a little deceiving because it hides some of the icons. Perhaps the folks in Redmond don't want you to be consciously aware of how cluttered this area can become. Don't let that stand in your way, however. If you click the small left-pointing arrow at the left side of the Notification area, the area expands to the left, allowing you to see the entire contents of the Notification area.

Each icon in the Notification area represents a utility program currently running in your system. You may see icons for any number of programs. How many do you see? Five? Ten? More? Some programs that you install on your computer are a bit egotistical — they think they're so important that they deserve a place of honor in your Notification area. When you install one of these egotistical programs, besides adding itself to your Start menu and your desktop, it stakes out prime ground in your Notification area. Good examples are video players such as QuickTime or RealPlayer. They (and their ilk) are notorious for this Notification area bullying.

Clutter, clutter, clutter. If you have a bunch of icons in your Notification area, your system is a prime candidate for cleaning. Get rid of a few of these babies, and you may find your system running leaner and faster than before.

Don't try to delete any of the Notification area icons yet. Some of the icons will go away as you remove old programs. You can also find out how to reclaim this prime area of your system by controlling what programs run when your computer starts; Chapter 13 provides this important information.

Cleaning Up: The Pros and Cons

If your system needs cleaning, you've come to the right place. *Cleaning Windows Vista For Dummies* is a great resource that you can use to get your system back to near-new condition. If your mind works like mine — I know that's a scary thought for some — then you will want to examine the pros and cons of cleaning your system, which can help you decide whether you want to clean your system right now.

The pros

You've finally reached the big time — the pros! Oh, sorry, wrong homonym. . . . In this instance, "the pros" mean benefits. Specifically, the benefits of cleaning up your system, which I list here:

✔ **Speed:** A clean system runs faster than one that needs cleaning. Do you remember when you first got your PC? You probably thought it ran very fast. If your system stays clean, you shouldn't notice it running any slower over time. Unfortunately, most systems don't stay clean and require your attention. Give your system the attention it craves — that is, do the cleaning — and it can run just as fast as it did the day you got it.

✔ **Efficiency:** If you're using a clean system, you can get through your work faster and therefore more efficiently. A clean system doesn't make you immensely more efficient — if it did, the self-help publishing market would shrink dramatically. You can still get sidetracked playing games or arguing religion and politics on various message boards, but with a clean system, you can do even those things more efficiently.

✔ **Reliability:** A huge benefit of a clean system is that it is more reliable than one that isn't. If you fail to clean your system, over time it goes from clean to cluttered to messed-up to unstable. Unstable systems crash. Unstable systems have a tendency to lose data. Unstable systems are a real pain. Clean your system, and you should see stability jump dramatically. No pain, big gain.

✔ **Stress reduction:** Do you like to sleep at night? Do you prefer having no worry? Believe it or not, having a clean system can reduce anxiety and provide a pleasant ease of mind. How so? Consider the worry that you'd have if your system were infected by a virus, or you weren't sure that the financial data on it was safe, or you didn't know what programs were running on the system, or. . . . You get the idea. Worry comes in all shapes and sizes. If you clean your computer, you have a better handle on what's on your computer and how it's being used.

✔ **Economics:** Cleaning your computer can save you money — sometimes lots of money. I suspect that hard drive clutter has helped boost the bottom line of hard drive manufacturers significantly over the years. Running low on space? Get a new drive. Computer running slow? Get a new system. Chances are, some of those new drives and new systems would have been unnecessary had the users done just a little housecleaning.

The cons

Every coin has two sides, and unless you're a bunko victim, the two sides aren't the same. I'm no bunko artist, so I'm pleased to point out that doing a cleanup also has its negatives. You need to be aware of these negatives, right from the get-go:

✔ **Time consumption:** Cleaning your computer takes time. You probably feel strapped for time right now, don't you? (Most people do.) Cleaning your computer can take anywhere from a trivial to a substantial amount of time. I've cleaned some systems — completely — in as little as two hours, but I've spent days cleaning other systems. How much time will your cleanup take? I can't answer that, but I can say be prepared for a time commitment and be patient. Your time will pay off in the end when your computer is running more smoothly.

Fortunately, you have some control over how and when to spend that time. You don't have to spend it all in a single block, although you could. You can spend the time over a period of days or weeks, as the time becomes available. Check out Chapter 2, where I discuss setting up a cleaning schedule to help you manage your cleaning time.

✔ **The learning curve:** Part of the time required to do the cleanup is rooted in another drawback: the learning curve. Figuring out how to use some of the cleaning tools takes time. If you're already comfortable with your computer and the cleaning tools, your learning curve is lower than for those who are unfamiliar.

✔ **The bother:** I won't lie to you — cleaning up your computer can be a bother. If you approach the task as a chore, then it will be bothersome. But I encourage you to fight the urge to procrastinate cleaning; don't put it off as you might other bothersome tasks. To borrow a phrase, remember that it's not just a job — its an adventure. Try to overcome the "bother factor" by looking on it as a learning experience. If necessary, spread the cleanup out over several days so that you don't max out your stress level in a single session.

Balancing pros and cons

You may come up with other pros and cons than those I present in the preceding two sections. Some may be specific to your particular situation. (Is your job in jeopardy if you don't clean up your computer? Is the valuable data on your computer at risk?) If you write the pros on the left side of a sheet of paper and the cons on the right side, you can easily see how they balance out — and then determine which side wins.

In general, I think that the pros outweigh the cons by a significant amount (hence, this book). I'm guessing you think so, too; that's why you're reading this book. Still, you may need to work on timing or attitude before you can bring yourself to actually do it. Just keep in mind that you may find having a clean computer beneficial in more ways than you can imagine.

Paying the price

If you're short on time, you may be tempted to pay someone else to clean your system. After all, you can pay someone to clean your car, your office, your house, and your yard. Why not have someone else do your computer cleaning for you?

Why not, indeed. You certainly can have someone else clean your computer, but chances are good that you won't like the price. Plan on paying anywhere from $50 to $150 per hour for computer cleaning. Do the math — if it takes two, four, six, or more hours to clean your computer, how much will you pay? Ouch!

Also, you should understand that cleaning isn't just a one-time thing. However, if you change your behavior, you won't have to clean as often or pay as much in the future. You can't pay someone else to change your computer behavior, which makes all you can discover while cleaning your computer yourself valuable.

Keeping Your House Tidy

Just like keeping your house tidy takes concerted effort on your part, keeping your computer system clean takes effort, too. Some people mistakenly think that caring for their computers should be as mindless and easy as caring for their TVs, and they don't even think about cleaning their computers. But if you read this whole chapter, you know that you need to clean your system — and that you can benefit from cleaning it. So, you're ready to jump right in and tackle the job. (You are ready, right?)

Throughout this chapter, I show you that you don't have to dread cleaning your system. Sure, this job takes some time, but it doesn't have to be an intimidating task. In fact, you can even clean your system over a period of weeks — a little here and a little there — and before you know it, it's done.

As you seek to clean up your system, the different areas you can focus on include

- **Your programs:** The entire purpose of your computer is to create an environment in which you can effectively use different programs. If your programs don't run well, the value of your computer decreases. If you concentrate on cleaning up your programs or making them run faster (the focus of Chapters 3, 4, and 5), you immediately increase the value of your system.

- **Your data:** Chances are good that your programs eat, sleep, and breathe data. Programs need data to run, to fulfill their purpose in life. If your data is messed up, then your programs may just refuse to work properly. Managing data can be a monumental task, but doing so effectively will free up space on your hard drive and allow your programs to run faster. Head to Chapters 6 and 7 to find out more on keeping your data clean.

- **Your e-mail:** We live in a well-connected world. If you use e-mail (and who doesn't?), you can clutter up your system without even realizing it. Spam and viruses routinely bombard your system through e-mail. If you manage your e-mail well (as I show you in Chapters 8 and 9), you can lessen clutter and make your system more secure.

- **Your Internet use:** E-mail isn't the only use for your Internet connection. As you browse the Web, your system routinely fills up with files that you don't even know about. Whether these files are benign or harmful, they all add to the clutter of your system. If you pay attention to what's stored on your system, you can take the steps to reduce the clutter and improve overall performance. Chapters 10 and 11 can help you tackle the Internet beast.

✔ **The operating system:** Ah, Windows. What can you say about Windows? Actually, you can say quite a lot — and not all of it bad! Windows Vista is a great operating system, and one of its biggest strengths is its configurability. In Part IV, I show you ways to tweak and prod Windows into running faster than it ever did before.

There are also some advanced things you can do, such as tweaking your hardware (or adding new hardware), improving your security profile, and — shudder — diving into the Registry. Such endeavors (which I cover in Part V) are usually relegated to the last, after you work through other, less advanced cleaning techniques. I recommend that you proceed into these areas with extreme caution.

How do you know when your system is finally clean? You know you've succeeded when your system runs smoother, faster, and more reliably than before. You know your computer is clean when you can finish your work quickly, without getting bogged down.

Chapter 2

Determining What to Clean and When

In This Chapter

▶ Practicing safe cleaning so you don't get burned

▶ Locating just the right cleaning tools

▶ Scheduling your cleaning tasks

▶ Answering the cleaning conundrum with an overhaul or new hardware

*W*hen you think about cleaning your Windows system, do you feel the walls closing in? Do you find it hard to breathe? Does everything start to spin and go dark?

If so, you've been sitting at the computer too long. Or maybe someone has spiked your drink. Or you sat in one position so long that you've cut off oxygen to your brain. Stand up. Stretch a bit. Go outside for a breath of fresh air.

You see, cleaning your computer is neither rocket science nor something even harder (like assembling your kids' Christmas toys after one-too-many egg nogs on Christmas Eve), but it involves multiple steps: creating lists, taking precautionary measures, finding helpful tools, making a cleaning schedule, and asking yourself (and then answering) tough questions, such as "Should I just wipe clean the system and start anew?" or "Do I need new hardware?"

After the fresh air and helpful stretch, read on and discover how you can approach these steps to get your computer back to its pre-messed-up glory.

How to Eat an Elephant

I'm sure you've heard the old joke, "How do you eat an elephant?" The answer, of course, is one bite at a time. You go about cleaning your computer system in the same way. (I could try to stretch the analogy by talking about elephants/computers and memory, but I'll gladly spare you the pain.)

Face it — you can do quite a bit to clean the average Windows system. Files proliferate, programs fall out of favor, viruses reproduce, e-mails cluster, and pop-ups populate. Throw in a little systemic neglect, and before you know it, you have a messed-up system that badly needs cleaning.

So how do you do it all? One bite at a time. Don't put off doing some cleaning today with the hope that you will have more time tomorrow. Truth be told, cleaning a Windows system is more about behavior than it is about one or two tasks. Granted, you need to do some remedial work to get your system back in peak condition. But after you do, keeping your system clean on an ongoing basis is much easier than doing the remedial work in the first place.

So, which part of the elephant should you chew on first? At the end of Chapter 1, you can find out the different areas of your computer system that you should clean. In general, you should work on the most accessible parts of the elephant first and then move on to the rest. (I give you ideas about setting up cleaning routines in the section "Creating a Cleaning Schedule," later in this chapter.) Following is a list of cleaning tasks that I recommend you do even if you're really pressed for time:

- ✔ **If you have only limited time available, get rid of unused and unneeded files.** Archive your old-but-still-valuable files to get them off your system. (You can read about archiving in Chapter 7.) When you have more time, you can go back and deal with your programs and your system as a whole. (Generally, you should get your programs under control before worrying about your data, but the key here is time restriction. Working on programs simply takes longer than does taming your data.)

- ✔ **If you have more time available, do a program inventory and remove the programs you no longer need.** (See Chapters 3 and 5, where I discuss creating an inventory and deleting unwanted programs.) You'd be amazed at how much clutter this can remove from your system. Then go back and clean up your data and archive your older information.

- ✔ **Get rid of malware and spam and get your Internet environment under control.** If you do this, you find that using the Internet can again become productive, rather than frustrating. (Part III covers a ton of territory in this regard.)

- ✔ **Closely examine what your computer loads without your knowledge.** This is one of the key places many people overlook, but Windows encounters instructions to automatically load different programs from a myriad of places (most on the Web). These programs can hog resources and slow down your system's overall performance.

    Of course, tracking down such unseen scoundrels can take a bit of time. When you have that time (and after you've done the other things in this list), jump in and try to figure out what's going on. Windows provides some utilities that can help, such as the Microsoft System Configuration Utility (affectionately referred to as msconfig), which I tell you about in Chapter 13.

✔ **If you really have some time to kill — or you just fancy yourself a masochist — you can wade into the murky waters of the Windows Registry.** The *Registry* is the centralized database that controls virtually everything that happens in the operating system. It's mind-numbingly complex and staggeringly obtuse for normal humans to deal with. However, you can do things in the Registry that you can't do in any other way. An entire chapter of this book (Chapter 20) deals with this very topic.

Working in the Registry isn't for the faint of heart. Make sure you double-check every action before you take it. One wrong step, and you can bring your system to its knees. (Don't be overly worried; Chapter 20 explains how to make backups of the Registry that are useful if you run into problems.)

After you've tackled the elephant that is your Windows system, you'll undoubtedly look back and be glad you went through the process. (You'll also be glad you're done, but that's another story.)

Precautions for Safety's Sake

It's a jungle out there. (It's too bad you ate your elephant; you could use it to help you get through the jungle.) In the jungle, bad things can happen to good people. Because you're good people, you may be interested in some things to help stave off or completely avoid the bad things.

Cleaning a Windows system necessarily involves moving things, adding things, deleting things, and sometimes renaming things. Any of these tasks, although necessary, can have unintended consequences. Heaven forbid you should delete a critical system file or wipe out the wrong data key in the Registry. (Refer to the previous bulleted list, where I define the Registry and explain its importance.)

These precautions can help you avoid the bad things:

✔ **Don't delete files without knowing what you're deleting.** If you're in doubt, simply move the file to a different folder or rename it. Then, if you restart your system (or the program) and find out you made a mistake, you can always move the file back or restore its original name.

✔ **Make periodic backups of your system.** (You've heard this before, right?) If you're getting ready to do a huge cleaning session, you might want to make a backup right before you start. If you want to rely on an older backup, you might want to have it close by in case you need it when you start your cleaning session.

- **Be careful how you delete programs.** In the wonderful days of DOS, in the misty past, programs usually consisted of a couple of files or all the files in a given directory. Not so in Windows. When you install a program, the installation program can move pieces and parts all over the place. When you run the program, it can move more of itself to still other places. Because programs can move around on you, the best way to delete a program is to use either the uninstaller provided with the software or the Add/Remove Programs applet in the Control Panel. Don't just delete the main folder for the program — pieces and parts will remain scattered hither and yon. (Hither is easy to find; yon is more difficult.)

- **Know what you're doing with the Registry.** The Registry is a largely incomprehensible place. Be careful when you're changing or deleting things in the Registry. In fact, I recommend making a backup of the Registry before you do any big changes or simply exporting a data key when you're getting ready to make more minor changes. Windows doesn't have a Recycle Bin for the Registry — if you delete something by mistake, you'll be glad you made a copy ahead of time.

  A *data key* is geekspeak for a branch in the Registry. You can find out more about data keys — and how to back them up — in Chapter 20.

- **If a new icon shows up on your desktop one day, don't double-click it.** If you don't know why it's there, someone (or some program) has possibly deposited it there. If you don't know what it does, why double-click it and run it? A safer course of action is to right-click the icon, choose Properties, and then examine what programs the icon runs.

- **Keep your original program discs accessible.** If you change the program's installation, you probably need the discs. If you delete a part of the program you shouldn't, you probably need the discs. If you want to reinstall the program, you probably need the discs. Just keep them close. And it wouldn't hurt to have any necessary *software keys* (those pesky ten-character — or longer — codes required to install or unlock your software) for the discs, either.

- **Use only programs from reputable sources.** This book talks about a lot of programs you can use to help with your system cleaning. You can download most of these programs from the Internet. Rest assured that the programs I suggest have been tested and are reliable. You can't make that same assumption with all the software you find on the Internet, though. If you download and run a program from a disreputable source, you could possibly infect your system with a virus or do some other system-crashing function.

I didn't list these precautions in any particular order. They simply give you some guidance as you start on your worthy quest through the jungle. But you already possess the best safeguard you can have: common sense. Trust your common sense, and it will help you through a large number of the problems you may face.

As you're cleaning your system, keep a notepad and pen nearby. Jot down each cleaning step you take, along with any oddities you observe. These notes could be helpful if you later need to track down a problem that crops up.

Finding the Right Tools

The Right Tools. Man, I loved that movie. Sam Shepard, Scott Glenn, Ed Harris, and Dennis Quaid were amazing. It had me on the edge of my seat, especially when . . . no, wait — that was *The Right Stuff.* (Dang it. *The Right Tools* would probably star Tim "The Tool Man" Taylor in a 1965 Ford Mustang convertible. Guess I'll have to wait for that one.)

You don't have to blast off into space to find the right cleaning tools. In fact, many of the proper tools are already on your system, provided with Windows. Others are third-party tools that you have to find on the Internet.

Finding Windows tools

You probably don't know about the tools already on your system because Microsoft just throws them in without any fanfare. In fact, on Windows Vista, these tools are downright hard to find.

Think I'm kidding? Follow these steps, and you can see what I mean:

1. **Right-click any blank area of the taskbar and choose Properties from the context menu that appears.**

   The Taskbar and Start Menu Properties dialog box appears.

2. **Select the Start Menu tab.**

   As shown in Figure 2-1, the bland little dialog box invites you to make a couple of configuration changes to your Start menu. (No changes here for you, thank you very much.)

Figure 2-1:
In this
dialog box,
you slice
and dice
your Start
menu.

3. **Select the Start Menu option and click Customize.**

   The Customize Start Menu dialog box appears, as shown in Figure 2-2.

Figure 2-2:
Ah ha! The
long-hidden
utility
features of
Windows
Vista.

4. **Scroll to the bottom of the Start Menu Items list.**

   You're looking for a section of the list titled System Administrative Tools. When you find it, notice that the Don't Display This Item option is selected. (Told you Microsoft made this hard.)

5. **Choose the Display on the All Programs Menu and the Start Menu options.**

6. **Close all the dialog boxes.**

   All you need to do is click OK a few times. This saves your changes.

Now, when you click your Start Menu button, a new Administrative Tools option appears, right above the Help and Support option. This option — which Microsoft hides because someone in Redmond feels you aren't ready for the responsibility — can help you clean up your system and access many helpful-yet-geeky tools. Some of these tools are explained later in this book, in various chapters. Other tools accessible through Administrative Tools are designed for heavy-duty system administration and aren't terribly useful when cleaning your system. Feel free to explore the tools to see whether they're beneficial to you.

Many other Windows tools are accessible only from the Run menu; I detail those tools at the appropriate places throughout this book. (I wouldn't want you to get too much power right away, without a proper explanation. There could be cosmic consequences.)

Finding third-party tools

Third-party tools are those provided by people or companies other than Microsoft. (You're the first party, Microsoft is the second party, and everyone else is third-party.) Many, many tools are available in your local computer store or on the Internet, each one promising to help you run your system faster, safer, smoother, and with less chafing than ever before. Some work well; some don't. You need to be careful that you don't fall for all the advertising glitz, however. The old adage that "if something sounds too good to be true, it probably is" readily applies here.

With that caveat in mind, you can go searching for tools in several places, if you're so inclined. I recommend trying these sites:

✔ **Tucows:** Once just a straight download site, Tucows has become much more. For that reason, I generally jump right to the Windows-specific section at www.tucows.com/Windows. For most folks, this site is the gold mine of downloadable software.

✔ **CNET:** One of those megasites (www.cnet.com), it includes not only downloads but also all sorts of reviews of products they want you to buy.

✔ **Shareware.com:** This site, at www.shareware.com, is actually run by the folks at CNET. You get many of the same results here that you do at CNET.

✔ **Major Geeks:** An interesting site with a military motif, www.majorgeeks.com is a site for, well, people who are geeks in a major way. A lot of different downloads help you do everything from *benchmarking* (a tech-geek word for speed testing) to working with multimedia.

✔ **Sysinternals:** Top-notch freeware utilities for Windows systems can be found at www.sysinternals.com. The utilities here are hard-core and totally geeky by definition. Really good stuff, though. (So good, in fact, that the site was purchased in July 2006 by Microsoft. Now when you access www.sysinternals.com, you're redirected deep into the bowels of the Microsoft site. The same great utilities are still there, however.)

I show you how to use a good number of third-party tools in the different chapters of this book. For instance, in Chapter 8 you get a quick overview of different spam-combating programs. And in Chapter 20, you can find out about different software solutions for cleaning the Registry.

These examples are just a portion of what's in store for you when it comes to third-party software. The point is, a lot of good third-party software is out there, and new stuff is rising to the top of the heap all the time. With a little looking around and checking out, you can find different tools that will help you clean your Windows system and keep it clean.

For a really cool bunch of online resources, refer to Chapter 23.

Creating a Cleaning Schedule

I've said it before and I'll say it again: Cleaning your Windows system doesn't need to be intimidating. Sure, cleaning can take some time to accomplish, but you don't need to do the cleaning all at once. You can break up the big job of cleaning into smaller, more manageable tasks, doing a little here and a little there until you're done cleaning completely.

Or are you?

In reality, cleaning is never done completely — it should be an ongoing endeavor. If you set up a schedule for your cleaning, your system can remain clean, and you lessen the chance of having a messed-up computer. Plus, your life will be happier, your kids smarter, and the sunshine brighter on your home. (I threw that in for the movie version of this book. It doesn't hurt to think ahead.)

So what type of schedule should you set up for cleaning? Well, the next few sections detail things you can do now (as in today), things you can do once a week, once a month, and every year. I'm sure you can find enough info in the following sections to create your own schedule.

Now. Do it now — right now.

Got some spare time on your hands today? The following list explains just five things that you can do in as little as 10 or 20 minutes to help make your system cleaner:

- ✔ **Take out the trash.** If the trash in your kitchen overflows, you either take it out, or the dog treats it as a toy box. Your computer probably has trash everywhere, and you don't even realize it — it doesn't overflow, and the dog doesn't care. To empty your computer trash, right-click your Recycle Bin (on the Desktop) and choose Empty Recycle Bin.

- ✔ **Eliminate unneeded e-mail messages.** Skip over to your e-mail program and empty the e-mails from three areas: Sent Items, Deleted Items, and Junk E-mail. (These names are typical in Outlook; the folder names may be different in your e-mail program.) For a detailed look at how to get a handle on your e-mail, refer to Chapters 8 and 9.

- ✔ **Delete unused programs.** Choose Start⇨Control Panel⇨Programs⇨ Installed Programs. Examine the programs listed there and see whether you can delete any. (**Hint:** If you don't use it any more, you should delete it.) Find out more about identifying your programs in Chapter 3 and getting rid of them in Chapter 5.

- ✔ **Clean out the Web cache.** The *Web cache* is your system's repository of temporary files downloaded from the Internet. You go through your Web browser to access the cache and delete anything you don't need. Exactly how you do this depends on the type of browser you have, but in Internet Explorer, you choose Tools⇨Internet Options to display the Internet Options dialog box. Select the General tab and click Delete in the Browsing History area. Chapter 11 contains details on how to tame the cache files.

- ✔ **Delete cookies.** *Cookies* are small data files stored on your system to customize your browsing experience on some Web sites. If desired, you can clean out the cookies stored by your browser. Some people like to get rid of stored cookies, but doing so generally doesn't save a whole lot of disk space. Deleting cookies carries a downside, so make sure you read through Chapter 11 before you clean them out.

There. That didn't take too long, did it? And, truth be told, you probably freed up several megabytes of space on your hard drive. Cool.

Once a week should do it

All across America, in offices large and small, people start watching the clock at about 2 p.m. on Fridays. Time seems to slow down and drag on forever as quitting time approaches and the weekend beckons.

Don't let your zeal for the weekend, however, stop you from doing a few clean-up tasks every week. Friday afternoons are a great time to do these chores, but you can actually do them any time during the week — it doesn't really matter. Follow this list to clean up your computer once per week:

- **Delete temporary files.** Temporary files tend to proliferate, for a variety of reasons, and do nothing but occupy space. Locate them, delete them, and then empty the Recycle Bin. Chapter 6 helps you with this process.

- **Make backups.** If you don't already do it daily, make backups of your data. Folks, a backup is cheap insurance. It isn't a matter of *whether* you need your backups, but *when* you need them because you *will* need them — so make backups! (Wow. Was that forceful enough?) After you make the backups, store them somewhere safe. Chapter 7 includes information about making and storing backups.

- **Clean out the root directory.** The *root directory* is a special place on each hard drive; it represents premier real estate in the file-storage world. Unfortunately, root directories also have a tendency to get cluttered up easily. If you take a look at them once a week and clean them out as necessary, it helps keep your operating system happy. You probably don't want to delete files willy-nilly, though; Chapter 7 contains the details on how to keep root directories in tip-top shape.

After you get good at completing these weekly tasks, they won't take you long at all. Plus, your system will be cleaner and your data more secure. Don't you feel better now? Is it quitting time yet?

It's the end of the month already!

The months click by, and the older you get, the faster they click by. You do certain things every month, like clockwork. You turn a page on the calendar. You reconcile your checkbook with the bank statement. You pay your mortgage or rent. You rake the gravel in your front yard. (Well, you do if you live in Arizona. Don't have gravel? Pity; you probably have to cut grass at least monthly.)

Add a few tasks to your monthly routine, and your computer system will remain clean and tidy:

- ✔ **Clean up your desktop.** The dreaded "icon creep" can result in more icons appearing on your desktop today than a month ago. Identify the ones you don't need and delete them. Chapter 12 has all the grungy details.

- ✔ **Archive project data.** If you're a project-oriented type of person, you probably finished up a few projects this past month. Why not archive the data associated with those projects so that it no longer clutters your hard drive? I discuss archiving data details in Chapter 7.

- ✔ **Eliminate spyware.** *Spyware* — software designed to report your computing actions to someone else — is a continuing plague on many computer systems. Spyware started as a way for unethical marketers to track what you do with your computer. Not cool. Now it has grown to include all sorts of pop-ups that sprout like crabgrass on your monitor. Very uncool. Your pop-up blocker may suppress the symptoms, but the underlying problem — spyware — is still there. Read Chapter 10 and eradicate spyware at least once a month.

- ✔ **Examine your startup files:** You may not know about this, but every time your computer starts, it automatically starts some programs. If something changes the programs that run at startup, you may not know about the change, either. Unless, of course, you check to see what starts running automatically. Review the information in Chapters 3 and 13 to find out how to identify and control these types of programs. Then, on a monthly basis, check out your startup files to make sure no surprises are lurking there.

- ✔ **Defragment your hard drive.** One thing you really benefit from every month is defragmenting your hard drive. As you add, change, rearrange, and delete files, information stored on the hard drive can become discombobulated. (Yes, that's a valid technical term — trust me, I know these things.) Information is stored in bits and pieces here and there so that Windows has to grab data from all over your hard drive when you open a file. That slows down the system. You can knock things back into whack by defragmenting your hard drive, which essentially puts pieces of individual files back together. When done, Windows can more easily and quickly access your files. Want to find out more about defragmenting? (Nod your head. Good.) Turn to Chapter 14 for all the nitty-gritty defragmenting details.

Defragment your hard drive at the end of the day. You can leave the program running on your work PC while you run home to decompress from the day. Or start the process on your home PC before you go to bed — sometimes, it can take a while to complete.

Now that your system is cleaner and tidier and your bank account is reconciled, aren't you glad that the month is over? Now you get to start all over again. . . .

Time for the annual clean-a-fest

Should old acquaintance be forgot and never brought to mind, we'll fill the hard drive with our drafts and sing of auld lang syne.

With appropriate apologies to Robert Burns, over the course of a year, many computer acquaintances can be forgotten. Or dropped. Or misplaced. Or whatever. Creating an annual checklist to keep your Windows system lean, mean, and clean is a good idea:

- **Review all data files on your computer and archive as necessary.** Perhaps the biggest annual task is doing a comprehensive review of the data files on your computer. If you've been doing monthly archives, you can now add other files to the annual pile and shuffle them off to archive media. Chapter 7 tells how to do just about everything you ever wanted to do with archives.

- **Review your Web browser's favorites list and delete items you don't use anymore.** Chances are good that what you considered your Web favorites a year ago no longer qualify as such. Keeping your favorites list pared down helps you find what you need faster, and that can be a huge benefit. Chapter 11 discusses, among other things, how to best deal with your Web favorites.

- **Visit manufacturers' Web sites to check for updates.** Take some time to visit the Web sites for the manufacturers of your system hardware. Check for new drivers for printers, scanners, cameras, and so on that have been released during the previous 12 months. Updating your drivers can improve speed and reliability. Chapter 13 discusses how to update (or remove) drivers.

- **Review your security precautions and update them as necessary.** It's a cruel, cruel world out there, and some of the perpetrators of cruelty are not content to remain "out there." Some of them want to get up close and personal with your computer. Your job is to stop them. Believe me — you don't want to encourage such relationships. You should, at least on an annual basis, make sure that you review your security precautions. Make sure you do your review with an eye toward major security changes in the past year and how you can be prepared for the coming year. Chapter 18 can help get you started.

✔ **Update your program inventory.** I recommend doing this on an annual basis. Work habits change; tools come and go. You need to make sure that your Windows system always reflects the way you currently use your computer. Chapter 3 walks you through the process of developing your program inventory and the benefits it offers.

Time for an Overhaul?

I know one technician whose standard answer to cleaning a Windows system is to reformat the hard drive and start all over again with a clean slate. Although that's one way to tackle the problem, it isn't necessarily the best way. It's akin to using a bazooka to swat a mosquito: effective but overkill.

Is a complete system overhaul advisable? Sure; there are times. But doing so should be your last resort and then only after you've thought through all the ramifications.

For instance, after you clean systems for a while, you get a feel for how long it takes to do the cleaning. You know what it takes to look through folder after folder, weeding out the files you no longer need. You know how long it takes to identify and remove programs, update drivers, and track down errant files. When you add up all those hours, you have a good idea of what it takes — time-wise — to clean your system.

Start adding up how long it takes to reformat your hard drive, reinstall Windows, locate and install your hardware drivers, dig out and reinstall your software, and back up and restore your data. Add up all those hours and you have a good idea of the time required to overhaul.

Compare the two time estimates. If the cleaning time estimate is within 10 percent of the estimate for an overhaul, go for the overhaul. Even if it takes a bit longer, you *do* end up with a fresher machine. You can get the complete skinny on overhauling your system in Chapter 21.

The kicker is that overhauling your system (or cleaning it thoroughly) does no good if you don't change the behavior that resulted in the messed-up system in the first place. Make sure that in the future you make cleaning an integral part of your everyday computing.

Is New Hardware the Answer?

You've got that gleam in your eye. I can see it; yep, that's it. You want a new computer, don't you? I can see you thinking that getting a new computer would sure make the job of cleaning up much easier — after all, the new system starts clean.

That's the problem, though — the new computer only *starts* clean. If you don't change how you use your computer, then your new system will be a sullied twin of your current system in short order. You need to know that it's behavior that messes up computers. (Have you heard this before?) If you keep the same behavior, you keep the same consequences of that behavior.

The same is true of adding individual hardware components to your system. Running out of hard drive space? If you add a hard drive without changing how you use the hard drive, you'll fill up the new one as well.

You might be thinking that I'm saying new hardware isn't the answer; I'm not. I'm just saying it isn't the easy answer you may assume it is. In fact, in Chapter 16, I describe how to justify, select, and implement a brand new system. Take a look at that information before deciding that getting a new system is the answer to your ills.

Part II
Programs and Data

The 5th Wave

By Rich Tennant

"How's the defragmentation coming?"

In this part . . .

Part II focuses on identifying what programs you have, how to make them run faster, and how to get rid of unnecessary programs. You also find out how to identify all the data on your hard drive as well as deleting or archiving data you don't need.

Chapter 3

Identifying What You Have

In This Chapter

▶ Determining what programs you really need

▶ Discovering what's really installed

▶ Figuring out when programs are running automatically

▶ Uncovering what programs are running right now

▶ Using the information you uncover

Do you know what programs are on your computer? Do you *really* know? Most people don't. Instead, they make assumptions. The problem with assumptions, of course, is that they can get you into trouble.

The first step toward cleaning your Windows system is to figure out what programs should be on your computer, compare that to what is actually on your computer, and determine what to do with the discrepancies.

This chapter helps you through this process. By the end of this chapter, you will be well on your way to regaining control over a computer system that's probably more out of control than you know.

Creating a Program Inventory

If you run a warehouse, you need to know what you have in stock; you need an inventory. When you have an inventory, you're better able to manage everything within the warehouse walls. Without the inventory, every day is a bigger chore than it needs to be and probably full of unwelcome surprises. (Running an uninventoried warehouse isn't just a job — it's an adventure! And if you do it on roller skates, it's a zippy adventure.)

Although a computer is much smaller than a warehouse, managing a computer isn't much different from a conceptual standpoint. When you take inventory in a warehouse, you're making a list of what is really there so you can compare it to what you believe should be there. When you take inventory of your computer, you start by figuring out what should be there. This list of what should be installed on your system is your computer inventory.

When figuring out your program inventory, you're probably tempted to click the Start menu and see what you have installed on your system. Don't! That comes later, after you figure out what the heck you do with your computer. (If you start by looking through the Start menu, what you find will improperly color your inventory. Trust me; you get better results by ignoring the Start menu for the time being.)

You can take either of two approaches to putting your inventory together: the think-tank approach or the laid-back approach. Read through the following sections and figure out which approach you want to use. There's no right answer; just pick the one that appeals to you the most, and then do it.

The think-tank approach

The best way to put together a program inventory is to think through how you use the computer. I call this the *think-tank approach* because you're putting your list together in one fell swoop, using sheer brain power to hammer out an inventory that reflects the way you use your computer. (Plus, you can impress the heck out of your know-nothing friends by telling them you belong to a think tank. If you tell them in a snobby voice, it sounds very impressive, indeed.)

To create an inventory using the think-tank approach, follow these steps:

1. **Turn off your computer, unplug the phone, grab a cold drink, and clear a place on your desk.**

   You can't think effectively if you're interrupted. (Despite what the personal productivity gurus try to sell us, multitasking is for computers, not for people.) Now you're ready; this is think-tanking at its best.

2. **On a fresh sheet of paper, start listing all the programs you need on your computer.**

   Think through the tasks you do on a regular basis and write down the names of the software you use to do those tasks. Do you do a lot of writing? Chances are good your inventory should include a word processor, such as Word or WordPerfect. Do you crunch numbers for a living? Then your inventory probably includes a spreadsheet program. Do you design Web pages? You probably have a page design program in your inventory. Write them all down.

3. **Include tasks that are easy to overlook, such as balancing your check-book or entertaining your mind.**

   There are probably more than a couple of utility programs you use on a regular basis, such as WinZip or Adobe Reader. These programs should be on the list, as well.

4. **Check your bookshelves and write down what you find, but only if what you find is what you really use.**

   Chances are good that you have software manuals or installation discs stored somewhere. (Of course, they may be buried under a half inch of dust, but rediscovering these old, dust-buried friends can be exciting.)

If you find items on your bookshelves that you no longer use, gently toss them into a corner. You can always donate them to someone lower than you on the corporate food chain, or maybe even sell them on eBay. Plus, you free up valuable space on your bookshelves.

Creating your inventory should take you about an hour only. If you find yourself taking more time than that, you're probably allowing yourself to become distracted. If you take much less time, then you're not successfully navigating the think tank and are probably missing some items.

The laid-back approach

If you like a more leisurely approach to life and your Windows system isn't so bollixed up that you can't use it effectively, you can put together your program inventory another way: Keep a journal.

Yep, you read right — keep a journal. A program diary. The steps for creating an inventory the laid-back way are, well, laid back:

1. **Put a small notebook next to your computer.**

2. **Over the course of a typical week, write down every program you use.**

   If you start the program, write it down. You don't have to write times and dates for using the programs, just the program name.

3. **At the end of the week, admire what should be a nice long list of programs.**

4. **If you find duplicates on the list, remove them.**

   For instance, you may have written a program name down on Friday, forgetting that you already wrote it down on Tuesday. When you're done, your inventory should contain nothing but a unique list of programs you used in your work.

If you decide to take this laid-back approach, you have some time on your hands. After all, you shouldn't move forward with the rest of your cleaning tasks until you have your inventory done. If your inventory takes a week to put together, what will you do with your free time?

I suggest going for a walk. Or, if you tend toward being a couch potato, catch a few reruns of *Lost* or *CSI.* Of course, you could read through the rest of this chapter, but don't do any of it yet — you really do need that inventory. Instead, bookmark this page so that you can come back in a week, after a few leisurely walks or a better understanding of Gil Grissom's quirky take on life at the Las Vegas Crime Lab. You should be ready to move along then.

Finding Out What Programs Are Installed

When you're done with your inventory, congratulate yourself and get another cold drink. Put the inventory away for a while, but don't forget where you put it. (You'll need it shortly.)

Grab another sheet of paper and start writing down what programs are actually installed on your computer. You can look in a lot of places to put this list together. All of those places involve your computer, so make sure you're comfortably seated in front of it as you work through the following sections. To find out what programs are installed on your system, look in these four main places: the desktop, the Start menu, the Control Panel, and your program folders.

You're doing nothing right now except exploring your system and documenting what you find. Resist the temptation to start removing programs, regardless of how strong that temptation is. You have plenty of time to remove programs later; Chapter 5 covers that task very nicely.

Inspecting your desktop

Does your desktop look like the public bulletin board at your neighborhood Piggly Wiggly? Do you have icons crowded together so tightly that it's hard to see the wallpaper in the background? If so, you have problems. Don't worry, though — help is coming!

Every program you installed on your system probably asked (in a very helpful manner) if you wanted a program icon placed on your desktop. If you said yes, it's no wonder your desktop is a mess. Even though it's a mess, it's also a good indicator of what programs are installed on your system. This is good.

Take a quick look at each area of your desktop; it contains important clues to the programs installed on your system. Pay particular attention to the following areas:

✔ **Icons:** Look at each icon on your desktop, figure out what program it belongs to, and write the program name on your piece of paper. Unless your desktop is a disaster area, you should be able to breeze through this task in just a few minutes. Ignore non-program items (such as folders or data files) unless they help you remember a program installed on your system.

✔ **Taskbar:** Taskbars are typically full of all sorts of icons, each associated with some installed program. Pay particular attention to the Quick Launch area, just to the right of the Start menu button. See Figure 3-1 for the taskbar. If there's an expansion icon to the right of the Quick Launch area, click it to see other icons in the area. Jot down the names of the programs responsible for these icons.

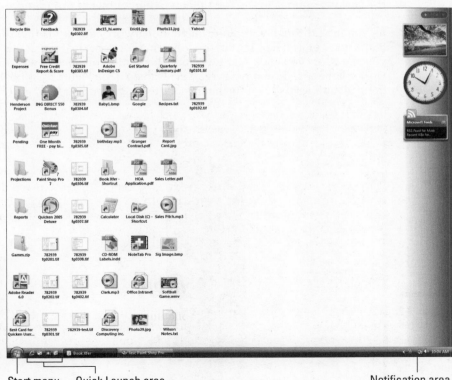

Figure 3-1:
Look for additional programs in the taskbar.

Start menu   Quick Launch area   Notification area

✔ **Notification area:** The Notification area, also called the system tray, is to the right of the taskbar (see Figure 3-1). Again, each icon here is related in some way to a program on your system. Write them down. If you don't know what program they belong to, hover the mouse pointer over the icon until you see a helpful reminder. If you see a left-pointing arrow at the left side of the notification area, click it to see all the icons stored therein.

You can find out more about cleaning up your desktop in Chapter 12.

Scrutinizing the Start menu

The Start menu is the gateway to your system. Unless your system is a Gateway, in which case the Start menu is the gateway to your Gateway. (Sorry; I wax philosophic sometimes.) Displaying the Start menu can tell you quite a bit about what you have on your system. Spend some time clicking the various options in the Start menu to find out what programs are installed.

As you look through your Start menu, don't worry about visiting the Control Panel just yet. (I cover that in the following section.) Instead, focus on what you see when you click All Programs. This option presents a whole new world of menus, probably several levels deep. (See Figure 3-2.) Look through them all and write down the names of the programs you find.

Figure 3-2:
Program menus accessible through the Start menu can extend several layers deep.

If you find the options available in your Start menu overwhelming, don't despair. Part of the reason you clean Windows is to reduce those feelings and help you get back in control of your system. You'll make it; hang in there!

Checking the Control Panel

Have you ever spent time in the Control Panel on your system? It's analogous to the cockpit of an airplane, giving you access to all the controls that make your computer work.

One area of the Control Panel specifically designed to help you figure out what's installed is the Installed Programs area. To access the Installed Programs area, follow these steps:

1. **Open the Control Panel.**

   Click Start⇨Control Panel and up pops the desired window.

2. **Click the Programs link.**

   Windows shows you a set of tasks you can perform related to programs on your system.

3. **Click the Programs and Features link.**

   A list of the programs that Windows thinks is installed on your system appears, as shown in Figure 3-3. This is the Uninstall or Change a Program window.

Figure 3-3: Windows Vista maintains a list of programs installed on your system.

4. **Scroll through the list of programs and write them all down.**

   Chances are good that there are quite a few programs listed here, but don't be fooled into thinking that the list represents every program installed on your system. It doesn't; that's why you're looking in places besides the Control Panel for installed programs.

5. **Close the Control Panel window.**

Peering in program folders

You should look in one final place to see what programs are installed on your system — the program folders. When you install a program on your system, the common convention is to install it in a folder called Program Files. This folder can contain dozens or hundreds of other folders, each of which is related in some way to a program installed on your system. To see what programs you have in your Program Files folder, follow these steps:

1. **Using Start⇨Computer, navigate to the Program Files folder and take a look at it.**

   On most systems, the Program Files folder is in the root directory of the C: drive. Figure 3-4 shows an example of a typical Program Files folder.

2. **Examine the name of each folder you see.**

   Most folders represent either the name of the program that uses the folder or the name of the publisher of a program you installed. For example, folders named ATI Technologies, Intel, and Intuit usually contain additional folders for programs from those companies. Folders named Microsoft Office, Microsoft Works, and Microsoft FrontPage all refer to individual programs. (Microsoft is really good at spreading its programs through a lot of different folders in the Program Files folder.)

3. **Look through the folders in the Program Files folder, writing down the names of any programs not already on your list.**

4. **Close all the folder windows.**

   When you're through looking around and taking notes, tidy up your screen by closing all the open folder windows.

 Over time, the Program Files folder can start to look like an old garbage dump, strewn about with folders that are no longer used. This happens because even though you delete old programs, the folders used by those programs could remain in the Program Files folder. Chapter 5 explains how to remove these pesky left-behind folders.

Figure 3-4:
The
Program
Files folder
contains
folders for
many of the
programs
installed on
your system.

Discovering What Programs Run When

Were you surprised by anything you found as you were putting together your program inventory? You find out shortly what to do with these lists, but first you need to figure out what programs run at various times on your computer.

Most programs that you use are started whenever you choose to start them, such as through the Start menu or a desktop icon. But a large number of programs run automatically when you start Windows. Sometimes, you may not even be aware that they're starting because they may run behind the scenes.

WARNING!

Programs that run automatically on your computer — especially those that don't make themselves known to you — are some of the biggest speed thieves in any system. Every program uses *resources* (memory and drive space). The more programs loaded at the same time, the more resources used for those programs.

You can configure programs to start automatically in Windows a couple of ways. Some of those ways are pretty technical; I cover them a bit later in this book (in Chapter 13). In the following sections, I examine a typical way that programs run: through the Startup folders on your system.

Starting up for all users

When Windows is first installed, one of the things it does is create a special Startup folder applicable to all the users on the computer. Anything placed in this folder is run and/or opened when you first start Windows. Sometimes real programs are stored in the Startup folder, and sometimes it's just a shortcut to a program elsewhere on your system.

To open the Startup folder for all users, follow these steps:

1. **Right-click the Start button (at the left side of the taskbar).**

2. **Choose Open All Users from the context menu that appears.**

   Word opens a folder window called Start Menu. Each item in the folder represents an entry in the Start menu. This folder is nothing more than a directory on your hard drive, the same as any other folder.

3. **Double-click the Programs folder and then double-click the Startup folder.**

   The Startup folder (see Figure 3-5) shows you what sort of programs are there (normally small "helper" programs used by other programs). For instance, my system has a program called Adobe Gamma Loader that Adobe software (Adobe Reader, in this case) uses to help "fast load" Adobe software.

Figure 3-5:
The Startup folder contains items that are loaded whenever Windows begins.

As you examine the items in the Startup folder, check them against your installed program list. You may discover additional programs that you didn't know you had. If so, add them to your list. If they're already on your list, mark down on the list that the program is part of the Startup folder.

Of menus and folders

The items in your two Startup folders appear in your Start menu — just choose Start⇨All Programs⇨Startup. You may be wondering why you weren't just directed to the Startup menu in the first place, instead of opening the individual folders.

The primary reason is because as you get ready to clean your system, you need to understand

when your programs are running. Because the Startup menu displays a combination of things from both the all-user and single-user Startup folders, you can't get the real facts on when a program is run just by looking at the menu. Instead, you must display the two individual folders.

Starting up for just you

Windows creates another folder — a Startup folder — just for your user account. Anything in this folder is started whenever you log in to your Windows Vista account.

On a single-user system, the Startup folder for all users and the Startup folder for your account are basically the same. Windows still maintains two separate Startup folders, and the contents of both are loaded and run whenever you start Windows and log in.

You can explore the contents of your Startup folder by following these steps:

1. **Right-click the Start button (at the left side of the taskbar).**

2. **Choose Open from the context menu.**

   Open should be the very first option on the context menu. Word opens a dialog box called Start Menu. Each item in the folder represents an entry in the Start menu. This folder is nothing more than a directory on your hard drive, the same as any other folder.

3. **Double-click the Programs folder and then double-click the Startup folder.**

These steps look very much like the steps required to open the Startup folder for all users, which I describe in the preceding section. The key difference, however, is that you choose a different option from the context menu. This option opens a different Start Menu folder — one just for your user account — than the Start Menu folder you can open by following the steps in the preceding section.

Check what you find against your installed program list. If you discover new programs, add them to your list.

Figuring Out What's Running Right Now

Ready for another surprise? Your computer is running programs right now. Yep; programs are running even though you probably didn't know it. (How dare they!)

The Windows Task Manager is a great tool for figuring out what programs are running on your system. To access the Task Manager, follow these steps:

1. **Exit all your programs, so that you have no buttons on your taskbar.**

   This step lets you have the clearest idea of what's going on.

2. **Right-click a blank area of the taskbar to display a context menu.**

3. **Choose Task Manager.**

   You see the Task Manager dialog box; the Applications tab should be selected. Look at Figure 3-6.

Figure 3-6:
The Applications tab lists any programs running on your system.

The Applications tab lists all the application programs that are currently running on your system. Because you exited all your programs before starting the Task Manager, the list of programs is likely empty. This is great, but it doesn't tell the whole story — programs are still running.

4. **Click the Processes tab shown in Figure 3-7.**

This tab shows any and all programs running right now. A bunch of information is available in the Processes tab, but right now you're interested in only the Image Name column. Here, you find a bunch of cryptic names of what's running. These names aren't terribly helpful, in and of themselves. You should still go through the list to figure out what the various processes are doing.

Figure 3-7:
The Processes tab shows everything running on your system, not just applications.

If the Task Manager is the heart monitor for your system (and it is), then the Processes tab is the most important element of that monitor. If you want to keep your system in tip-top shape, you should become intimately familiar with the Processes tab. Nothing sneaks by it. Period.

The names used on the Processes tab are not terribly helpful (they remind me of the old DOS filenames), so don't feel bad if you need some help figuring out what each of them does. When I need help on a process, all I do is copy the name and search for it in Google.

For instance, one of the processes running on my system is WUAUCLT.EXE. This name didn't look familiar, so I fired up Google (www.google.com) and searched for that name. I was amazed that there were over 978,000 matches to what I considered an obscure term (see Figure 3-8).

Figure 3-8:
You can use Google to search for the names of processes running on your system.

Looking at just the first couple of matches, I was able to determine that WUAUCLT.EXE is a safe program installed by Windows itself. Thus, it's okay to leave the program running in memory.

When searching through Google for process names, if you see any that are identified in a Google search as spyware or a virus, make special note of that process name. (You may want to check a few sites to ensure that the program is widely recognized as spyware or a virus.) These programs are invalid and can seriously degrade the efficiency and reliability of your system. You can find out how to handle invalid programs in Chapter 10.

If one of the running processes you search for isn't a part of the Windows operating system, but is instead used by a Windows application, add that application name to your installed program list. (If the program is running on your system, that's a pretty good indicator that it's installed on your system.)

Making a Game Plan

Now that you're done looking through your system, grab the lists that you made and set them side by side. Your next task is to compare the program inventory (what you need) against the program list (what you have). Hopefully, everything on your inventory is also listed on your installed program list. If not, you may want to figure out how the program ended up on your inventory. (Perhaps you thought you had something installed but confused your system with a different system in your office.)

In comparing lists, you may discover some programs that you forgot you need. In that case, add those programs to your inventory. The more likely scenario, however, is that your installed program list is much longer than your program inventory.

Unused programs, or those you no longer need, are a prime source of clutter on any computer system. These programs are prime candidates for removal from your system; keep this in mind.

Hold on to the lists you created; they serve you well as you focus on cleaning your Windows system. The remaining chapters in Part II, in fact, rely heavily on these two documents — you may want to keep these lists close by.

Chapter 4

Making Your Programs Run Faster

In This Chapter

▶ Applying a little common sense to your programs

▶ Accessing large data files faster

▶ Ensuring program compatibility

▶ Making games run faster (with less clutter)

▶ Considering multimedia software

Don't you feel special! You're finally taking control of your computing life, grabbing it by the proverbial horns. You have your *program inventory* — a list of what you want on your system — and you have your *installed program list* — what you have on your system already. (If terms like program inventory and installed program list leave you scratching your head, you need to make a quick detour to Chapter 3.)

In all likelihood, your program inventory is a subset of your installed program list. Now's the time to focus on the program inventory because you want to run those programs — and run them well.

This chapter introduces you to different ways to make your installed programs — the ones you care about — run faster than ever before. Your overall computer speed improves as you clean your Windows system, but you can also speed up individual programs.

Common Sense for Programs

An *oxymoron* is two or more words that together form a phrase but otherwise seem to contradict each other. Classic examples include military intelligence, jumbo shrimp, amicable divorce, and Microsoft Works. (Thousands of such examples abound in the wild, grazing peacefully, almost gleefully, on the English language.)

Add to the list "common sense." Common sense is, more often than not, quite uncommon. With that in mind, I've put together a few common-sense concepts you can follow when trying to speed up your programs. Applying these ideas continues to benefit you as you further scrub your Windows system clean.

Turn off whiz-bang features

People like whiz-bang. They have the same reaction to whizzes and bangs as they do to fireworks on the Fourth of July: "Ohhh! Ahhh!" It makes them feel good about their computer systems.

You're not that way, right? You're more interested in uncluttering your life, cleaning your Windows system, and making things run as smoothly and quickly as possible. You're a pragmatist — keeping your focus razor sharp, ready for a no-nonsense approach to computing.

Right.

We all fall victim to the lure of whiz-bangs once in a while. (Including the folks in Redmond.) We like to see our icons displayed in millions of colors, twirl around while waiting for us to click them, and have a cute animated pet follow the mouse pointer around the screen. These niceties come at a price, however.

The short of it? If you want your programs to run faster, turn off any whiz-bang features you have, unless you absolutely need them. Such features can tax your system and therefore slow it down.

Watch out for networking "gotchas"

If your computer is connected to a network, you can share information and resources easily with other people. If everything is configured properly, you can easily access information on their machines, and they can access it on yours.

Therein, of course, lies the rub. If your network is set up so that your machine is providing information or resources to others on the network, your system can slow down dramatically during times of peak network usage. The following list highlights just a few scenarios where your computer gets sluggish:

✔ While your co-workers access files on your system, less CPU time is available for your tasks because your computer is busy servicing the requests of your co-workers.

✔ If your system is doing double-duty as the network print server, you can — and will — see drastic slowdowns as the print jobs are serviced.

✔ On networks, people can deposit information on your system that you have no control over. I'm not talking about viruses (although that could be a concern), but about actually storing files on your system. The trouble with this scenario is twofold:

  • All that extra information clutters up your computer, causing it to run slower.

  • If the people dropping off stuff aren't terribly tidy information managers, your system can get cluttered up in a real hurry. Trying to track down what's safely deleted and what isn't can become a nightmare.

For more information about how to unclutter your network life, see Chapter 19.

Never upgrade unless you have to

"Really? Never upgrade? Wow. But I thought I always needed the latest and greatest version of my software." No, you don't. My firm conviction is that software vendors (not just Microsoft) want you to always have the latest version of their software. If I were working for a software vendor, I would want you to have our latest software, as well. If you ask vendors why they want you to upgrade, they won't say, "So we can enhance our bottom line." Instead, they focus on new features, increased productivity, or fewer problems.

Weren't these the same reasons they gave you for upgrading to the version you currently have? Yep. It's all part of the game — the game to get you to keep upgrading. The problem with upgrades is that they usually include features that you got along just fine without for years and probably won't use now even though they're included. These features add to the software's bloat, making it fatter, slower, and more resource-hungry than ever.

When you upgrade software, you run the risk of cluttering up your system with pieces and parts of programs left behind in the upgrade process. Upgrading only when you need to helps minimize this process and makes cleaning Windows easier. (I'm not ranting against software companies; they have a right to sell their wares and attempt to convince you that your life is happier, safer, sexier, and more fulfilling after you get the latest version of Widget Whacker Deluxe. You just need to look at software differently than how the software companies want you to.)

You don't *always* need to upgrade

Case in point: Microsoft Word. (I'm not picking on Word; I'm just using it as an example in thinking about upgrades.) The latest version is Word 2003, and it's sold as part of the Office 2003 suite. I still know people who are using Word 97 with absolutely no decrease in happiness, safety, or prosperity. They skipped the upgrades to Word 2000, Word 2002, and now Word 2003, and in the process saved well over a thousand dollars. The fact of the matter is, they were able to do everything they wanted by using the older version of Word: So why upgrade?

So when do you *need* to upgrade? You should upgrade at these times:

- ✔ If you're developing your own products that rely on the newest versions of the software
- ✔ If you must remain compatible with people or companies using the newer versions

But never, never, never (did I say never?) upgrade unless you have to. Make sure you have a solidly thought-out reason for upgrading before you plunk down your hard-earned cash.

Speed up specific software

Entire books could be written about how to speed up individual software programs. Don't let the plethora of available information stop you from reading through the following sections, particularly if you have some of this software installed on your system.

Software travels in packs, never alone. When you install software on your system, additional "helpful" programs are often installed along with the primary application. These additional programs can affect the speed at which your computer works, and they can clutter up your system. Be alert to what is really installed on your system!

Microsoft Office

If you have Office 97 installed on your system, chances are good that a utility program called Find Fast is also installed on your system. This program allows Office applications to find files a bit faster, but it gains this search speed by performing background indexing of the files on your hard drive. The downside is that at times the background work done by Find Fast can bring your system to its knees.

The only solution is to remove Find Fast completely. (Most people never need the program anyway.) To remove it from your system, perform the following general tasks:

1. **Delete the Find Fast shortcut from the Startup folder.**

   Locating the Startup folder is discussed in Chapter 3.

2. **Double-click the Find Fast icon in the Control Panel and delete any indexes listed there.**

3. **Restart your computer and search for a file named** `findfast.cpl`.

   Only one of these files should be on your hard drive; the file is the Control Panel applet for the program. Feel free to delete it, but only after you complete Step 2.

Just three short tasks, and you're on your way to a leaner, meaner machine. You should notice an immediate improvement in your system's responsiveness.

Recent versions of Office (Office 97, 2000, 2002, 2003, and 2007) may add another icon called Windows Office to your Start folders. No, this program doesn't start Office itself, but it spends a bit of time initializing different parts of your system so they work quicker with Office. The shortcut runs a program technically called the Office Startup Assistant. This program takes up some resources, but it isn't the resource hog that Find Fast is. If you use Office only sparingly (once a day or less often), feel free to remove the shortcut from your Startup folders.

Another tip for making Office run faster is to check how you have your Office applications configured:

- ✔ **Make sure that the Fast Save feature in Word isn't turned on.** With this feature on, your individual documents save slower in the long run, and you risk corrupting the documents. In Word, choose Tools⇨Options; then clear the Allow Fast Saves check box on the Save tab.

- ✔ **Minimize the number of external links in an Excel workbook or a Word document.** *External links* (links to resources outside of the workbook or document) are refreshed whenever you open the workbook or document, slowing down how quickly you can start using the data.

- ✔ **Don't save your data on floppies.** Floppies' limited space makes them poor candidates for storing files, and they're much slower and less reliable than hard drives. (Obviously, saving data on floppies won't be an issue if your computer doesn't even have a floppy drive — and most don't these days.)

> ✔ **Turn off the graphics display in your document or workbook.** You probably won't want to turn off the graphics display in PowerPoint because the graphics are typically integral to your presentation. In Word, you choose Tools⇨Options and select the Picture Placeholders check box on the View tab. In Excel, you choose Tools⇨Options and select the Show Placeholders check box on the View tab.

Microsoft Outlook

I know, I know . . . Outlook is technically part of Microsoft Office, so you were expecting it in the preceding section. Ha! Fooled you.

Outlook has become a staple on many people's computers, running everything from appointment calendars to task lists, all while also handling e-mail. Because it does so much, Outlook is a real resource hog. One feature of Outlook that is especially piggy deserves some close scrutiny: Journaling.

When the Journal feature is turned on, an Outlook journal entry is written every time you make changes to files in other Office applications, such as Word and Excel. Unless you really, really need this feature, turn it off. For most people, it does nothing except slow down how you use the system, bog down your applications, and suck up hard drive space.

In Office 97, journaling is turned on by default. In later versions of Outlook, journaling is turned off by default, but the feature could inadvertently get turned on (by other users, macros, gremlins, and so on). To make sure that journaling is disabled, follow these steps:

1. **Within Outlook, choose Tools⇨Options.**

   Outlook displays the Options dialog box.

2. **If you're using Outlook 97, display the Journal tab. If you're using a later version of Outlook, display the Preferences tab and click the Journal Options button.**

   The Journal Options dialog box appears.

3. **Clear the check boxes in the Also Record Files From area of the dialog box.**

4. **Close all the open dialog boxes.**

Quicken

All the versions of Quicken that I've seen have a feature called Billminder. This feature is installed automatically when you install Quicken. It runs every time you start your computer, whether you plan to work with Quicken or not.

TECHNICAL STUFF

For the VBA macro writer . . .

Macros are used to perform repetitive tasks quickly so you don't have to do them manually. As the macro completes each of its tasks, the program (such as Word or Excel) updates the screen to reflect the changes made by the macro. This updating, because the macro is working so quickly, often makes the screen look like it's gone haywire. You can speed up the macros by turning off screen updating. Just add the following line at the beginning of the macro:

```
Application.ScreenUpdating =
    False
```

After your macro is complete, set the Screen Updating property to True.

Billminder reminds you of upcoming bills and obligations, with an eye toward helping you remember the ways in which you've spent your money. Do you need it? You can make up your own mind, but most people I know don't use Billminder, which means for them it uses resources that are best freed up for other purposes.

Follow these steps to make sure that Billminder doesn't run every time you start Windows:

1. **Choose Start➪All Programs➪Quicken.**

   You should see a submenu that lists Quicken-related programs.

2. **Choose Billminder.**

   The Billminder program starts up, which you can see in Figure 4-1.

3. **In Billminder, click Options to display the Billminder Options dialog box.**

4. **Clear the Enable Billminder on Windows Startup check box and click OK.**

5. **Exit Billminder.**

In some versions of Billminder, these steps may not work as noted. In that case, you can simply open the Startup folders on your system and delete the Billminder icon.

The biggest thing you can do to increase Quicken's speed is to decrease the size of the Quicken data file. If you're a long-time Quicken user, your files probably still contain a bunch of old data. This info is great for those times you want to get misty-eyed over the good old days, but it really is an anchor when trying to slice and dice the current data.

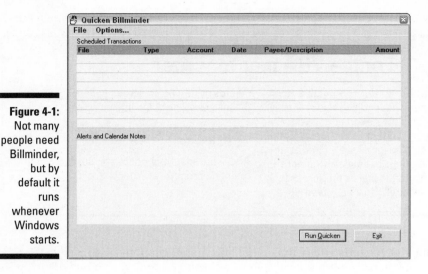

Figure 4-1:
Not many
people need
Billminder,
but by
default it
runs
whenever
Windows
starts.

Use Quicken's Copy File feature to move part of your data file into a separate data file. (Yes, you use a "copy" feature to move something. Go figure!) The feature allows you to specify a date range for items you want moved. More information on the Copy File feature is available in the online Help system for Quicken.

Speeding Up Access to Large Data Files

Have you ever worked with word-processing documents that are 1,600 or more pages? How about spreadsheets with 10,000 rows of formulas? Or databases with 35MB of data?

Computers have made it possible to amass huge quantities of data, and sometimes even process it! (Just finding what I want in an avalanche of data is my biggest stumbling block in processing.) If you're running programs that process huge data files, you'll find the next few sections helpful. They outline some specific things you can do to make your system run faster.

Change your hardware

I get a bit tired of people who tell me that the answer to life, the universe, and everything is to get new hardware. (In reality, the answer is 42.) After some investigation, I typically find that those people either (a) have no concept of money or (b) have a vested interest in selling the hardware. Drives me crazy.

Buying new hardware is *not* the answer to every problem, but it can help alleviate some problems, such as dealing with large amounts of data. Here are three options to consider if you determine that you really need the new hardware:

- ✔ **Add more memory.** The single biggest bottleneck in many Windows systems — especially those that process large amounts of data — is memory. Adding more memory can significantly speed up your overall system.

- ✔ **Use faster hard drives.** Fast internal hard drives are relatively cheap these days. For instance, you can routinely find 100GB, 7,200 RPM drives for under $100. Increasing the drive size doesn't increase the price that much, with 250GB (or larger) drives selling for under $200. (I even found a 300GB, 7,200 RPM drive on sale for $80.)

- ✔ **Use a flash drive.** *Flash drives* are amazing little devices that act like a hard drive but are really fast memory. They usually plug into your system by using a USB port and come in varying sizes. Lacking mechanical parts, they're much, much faster than physical hard drives.

I discuss new hardware in more detail in Chapter 17.

One sure sign that more memory or a larger hard drive would be helpful is when your system spends a lot of time accessing your hard drive. Most systems have a disk-access LED on the front of the computer case. Watch it sometime, particularly as you switch from one program to another. If you notice a response lag and the LED flashes for extended periods of time, that means that Windows is swapping memory out to the hard drive to make room for the program you're switching to. Adding memory reduces the need for swapping, and a faster hard drive makes any necessary swapping faster.

Reconfigure your data

If adding memory or changing your hard drives isn't a viable solution, you may want to rethink how you use the data within your programs:

- ✔ If your e-mail client is keeping track of thousands of old messages, archiving a few of them (thereby reducing the work that the client has to do) may be worth your time.

- ✔ If you're using a database program for your customer management tasks, you may want to export your old customer data into a separate database file. That way, as you're working with newer data, your system won't be slowed down because of the older, unused data.

Your ability to reconfigure your data depends, of course, on your needs and your software's capabilities. You should evaluate your needs to determine whether reconfiguration is viable, and you should check your software to see whether exporting or archiving is available.

Reconfigure your program

When companies write programs, they do so with a target audience in mind. The company has to make certain assumptions about the software user, such as the type of machine being used, the condition of data, the way the user works, and so on.

One assumption concerns the size of data files you're using with the software. Most software is written with the expectation of using small- to medium-sized files. If you start using larger data files and notice that the software becomes sluggish, you need to examine different configuration settings for your software. (I'm talking configuration within the software itself, not within Windows.)

As an example, some software has an automatic backup or autosave feature. This is a great safety feature to have, depending on the value of the data you're using. The feature may be set up so that every five minutes or so, your data is automatically saved. The problem creeps in if you're using such a feature with large files. If saving a file takes 30 seconds or longer, frequent saving can disrupt your workflow. You may want to reconfigure the software so that it forces a save less frequently or not at all if you're well-disciplined and save the file yourself.

Programs commonly save temporary files to your hard drive while you're working within the programs. If the temporary files are related to the size of your main data file, your system may fill up with temporary files and cause problems — particularly if the software doesn't properly delete the files. (See Chapter 6 for more information on identifying and getting rid of temporary files.) If possible, you may want to configure your software so that it saves its temporary files in a set location. This configuration makes getting rid of the temporary files a breeze.

Are We Compatible?

Do you have a program on your program inventory that doesn't appear on your installed program list? Is the program on your wish list, but not installed, because it won't run under Windows Vista? Well, Bucko, fasten your seat belt because I'm gonna tell you how you can make that program run just fine under Vista! (Wow. This is exciting.)

It wasn't that long ago that every new version of Windows meant more and more programs had to be put out to pasture — they just wouldn't work with the new versions of Windows. As a partial solution to that problem, Microsoft developed something euphemistically called the Windows Application Compatibility mode. (This feature was first introduced in Windows XP and has, thankfully, been continued in Windows Vista.) Despite the totally geeky name, the feature is really very cool.

Suppose that you try to install a program under Windows Vista, or you did an upgrade to Vista and a previously installed program stopped working correctly. Chances are good that the program worked fine under a previous version of Windows, but under Vista it simply goes on a permanent vacation. (Perhaps it doesn't really go on vacation, but simply acts stupid all of a sudden.)

To try to correct this situation, here's what you need to do:

1. **Right-click the program icon that you want to fix and choose Properties from the context menu.**

   Make sure you right-click the actual program icon, not a shortcut to the program. To find the program icon, you may have to browse through your hard drive. If you're trying to run an installation program for an application, locate and right-click the icon for the setup or install program.

   Windows displays the program's Properties dialog box. You should make sure the Compatibility tab is displayed, as shown in Figure 4-2.

Figure 4-2:
You can easily miss the Compatibility tab, unless you know where to find it.

2. **Select the Run This Program in Compatibility Mode For check box.**

   When you click the check box, the drop-down list under the check box becomes active.

3. **Using the drop-down list, select a version of Windows with which you know the program works.**

   You can choose from Windows 95, Windows 98/Windows Me, Windows NT 4.0 (Service Pack 5), Windows 2000, Windows XP (Service Pack 2), and Windows Server 2003 (Service Pack 1). If you don't know which one to choose, pick the version of Windows that you had before you upgraded to Vista or refer to the system requirements on the program's software package.

4. **If desired, make other selections in the dialog box.**

   You can choose to limit the display settings or modify the input settings. These changes are typically only necessary for very old programs or for some games.

5. **Click OK.**

6. **Double-click the program icon to run the program.**

   Windows Vista sets up a virtual environment that closely matches the version of Windows you specified in Step 3. Your program should work fine, and it'll probably run even faster than it used to in the old version of Windows.

Not all programs are appropriate to use in a Windows Vista environment, even in Windows Application Compatibility mode. Some programs — particularly system tools — are designed for specific operating systems and can cause problems for you even if you run them in a compatibility mode. Programs such as anti-virus software, firewalls, CD burners, and backup software that aren't designed specifically to work with Windows Vista may operate at such a low level that they're essentially incompatible with the Windows Vista low-level routines. Programs such as these should not be installed, even using compatibility mode.

Playing Games

At the risk of seriously dating myself, I remember the days when the ruling games on PCs were Scott Adams' adventure games. You could fit the whole thing on a single diskette. Then along came arcade-style games, including the one that changed everything: Doom.

Now, computer game publishers hire scriptwriters, songwriters, orchestras, and actors. It isn't unusual for a computer game to require ten CDs or to ship on one or more DVDs.

Games also push computer systems to the limits. Realistic scenery, 3D images, great music, and a lot of special effects all tax a system. If you walk into a computer store, you find computer systems optimized for computer games. (The price is also optimized — all that horsepower doesn't come cheap.)

What does that have to do with clutter? Game players tend to gravitate around a limited number of games, and the games tend to suck up a lot of time. The game publishers know this, so some of them assume their particular game is the only one running on your system. When a game (or any program, for that matter) thinks it has complete run of a system, the upshot is that installing the game can cause problems when you want to run other software.

If you have multiple game players in the house and everyone is sharing the same system, games also can cause conflicts with each other. Plus, you may have one gamer who likes to install every new game that comes along, play for a couple of days, and then install the next new game. Immediate clutter and a potential mess.

Eliminate most clutter immediately

Kids and computers seem to be drawn to each other. (Perhaps they're mutually magnetic.) One thing that kids are prone to do is to install games on a computer. If having a bunch of games installed on your computer drives you nuts, you can do one of several things:

✔ **Set rules for installing software.** If you paid for the computer, you own it. Be authoritarian and set rules about what can be installed and how that should happen.

✔ **Limit computer use.** The chances of your children installing rogue programs increases exponentially relative to your proximity to the computer. If you set guidelines for when the computer can be used, you help safeguard your programs and your data.

✔ **Lock your computer.** If you're away from your computer for a time and you want to lock it, press the Windows key+L. (Pretty cool, huh?)

✔ **Create an account for your kids.** Windows Vista allows you to create a user account, on the computer, that limits what kids can do. (Such accounts are beyond the scope of this book, but any good user's guide to Vista should be instructive on how to do this.)

✔ **Get a computer for the kids.** That way, if they want to muck up their computer, it won't affect yours in the least.

Setting ground rules and taking sensible precautions can help you manage what's on your machine, thereby reducing clutter and the chance of your system getting messed up.

These tips can help your games run faster and with fewer problems:

- **Install only the games you actually play.** Don't use your system as a repository of every game ever published, thinking you'll get to them someday.

- **Make sure you have a fast CD-ROM drive.** Many games don't install everything they need on your hard drive; they reference the CD-ROM quite often. Make sure you have a fast CD-ROM drive with a large buffer, so you can get the performance you need.

- **Make sure you have a DVD drive.** Some games — particularly the larger and more elaborate ones — are being distributed on DVDs. Make sure you have a DVD drive installed. (Besides, you can watch movies if you get tired of games.)

- **Install your games on a fast hard drive.** A hard drive designed for multi-media use should work just fine. Also, install the games on a different drive than the one on which you installed Windows. That way, operating system requests that require hard drive access won't interrupt what the game hard drive is doing.

- **Get a video card optimized for games.** Some games require specific capabilities in your video card, so make sure you check that out.

- **Install the proper video drivers for your video card and for Windows Vista.** Some games require specific technologies, such as OpenGL. These technologies are typically implemented through the video driver, not through Windows. Installing the proper video driver for your needs solves a lot of potential game problems.

That should do it. You can try out a lot of other things, but the preceding list identifies what things most often affect the speed at which your games operate.

Pushing the Envelope: Multimedia Editing Programs

As Olivia Newton John might have said (had her singing career not tanked prior to the digital revolution), "I wanna get digital, let's get into digital." Everything these days is digital — digital video cameras, digital still-shot cameras, digital audio recorders, digital mixers, and so on.

All that digital equipment stores tons of information and can plug into your computer. Everyone wants to store, edit, play, and share all that digital information. New software is appearing all the time, promising the ability to slice and dice multimedia information 12 ways to Sunday.

The problem with having all that digital information on your computer, of course, is that it's huge, huge, huge! I'm not talking about popularity, but about the size of the files created for digital multimedia. Many things can affect the size of multimedia files, including quality, resolution, and audio or video speed. CD-quality audio can take 50KB of disk space per second. Video throws the storage needs through the roof, often running at 6MB per second. That's huge!

Say that you shoot two hours of digital video of your parent's 50th anniversary. You get everything — the grand entrance, the arrival of the siblings, the arrival of your aunts and uncles, the arguments, the food fight. Hmmm . . . That's 7,200 seconds, or anywhere from 36GB to 44GB of data. Ack! Just for a single event!

As you can imagine, programs that allow you to fold, spindle, mutilate, and otherwise process such huge files can place quite the burden on your computer system. Top-notch programs push the envelope, trying to squeeze all the performance out of your system that they can.

The following points are the best two ways to speed up those programs:

- **Make sure you have lots and lots and lots of RAM in your computer.** The more memory you can install, the better. If your motherboard can handle it, install 1GB or more of RAM. (Actually, Windows Vista says that it requires 1GB of RAM, although it will run sluggishly fine with less.) Windows Vista can handle the added memory just fine, and the addition helps with editing Mom and Dad's anniversary party, so the finished video doesn't include Uncle Joe showing up with his walker and his surprise 20-something bride.

- **Make sure you're using the fastest video card you can, along with a fast hard drive designed for multimedia use.** Yes, they do make hard drives just for multimedia use. If you have one of these babies, you won't be sorry when it comes time to do gymnastics with gigabytes of data.

Chapter 5

Getting Rid of Old Programs

· ·

In This Chapter

▶ Figuring out which programs to delete

▶ Selecting an appropriate plan of attack for removing programs

▶ Finding third-party resources for program removal

· ·

Creating your program *inventory* — those programs that you need to have on your system — is the focus of Chapter 3. In Chapter 4, I show you how to make your programs run faster. In this chapter, you focus on the programs you want to get *off* your system. Unneeded and unwanted programs should be removed and tossed into the dustbin of personal computing history, and you're about to discover several ways you can do that.

Identifying Candidates for Removal

"Off with their heads!" Wouldn't it be cool if you could get rid of unwanted programs with as much ease as the Queen of Hearts got rid of unruly subjects in *Alice's Adventures in Wonderland?* You could swagger around, giving orders all day long with the assurance that your every whim would be carried out at your very decree. (And you could attend some very interesting croquet matches.)

It's not that easy in the Windows world. Before you can behead a program, you have to track it down, figure out the best way to axe it, and then make it happen. Unlike the decree-wielding Queen of Hearts, you serve as investigator, judge, jury, and executioner — you don't just give the orders: You have to do all the work yourself, too.

So, put down your scepter for a moment and grab your investigator's notebook. You're going for a trek that leads you to all the places where you can identify different programs that need to be removed.

Unused programs you installed

The first order of business is to look for programs that you once installed, but no longer need. In Chapter 3, you put together your program inventory and your installed program list. If you compare the two lists, you may see some programs on the installed program list that don't appear on the program inventory. Highlight these programs; they're prime candidates for removal.

If you didn't put together an installed program list and a program inventory, you have a bit more work to do. You need to go through all the programs on your system — the ones you previously installed — and figure out which ones you no longer need. Jot down the program names on a piece of paper so that you know what to delete.

Preinstalled software

One of the things (among many) that drives me crazy is preloaded software. You buy a computer from Dell, HP, Gateway, or any number of other retailers, and they throw in a boatload of software, already installed on the computer. The problem is that most of the software is of very little value. Sometimes, all of the software is of no value. It's easy to fill up a computer with no-value software and tout what a great deal I'm getting. Hogwash!

Did your computer come with a lot of software preinstalled? If so, I'll bet you don't use most of it. Take a look at what was installed when you got your system and add the unused software to your list of removal targets. Don't worry; removing preinstalled software won't make your computer stop working, void your warranty, or subject you to criminal prosecution. (Unlike those stupid little tags on mattresses that I'm still scared to remove.)

Stuff you find in the Program Files folder

Most mild-mannered programs (not to be confused with those arrogant programs that think they own your computer) are polite enough to install themselves in your Program Files folder. That's pretty cool, really — that means you can poke around in the folder and discover information about programs installed on your system.

On most systems, the Program Files folder is accessible from the C: drive. Just open the C: drive and double-click the Program Files folder. Voilá! You have found the secret clubhouse of all your programs. (The mild-mannered ones, at least.) Figure 5-1 shows an example of a typical Program Files folder.

Most of the folders in the Program Files folder are named after either the program that created the folder (such as Microsoft Money) or the software company that publishes the software that created the folder (such as Intuit or Adobe).

Take some time to browse through the different folders. See if you can figure out which software program installed each folder. If you find software you want to remove, write the program name on your list of deletion targets.

Windows security at its best

Depending on how you have your Windows Vista system set up, you may run into what I call the mother-hen security feature when you try to display the Program Files folder. Like a busybody mother hen, Windows refuses to show you the contents of your C: drive and then of your Programs Folder. Instead, you see this ominous message:

```
These files are hidden. This
    folder contains files that
    keep your system working
    properly. You should not
    modify its contents.
```

Ignore the clucking mother hen. Click the Show the Contents of this Folder link and the warning goes away, never to return for that particular drive or folder. Instead, you're greeted with the contents you wanted to see in the first place.

Don't delete anything in the Program Files folder quite yet. Deleting items can sometimes cause unintended problems and should only be a last resort. In the section "The brute-force method," later in this chapter, you can find out when it's okay to delete things in the Program Files folder.

Four Ways to Remove Unwanted Programs

An old saying states that "all roads lead to Rome." This was first uttered by an Italian peasant who didn't have a clue concerning geographic realities. Since that fateful day when the peasant misled an unsuspecting traveler, others have translated this saying to mean that you can reach the same goal multiple ways.

So it is with removing programs: You can get them off your system several ways. The methods follow in order of preference:

1. Use the application's uninstall command.

2. Use the Windows Control Panel.

3. Use third-party removal software.

4. Use brute force to wrench it from your system.

I recommend that you try each method, beginning with the first and moving toward the last. The best method to use for removing programs is the one that is successful for you, with the least amount of work necessary. With that in mind, consider the following sections where I discuss each of these removal methods.

An application's uninstall command

Most well-behaved programs provide a way to get themselves off your computer with almost as much ease as you put them on. You normally won't find the uninstall command in any of the application's menus, but as a separate program, installed at the same time that you installed the application.

To remove a program by using its uninstall command, follow these steps:

1. **Choose Start⇨All Programs and navigate through the menu until you locate your program's menu option.**

   When you open the submenu that actually contains the options for the program, you often see other choices, as well. See Figure 5-2.

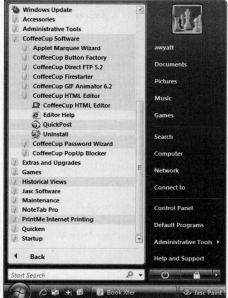

Figure 5-2:
Look for
uninstall
commands
by using the
Start menu.

2. **Examine the choices available; one of them should clearly be marked as an uninstall program.**

3. **Run the uninstall program and follow the presented instructions.**

Even if your program has an uninstall command, that command might not have been added to the Start menu. If you can locate the program folder for the application (quite possibly in the Program Files folder), you may find an uninstall program in it. Do a little bit of snooping in Program Files, using the techniques described in the preceding section, to find out if this is the case. You can then run the uninstall program from wherever you find it.

Some programs aren't as accommodating in getting themselves booted from your system. For instance, the program may require you to visit a Web site or jump through some other hoop in order to remove the program. The program's Help file is a good place to check for a nonstandard removal method. A section in the Help file may talk about how to remove the program. A Readme file may have been installed on your system when you first installed the program. If you read the Readme file, you may discover instructions on how to remove the program.

The Installed Programs area of the Control Panel

The Control Panel is the nerve center of Windows, and it allows you to change all sorts of configuration settings. The Control Panel also includes an area that allows you to add or remove programs from your system. This area, appropriately enough, is called Installed Programs. (I've often marveled at Microsoft's ability to come up with catchy names.)

If you open the Control Panel, click the Programs link, and then click Programs and Features, you'll see a listing of which programs Windows thinks you have installed on your system. See Figure 5-3.

You should be aware that the Installed Programs area doesn't necessarily list all the programs installed on your system, and it may include programs that you already removed from your system. This occurs because Windows lists only programs registered in a specific area of the Registry. If, during installation, a program doesn't properly inform the Registry of its existence, that program won't show up in the list. Likewise, if an uninstall program doesn't clean up the Registry or you remove a program manually without editing the Registry, the program may still show up in the list. I further discuss the Registry in the section "Cleaning up the Registry," later in this chapter, and also in Chapter 20.

To remove a program, scroll through the list of available programs until you find the program you want removed. When you click the program name, the options at the top of the Control Panel window change to display a new option: Change/Remove. Click the Change/Remove button, and Windows tries to remove the program from your system. Removing the program usually involves running the same setup program that you used to install the program.

Figure 5-3:
Windows keeps track of the programs installed on your system.

Programs have a tendency to travel in packs. When you remove one, make sure you look for others that may be related to that program. If you find ancillary programs in the list, delete them right after you delete the main program.

Third-party software

Ah, the sweet smell of capitalism at work! Isn't it wonderful that you can find a piece of software to fulfill almost every perceived need? You can find software for everything from keeping track of your rubber-band collection to modifying desktop icons to hacking into NSA supercomputers.

With all that variety to choose from, you might be wondering if anyone's developed software that removes recalcitrant software from your system. The answer is a resounding "Yes!" One that I've found helpful for Windows Vista is Cleanse.

Cleanse is a general system cleaning utility, published by Zards Software (www.zardssoftware.com). The program's main function is to remove programs from your system. All you need to do is start the software and you are shown a complete list of programs installed on your system. You can then select the application you want to remove and make it go away. One of the really nice things about Cleanse is that it doesn't just stop at removing the software; it also looks through the Windows Registry for leftover artifacts and then looks through your hard drives for orphaned files.

Windows Vista is brand new. As it becomes more entrenched, you'll see additional programs from innovative software publishers. Don't be afraid to periodically search the Web, looking for programs (like uninstallers) that work with Vista. You may be pleasantly surprised with what you find.

The brute-force method

In the old days of computing, things were different. (Let me hobble over to my rocking chair for a moment. Hand me that shawl, will you, son?) When you installed a program under DOS, it went into a single directory, and life was wonderful. If you needed to delete the program, you just deleted the directory. Everything related to the program was deleted from your system in one swoop.

Not so any more. Today, only rarely are programs installed in a single place on your hard drive. Instead, installation programs act like that little spreader device on the back of salt trucks — the salt comes down the chute, hits the rotating blade, and is spread everywhere. Modern installation programs often place program pieces not only in the program folder, but also in your system folder, your profile folder, a drivers folder, and various other places. In addition, programs add things to the Registry, that central repository of all things most important to Windowsdom.

Thus, deleting a modern program from a Windows system involves two very important steps:

1. **Locate the files that make the program work.**

2. **Clean up the Registry.**

The brute-force removal method should be the last way that you try to remove programs. Often, programs install pieces of themselves in multiple places on your hard drive. Just because you delete the main program file and remove it from the Registry doesn't mean that all the far-flung pieces and parts have been removed. The orphan pieces likely won't interfere with the operation of your other programs, but they do — over time — clutter up your hard drive and occupy disk space. Therefore, brute-force removal involves a third step: doing away with the bits and pieces.

Locating and removing the program

In the section "Stuff you find in the Program Files folder," earlier in this chapter, I show you around the Program Files folder. This folder is the traditional "main place" where programs are installed on a Windows system. In this section, I send you exploring again — this time looking for any folders that obviously belong to the program you want to delete.

To locate an unwanted program and then remove it by brute force, follow these steps:

1. **Right-click shortcuts or menu items and choose Properties.**

   Remember that program shortcuts are in folder windows, and menu items are on, well, menus. Right-click them, and the context menu should include a Properties option you need to select. Figure 5-4 shows an example of the Properties dialog box that's displayed. Looking in the Target box, you should be able to see where the shortcuts point.

   Pay particular attention to the Target field. This field normally shows the complete path and program name executed by the shortcut or menu item.

2. **Write down the full path so that you have it after closing the dialog box.**

   Don't waste trees unless you have to. Open a Notepad window and copy the contents of the Target field to the Notepad window. That way, you don't have to worry about transcription errors.

Figure 5-4:
The
Properties
dialog box
can give
clues about
where a
program is
stored.

3. **When you're satisfied that you located the folder containing the program files, open that folder.**

4. **Note in your Notepad window all the program names in that folder.**

   You need those filenames when you clean up the Registry.

5. **Delete the items in the folder that are related to the program you want to remove.**

   If the entire folder is used for the program, delete the entire folder.

   If in doubt concerning what you're about to delete, don't delete it. Instead, move it to a different place on your hard drive or rename it. Doing so allows you to see whether your change makes any difference to Windows. If you run into problems, you can always move back the file or folder or give it its original name.

You've completed the first part of brute-force removal. Continue the process with the steps in the following section.

Cleaning up the Registry

You must clean up the Registry after deleting program files; see the preceding section to find out how to delete program files. The idea is to get rid of all Registry references to the deleted program. You do this by using the Registry Editor to search through the Registry.

Editing the Registry is, by nature, pretty technical. You've no way around it, though. If you're going to remove a program manually (that is, by brute force) from Windows, you must go through the Registry and remove the program there, as well. This section talks about how to search for and edit information in the Registry, but detailed information about cleaning the Registry is in Chapter 20. (Also pay attention to the safety tips about working with the Registry, in Chapters 2 and 20.)

Manually cleaning the Registry in this way is a perilous adventure, but one you can easily complete if you're very careful. Make sure you delete only those programs that you're sure should be deleted and (as stated elsewhere in this book) make sure you have a backup of the Registry in case a problem crops up.

Grab the list of programs that you created in the preceding section and follow the steps given here after making a backup of the Registry:

1. **Choose All Programs⇨Accessories⇨Run from the Start menu.**

   Windows displays the Run dialog box.

2. **Enter** regedit **in the Open field and click OK.**

   The Registry Editor starts, opening a window like what's shown in Figure 5-5.

Figure 5-5:
The Registry Editor is a power tool in Windows.

3. **In the left window, collapse the Registry tree by clicking any of the arrows beside the subfolder.**

   The tree may already be collapsed, in which case you're done with this step. When collapsed, the tree should look like what's shown in Figure 5-5.

4. **Select Computer at the left side of the screen and press Ctrl+F.**

   The Find dialog box is displayed, as shown in Figure 5-6.

Figure 5-6:
Using the
Find dialog
box, specify
exactly for
what (and
where) you
want to
search.

Find

Find what:

Find Next

Cancel

Look at

☑ Keys
☑ Values
☑ Data

☐ Match whole string only

5. **In the Find What field, enter the program name you want to search for.**

   Enter the program name from the list you compiled in the preceding sec-tion. Enter the program name, along with any filename extension, such as .exe, .dll, or the like. Don't enter the full path name for the pro-gram. You should also leave the Keys, Values, and Data checkboxes selected in the Find dialog box.

6. **Click Find Next.**

   If the Registry Editor finds a match, it expands the tree in the left window to show where it found the match. It displays the matching data in the right window.

7. **Delete the information the Registry Editor located, if appropriate.**

   Before deleting, examine the information, as well as other information in the key where the match was found. You can delete the item by pressing the Delete key.

8. **Press F3 to find the next occurrence of the program name.**

   If the Registry Editor finds a match, it expands the tree in the left window and displays the matching data in the right window.

9. **Repeat Steps 7 and 8 until you find no more program references to delete.**

10. **Repeat Steps 3 through 9 for each program that you listed in the preceding section.**

11. **Close the Registry Editor.**

Congratulations! You deserve a break. Take a deep breath and get another cup of coffee before proceeding to the following section, where I describe the final part of brute-force removal. (Relax, it's the easy part.)

Sweeping away loose ends

A good cleaning job is never done. Work, work, work — it never ends! In order to finish up, you have a couple of other things to "sweep up." Specifically, you need to delete any shortcuts — desktop or menu — that point to the programs you just deleted:

- **To delete a desktop shortcut:** Click the shortcut once (to highlight it) and press Delete. Alternatively, right-click the shortcut and choose Delete or simply drag it to the Recycle Bin.

- **To delete a menu item:** Right-click the menu item and choose Delete.

Deleting a shortcut from the desktop, or removing an option from a menu, does *not* delete the whole program. You've only removed a way of accessing the program, not the program itself.

Eliminating Remnants of Failed Programs

A *failed program* is my name for a program that never did get quite installed correctly or working correctly. Perhaps the failed program is one where you got halfway through the download and the dog yanked your Internet connection from the wall. Or it could be one where you got most of the way through the installation program and it unexpectedly exited. The reasons for failure could be myriad, and all such failures lead to a cluttered system.

If you want to reinstall your failed program, you should have no problem — just start the install process again. (Some install programs are even smart enough to figure out that you completed a partial installation before.)

If you decide that you want to get rid of the failed program, put on your detective's cap and start looking around for what the program added to your system. You can find what the program added in a couple of ways: Either look for a log file or, if you can't find the log, manually search for files.

Many installation programs create log files that tell what was done during the installation process. If you can find the log file, you can read it to discover what was done and then manually undo what was done. (Log files can typically be opened with Notepad or some other text editor.)

Installation log files can be in any number of places. If you downloaded a pro-gram to your hard drive prior to installation, the log file could be in the same folder where you placed the downloaded file. If the installation program already created a folder for the program, the log file could also be there. Or, the log file could be in a temporary folder that the install program used. Check the various `Temp` folders on your hard drive to see if anything is there.

If you can't locate the log file, do a search for the files by following these steps:

1. **Click the Start menu button.**

   The Start menu appears. (What did you think would happen?)

2. **In the search box at the bottom of the Start menu, enter *.*.**

   The asterisk-dot-asterisk notation dates back to the early days of DOS. It's geek shorthand for "find all files."

3. **Click See All Results.**

   Windows displays the Search Results in Indexed Locations dialog box, as shown in Figure 5-7.

Figure 5-7: Use the Search Index dialog box to find files and folders.

4. **Click the down-arrow next to the Advanced Search link, at the right side of the dialog box.**

   Windows displays the advanced filters near the top of the dialog box.

5. **Click the Location drop-down list and choose Local Hard Drives.**

   You want to search more than just what Windows has indexed. You'll also want to click the Include Non-Indexed, Hidden, and System Files check box.

6. **Click the Date drop-down list and choose Date Modified.**

7. **Click the Any drop-down list (just to the right of the Date Modified drop-down list) and choose Is.**

8. **Click the date drop-down list (just to the right of the Is drop-down list) and select today's date.**

   This step assumes that you tried to install the failed program today. If not, wrack your brain to figure out when the failed installation took place and enter that date. You pick the date from the calendar that appears when you click the date drop-down list.

9. **Click the Search button.**

   The button is at the very right side of the advanced filters area.

Windows goes to work, feverishly trying to locate any files that were modified whatever day you specified in Step 8. When the search is completed, take a look at what it located. The results may lead you to the pieces of the failed program that were installed.

After you find the pieces, figure out whether it's okay to delete those pieces. If in doubt, rename or move the pieces to a different folder and restart Windows. If you experience no repercussions from making the change, you can easily delete the files for good.

Chapter 6

Data, Data Everywhere

In This Chapter

▶ Giving temporary files the boot

▶ Hunting for orphan data

▶ Using the Disk Cleanup tool

▶ Doing away with duplicate data

▶ Dealing with multimedia files

▶ Discarding Recycle Bin contents

*W*hen I was a kid, we lived in the last house on a dead-end street. There was a chain-link fence at the end of the street, and just past the fence was a huge three-story house. All the kids in the neighborhood knew there was a little old hermit lady who lived in the house, along with her cats.

When the lady died, her grown kids came by and started cleaning out the house. I remember watching as they placed a huge refuse container in the yard — the big type that had to be brought in with a semi. I can still envision people standing at the second-story windows, shoveling years of collected debris out the windows and into the refuse container. Magazines, newspapers, cat food cans, and who-knows-what, all shoveled out for days on end.

Those childhood years are gone, but I firmly believe that I have a little old hermit lady living in my computer. She, along with her dozens of cats, collects things and clutters up my hard drive with heaven knows what. My little old lady is a packrat, keeping things for years and years.

Truth be told, you probably have a little old hermit lady living in your computer, as well. How does all that data get on your system? Some say it breeds, on its own, during quiet times on the computer. That's doubtful, although it may seem that way.

Instead, data files collect all on their own. How many programs are on your program inventory? (See Chapter 3.) Each of those programs has its attendant data files, and each of those programs creates additional data files. In addition, you probably download data files and you might have co-workers who send you data files to review or use.

Over time, the collected mass of data can be staggering. It's probably time to open the second-story windows, back up the dumpster, and start shoveling things out. The purpose of this chapter is to help you identify data, determine whether you need it, and then get rid of what you no longer need. Chapter 7 helps you organize and manage the data that's left after your winnowing process.

Finding Temporary Files

Have I told you that programs create data? In case I haven't, let me tell you — programs create data. Even when you don't think they're creating data, they often are. Large application software is the biggest culprit in file creation. Not only does the software create a document, a workbook, a spreadsheet, or a graphic, it also often creates temporary files.

Temporary files are intended to be just that — temporary. They're intended by their creators to store data for a short time and then be deleted. Sometimes, they overstay their welcome, however. They become permanent residents of a hard drive, sitting quietly, not bothering anyone, and occupying space. Sometimes, a lot of space.

Temporary files collect on your system when the program that created them never gets around to deleting them. Perhaps the program was ended abnormally, before it could delete the files. Perhaps the program has a glitch that precluded the deletion. Who knows? The only thing you can be sure of is that the unneeded temporary files are cluttering up your system.

Hard drives, they are a-growin'

Hard drives continue to get bigger and bigger. My first hard drive (for my original IBM PC computer) was a 10MB drive. It was the size of a large shoebox and sat on the desk next to the computer. I thought I was in heaven.

Last week, I stopped by my local computer store and went browsing through the hard drive section. The smallest drive they had was 80GB (8,000 times larger than my first hard drive), and 300GB drives were common. I even found a couple of drives that could hold a terabyte of data. (A *terabyte!* Wow!) Our hard drives continue to collect more data than I could ever have imagined when I was bursting with joy at my original 10MB hard drive. Left unchecked, it's easy to sink like a stone in a sea of data. But getting a bigger hard drive isn't the whole solution to dealing with this sea of data. First, you should consider ridding your hard drive — no matter how big it is — of any data you just don't need anymore. That's what this chapter is for. Head to Chapter 17 if you determine that you really do need a bigger hard drive.

The best approach is to track down temporary files and make sure they're under control. You should search for both folders and specific types of temporary files. After you find the files, you can determine whether you want to delete them.

Locating and deleting files from temporary folders

Temporary files cluster together in temporary folders. The folders are temporary; they're used just as repositories for temporary files by individual programs or by the operating system itself. If you locate the temporary folders on your system, you can find a bunch of temporary files for possible deletion.

To locate the most likely candidates for temporary folders and then to delete their contents, follow these steps:

1. **Click the Start menu button.**

   The Start menu appears.

2. **In the search box, at the bottom of the Start menu, enter** temp.

   Folders using the letters temp in them are the most common repositories of temporary files. You may discover other likely candidates for folder names, depending on the software installed on your system. Don't be afraid to try searching for other folder names, as well (such as those containing the letters tmp).

   As you type temp, the menu is replaced with some search results. Pay no heed yet; these are nothing but preliminary results.

3. **Click See All Results.**

   Windows displays the Search Results in Indexed Locations dialog box. This is the place where you want to do your real searching.

4. **Click the down-arrow next to Advanced Search, at the right side of the dialog box.**

   Windows expands the top portion of the dialog box, giving you a lot more choices on how you can do your search.

5. **Using the Location drop-down list, choose Local Hard Drives.**

   This action tells Windows you want to search all of the hard drives installed in your system.

6. **Choose the Include Non-Indexed, Hidden, and System Files check box.**

   Why limit yourself to Windows' index? You want to search through everything.

After a short time, you should see a number of different folder and file names start popping up in the search results. (Windows should display these results automatically. If it doesn't for some reason, click the Search button.) You could have only a few results, or you could have many. I had 124 matches on my main system. That's quite a few potential temporary file folders.

Some of the matches aren't applicable because you may get folder names such as `Templates` or `systemprofile`. (Both contain the letters *temp*.) Other matches are clearly designed to hold temporary files, with names such as `InstallTemp`, `WUTemp`, or `Temporary Internet Files`. The bottom line is that each of these folders may contain old files that you can get rid of.

After you've figured out potential candidates for get-riddable temporary files, you should open each folder, examine its contents, and decide whether you need to keep the files.

If you decide to delete them, delete only the files inside the folder, not the folder itself. Instead, rename the folder, such as `keeptemp` or `keepInstallTemp`. Then, when you later restart Windows and use it for a while, you can see whether your system generates any errors. If not, you know you can fully delete the folder.

If you don't like all the extraneous information that shows up in the Search Results dialog box, try doing your search from the command line. Open a command line window (Start⇨All Programs⇨Accessories⇨Command Prompt) and issue the following two commands, each on its own line:

```
cd\
dir temp.* /ad /s /b
```

The result is a short list of all the directories named `Temp` on the current drive.

Finding and eliminating specific files

The first step in looking for temporary files is to quit all of the programs you're running. Get out of them all; no exceptions! You never know whether those programs are creating temporary files. If so, you won't be able to delete the files. If you exit the programs, they should get rid of the temporary files with which they were working. The result is fewer "false positives" when doing your search.

Also, make sure that no network users are using anything on your system. If files on your system are accessible through the network, those files' users could be creating some of your temporary files. For instance, if a Word document is on your system and someone opens it from a remote system, their Word program creates a number of temporary files on your system while working with the document.

The key to locating temporary files is to recognize that they often have characteristics in common. Use the Windows Search feature to locate the different files on your system that have these characteristics:

- ✔ **.tmp extension:** By far, the most common indicator of a temporary file is one that ends in the .tmp extension. If you see a file called MyDoc.tmp, you're pretty well assured that's a temporary file, ripe for deletion.

- ✔ **Tilde (~) as first character:** Not content with conforming to the .tmp extension standard, some programs create temporary files that begin with a tilde. For instance, you may see a file named ~DF3E05.tmp or ~$Report.doc.

- ✔ **Zero file length:** Sometimes, a program may create temporary files and put nothing in them. Because these files have no characters, they have no size. They do nothing but take up space in the folder; feel free to delete them.

- ✔ **.bak extension:** Technically, these files aren't temporary. Instead, they're backup files, often created by software. If the file is old, chances are good that the file is no longer needed and you can safely delete.

- ✔ **.old extension:** When programs update some files, they rename the original file with the .old extension. If you see files such as setup.old or channel.old, delete them.

After you search for and find files with these characteristics, feel free to delete the files — after determining that it's safe to do so — to free up space on your drive.

Tracking Down Orphan Data

When someone mentions orphans, do you have visions of Annie pop into your head, or perhaps Oliver Twist? Orphan data is not nearly as musical or literary. Instead, *orphan data* is information stranded on your computer when the program that created it was deleted from your system.

In Chapter 5, you can find out how to rid your system of old programs. Perhaps some of those programs left data on your system — data you no longer need. That data is what you need to track down and remove.

You can track down orphan data by using a number of techniques. These techniques aren't magical, but they do take time and require that you put on your detective's hat and do a bit of digging:

✔ **Look for folders.** Some programs create their own folders for storing data. When you remove programs, the data folders are often left behind, chock full of files. Use Windows Explorer to snoop through your hard drive's folders, with an eye toward locating possible folders you no longer need.

✔ **Look for extensions.** Different programs work with different types of files. These file types are most often identified by the filename extension used for the file. If a program you removed used files with the .xyz extension, you can easily search for such files. If the program used a more common filename extension (such as .doc, .jpg, .txt, and so on), you need to not only locate the files, but also determine whether other programs on your system need them.

✔ **Use the process of elimination.** Account for what you need. Whatever's left is a candidate for removal. Get a printout of the filenames for the data on your drive. Look through the filenames and cross off those with which you're familiar. By process of elimination, you can target files.

If you have orphan data and think you may someday need it again, copy it to a long-term storage medium, such as a CD-ROM or a Zip disk. That way, you can get it off your system but still access it. Chapter 7 provides guidance for how to archive data you no longer need.

Doing a Disk Cleanup

Windows includes a tool that has the express task of helping you clean your hard drive. Bearing the moniker Disk Cleanup tool, you might think that it can be helpful in taming your data.

In reality, the Disk Cleanup tool just barely scratches the surface in helping clean up your data. Don't take that as a negative statement of the program — it's not. The tool is a great place to reclaim some easily reclaimable hard-drive space. The most common areas checked by the program follow:

✔ **Temporary Windows files:** As Windows goes about its regular business, it periodically creates temporary files. If all goes well, those files are deleted when no longer needed. If (for some strange reason) they aren't, the Disk Cleanup tool identifies them as targets for deletion.

✔ **Temporary Internet files:** While browsing the Internet, a lot of temporary files are automatically downloaded to your system. Getting rid of these files can free up disk space, but it can also make accessing your favorite Web sites just a bit slower until the temporary files are again downloaded. (They should still be deleted because the temporary files include many from sites you may never visit again.)

✔ **Temporary program files:** Many programs create temporary files and place them (appropriately enough) in a system folder for temporary files. The Disk Cleanup tool targets temporary files in this folder for deletion, but only if they haven't been modified in the past week.

✔ **Downloaded program files:** This doesn't mean the latest shareware you downloaded. It refers to controls and applets that are downloaded as part of the Web pages you visit.

✔ **Recycle Bin:** Delete a file? Bam! It ends up in the Recycle Bin faster than Emeril can chop an onion. If you're the type who forgets to empty the Recycle Bin, the Disk Cleanup tool is pleased to point out your character flaw.

✔ **Setup log files:** While installing various Windows pieces and parts, the system keeps track of what it does through log files. After a time, these files can be safely deleted.

To run Disk Cleanup, follow these steps:

1. **Choose Start➪All Programs➪Accessories➪System Tools➪Disk Cleanup.**

   You see the Disk Cleanup Options dialog box (Figure 6-1), which asks you if you want to clean only your files or files from all users on the computer. Dare I say which one you should choose?

Figure 6-1:
Disk
Cleanup
asks what
you want
to clean.

2. **Click Files from All Users on This Computer.**

   If you have more than one hard drive in your system, you may be asked to specify which disk should be cleaned up. If so, pick a disk and click OK. The Disk Cleanup tool starts looking through the contents of your system, calculating how much space it can reclaim. After a time — the exact amount of time depends on how much data is on your system — you see a dialog box from which you can pick what you want to clean. See Figure 6-2.

Figure 6-2:
Choose what you want Disk Cleanup to work on.

3. **Scroll through the Files to Delete list, highlighting items to find out more about them (cursory explanations appear in the Description area) and selecting the check box of each item you want to delete.**

   Pay attention to the disk space at the right side of the dialog box (under the Files to Delete list) — it gives you a good clue as to how much of your disk drive is occupied by each item.

4. **When you're satisfied with your choices, click OK.**

5. **Disk Cleanup asks if you want to proceed; you must click Delete Files to continue.**

   When you click Delete Files, the deletions commence. Depending on what you asked Disk Cleanup to do, the actual cleanup can take a few minutes to complete.

When you tell Disk Cleanup to delete files, those files are deleted for good. They aren't moved to the Recycle Bin, as typically happens when you delete other files. Make sure you really want to delete the files that Disk Cleanup is proposing to delete.

Help! Send disk space — quick!

If your insatiable desire for data outstrips your capacity to store that data, you could run out of hard-drive space. When you start running low on disk space, Windows Vista gets nervous and warns you about the situation:

✔ When you have only about 200MB of free disk space, a message lets you know. This message appears once during each Windows session.

✔ When you have only about 80MB of free disk space, a similar message is displayed, appearing once every four hours — up to two times per Windows session.

✔ When you have only about 50MB of free disk space, a message appears every five minutes.

✔ When you have only about 10MB of free disk space, Windows automatically calls up your local computer store and orders a new hard drive. The drive is installed by elves while you're asleep.

The last item would be pretty cool, but Windows hasn't quite gotten there — yet. (Microsoft has started hiring elves in preparation for the next version of Windows.) If you see a low disk space message, start getting rid of some files! If you click the message, the Disk Cleanup tool runs automatically.

Finding and Eliminating Duplicate Data

Duplicate duplicate data data can can be be a a problem problem on on any any system system. (Is there an echo in here?) One of the problems with data is that, over time, you can end up with multiple copies of the same file on your system. It's easy to do:

✔ You copy a file, instead of moving it, from one drive to another.

✔ You create a copy with intentions of later deleting it, but forget to do so.

✔ You download a file, give it one name, and then download it later under a different name (same file; different name).

On my system (and I suspect on yours), it's particularly easy to end up with multiple copies of graphics files, audio files, and database files. Unfortunately, the tools that come with Windows don't provide an easy way to find duplicate files. You can compare graphics or audio files sizes, but this is a very tedious task.

Instead, I recommend that you turn to a third-party software program to help track down duplicate files. Finding duplicate files normally isn't a task relegated to a stand-alone program. Instead, the task is most often a feature in a larger utility application.

Anytime you start deleting a bunch of files (as is the case when you search for and remove duplicates), you should have a current backup of your system. If you mistakenly delete a file you shouldn't have deleted, you can use the backup to restore it. To minimize the chances of needing the backup, carefully examine any file you're about to delete to ensure it's something that really should be deleted.

A number of programs on the market include the capability to find and flag possible duplicate files. Some of the programs will work with Windows Vista, but not all of them will. You'll want to double-check to make sure that the program you're considering will work properly with your version of Windows.

One program that I've found and grown particularly fond of (in a purely platonic sense, of course) is CloneMaster, from SoftByte Labs, Inc. (www.softbytelabs.com). The software isn't a "do it all" package; it's specifically for identifying and removing duplicate files on your system. You can download an evaluation version that's good for 30 days, after which you'll need to pay a nominal fee to fully use the program.

To find duplicate files with CloneMaster, follow these steps:

1. **Start CloneMaster by choosing Start⇨All Programs⇨SoftByte Labs⇨ CloneMaster⇨CloneMaster.**

   The main screen appears, as shown in Figure 6-3.

Figure 6-3: CloneMaster allows you to configure what's checked on your system.

2. Specify where you want to look for duplicates.

The easiest way to check your whole system is to just expand the Computer option at the left of the program window (click the plus sign beside it) and select a check box next to one of your disk drives. If you want to be more selective in what you compare, you can drill down and select any other folder you want.

3. Click Start Scanning.

CloneMaster goes to work, looking for duplicates. Depending on the number of files, this process can take quite a while to figure out potential duplicates. If you have a cluttered drive, you may want to run the program over your lunch hour or while you're in a meeting. (Given the fact that CloneMaster does an exact, byte-by-byte comparison of files before considering them duplicates, the software is pretty darn fast.)

When the program is done searching, you see the duplicate files window, shown in Figure 6-4.

Figure 6-4:
Potential duplicate files are neatly organized in a window.

It's not unusual for CloneMaster to find hundreds, if not thousands, of potential duplicate files.

4. Click a file at the left side of the screen.

CloneMaster displays, at the right side of the screen, the duplicates of whatever file you selected at the left side of the screen.

5. If you identify a file you want to delete, select the file at the right side of the screen and press the Delete key.

CloneMaster moves the deleted file to the Recycle Bin, the same as any other deleted file.

It may take a while to go through all the duplicates, but you'll have a much cleaner system after you finish and empty the Recycle Bin. If there are too many duplicates in your list, you can always display the Scan Settings tab and again scan a different area of your system.

What to Do with Multimedia Files

As I discuss in Chapter 4, multimedia files can be huge. Because of their size, multimedia files present a special problem when it comes to storage needs.

If you're working with multimedia files, consider these ideas for handling the amount of data you're faced with:

- **Get a new hard drive.** You can easily add a new hard drive to your system. Better, you can get a huge-capacity hard drive designed for multimedia use. Place your files on that drive so they're accessible as quickly as possible.

- **Archive often.** When you're done with an audio or video file, get it off your hard drive and onto a longer-term storage medium, such as a CD-ROM or DVD. (Chapter 7 focuses on how to archive information.)

- **Be selective about what you keep.** Keep your original and final files (the ones you slaved on for weeks), but you should consider getting rid of anything in between. Different versions of the same file are prime candidates for removal.

- **Get illegal files off your system.** Audio and video file swapping still enjoys a thriving underground. Some of this content is illegal. If you have any question about the files, get them off your system completely. Some swapping software makes your multimedia files automatically available to others, which means that the attorneys for the RIAA can locate the files and press charges. Trust me — you don't want the pain of a lawsuit.

Empty the Recycle Bin Often

When you use the Disk Cleanup tool described in the section "Doing a Disk Cleanup," earlier in this chapter, the tool proposes to delete the files in your Recycle Bin. Many people forget they have data there. When you delete files and other objects from Windows, those things are normally stored in the Recycle Bin.

To see what's in your Recycle Bin and then to delete files from it, follow these steps:

1. **Double-click the Recycle Bin icon on your desktop.**

   A standard folder window opens, and you can see the last gazillion files you deleted. Remember that everything in your Recycle Bin is still occupying space on your hard drive. It's a good idea to regularly empty the Recycle Bin.

2. **Select one file and press the Delete key to delete files individually.**

   Choose File⇨Empty Recycle Bin to delete all the files in the bin. I prefer to periodically right-click the Recycle Bin icon and choose Empty Recycle Bin because it's quick and easy.

Resize the Recycle Bin

The Recycle Bin is a flexible place, willing to enlarge itself, as necessary, to accept your recently deleted files. By default, the space allocated by Windows for the Recycle Bin is up to 10 percent of your hard-drive space. If you think about it, that's a ton of space.

Say you have an 80GB drive — not uncommon in today's computing environments. That means that the Recycle Bin can possibly occupy up to 8GB of your drive. That could be a huge number of files and is probably more than you would ever need.

The Recycle Bin is constructed so that it keeps whatever ends up there until you manually delete it (or until the allocated disk space fills up). If the disk space fills up, the oldest files in the Recycle Bin are deleted to make way for the newer items. If you have 8GB (or more) set aside for the Recycle Bin, the sheer size of the allocated area means you're wasting a lot of disk space.

The solution is to change the amount of disk space allocated to the Recycle Bin by following these steps:

1. **Right-click the Recycle Bin icon and choose Properties.**

   Windows displays the Properties dialog box for the Recycle Bin.

2. **Specify a maximum Recycle Bin size in the Maximum Size control.**

   Unless you have a specific need to have a large Recycle Bin (for instance, if you routinely delete huge multimedia files and you want to make sure they fit in the bin), set the size to something relatively low, such as 500MB or 750MB.

3. **Click OK.**

How does resizing the Recycle Bin help unclutter your system? Simple: When Windows doesn't need to track as many deleted files, the operating system is more responsive.

After you empty the Recycle Bin (or delete an item from it), those files are gone for good. If you have any question about actually deleting a file from the Recycle Bin, restore the file and move it to a different place on your hard drive for a short time. If everything works out and you actually want to delete it, you can then do so.

Some third-party system software programs, such as antivirus software, may set up their own Recycle Bins, in addition to the Windows Recycle Bin. You should check the documentation that came with your software to see if that software has its own Recycle Bin. If so, make sure you periodically check that Recycle Bin and empty it, as well as the primary one.

Chapter 7

Organizing and Archiving Data

In This Chapter

▶ Figuring out an organization scheme
▶ Keeping your root directory clear
▶ Using default folders
▶ Archiving older data

*W*ith so much data on your system, you need some way to organize it. I'm not talking about organizing with files and folders; that's a no-brainer. Files and folders are the building blocks of any system. I'm referring to how you use files and folders to organize your data so you can more easily access it.

Fortunately, you can take complete control of how your data is stored on your system. This chapter presents ideas for making sure your data is stored on your hard drive in an orderly fashion. If your data is stored willy-nilly, your system needs help. (Willy-nilly is Swahili for "cluttered.") By imposing an organizational plan on your system, you reduce clutter and increase your system's efficiency.

In addition, this chapter focuses on the importance of archiving and backing up your data. Archives and backups are two important parts of any data-management scheme. If you archive regularly, your hard drive is cleaner and backups are easier. If you back up regularly, you decrease your chances of losing data due to unforeseen problems.

Organizing Your Data

Organized data — the term brings to mind visions of a small union hall, where twice a week your data meet to make sure their collective voice is heard. If they don't get what they think is fair, they go on strike, picketing for better storage conditions for data everywhere. Your applications stop working because they refuse to cross the picket lines.

Okay, I know that data can't actually organize and go on strike. But if you fail to organize your data, your hard drive *will* become cluttered, you *will* lose track of your data, and it *will* seem like your data has indeed organized against you. You create a better scenario when you organize your data (without the union hall and pickets) so that your system can run as smoothly and efficiently as possible.

Organizing your data is more art than science. You need to think through how you want your data organized, figuring out the scheme that's best for your needs. You probably don't want me coming and organizing your kitchen — not because I can't organize a kitchen, but because the kitchen would then reflect *my* personality, not yours. Likewise, I can't organize your data for you. I can, however, provide pointers and insights that help as you wade through the process. The following sections examine organizational issues you should keep in mind.

Adding and partitioning hard drives

Multiple hard drives on a system are a really good idea because having multiple drives enables you to more easily organize different types of data. Consider the drive setup shown in Figure 7-1. It shows that the system has two hard drives, C: and D:. This arrangement allows one drive (C:) for Windows and any programs you want to install on the system and the other drive (D:) for your data. The benefit of such an organization scheme is simple: With your data all on one drive, backing up is a snap. You can effectively ignore drive C: backups because you can reinstall programs from the original CD-ROMs. On a single drive, your data is easy to access, back up, and restore.

Figure 7-1:
This system has two hard drives available.

You could actually install more than one physical hard drive, or you could partition a single physical hard drive so Windows treats it like multiple hard drives.

A *partition* is a logical division of a physical hard drive. Each physical hard drive can have multiple partitions, each of which is treated as a separate drive by Windows. A hard drive is partitioned when first installed and seldom changed from then on. If you want to change the partitions on a drive that already has data on it, use a third-party utility, such as Partition Commander 10 from VCom (www.v-com.com).

I find the optimal system one that includes three drives. The first drive is for the operating system, the second for programs you install, and the third for data. Most of my systems have drives C:, D:, and E:, organized for this very purpose.

If you have only a single drive on your system, don't fret. You can still organize your data efficiently.

Creating a folder structure

In the Windows Vista world of data management, folders really should demand your attention because they are the primary organizational tool for the operating system. Ponder these points as you prepare to create a folder structure:

- ✔ **Determine how to use your folders (you have an unlimited supply) in the most effective way possible.** Some people, for instance, organize their data by project, with a separate folder for each project. Some people organize by application, with a separate folder for data created by each program they use. Still others organize by topic or date.

- ✔ **You can't create a folder structure the wrong way unless your method resembles the junk drawer in my kitchen.** If your hard drive is becoming a catchall for everything you throw there, you don't really have an organization scheme. Other than that, there isn't a right or wrong way to organize.

- ✔ **Your hard drive's organization should reflect the way you think and the way you use the computer.** If your thinking leans towards projects, then organize by project. If your thinking reflects a different model, then organize around that way of thinking.

With those points in mind, follow these steps to put your data into a logical folder structure:

1. **Determine what major divisions you want to use and make a folder for each.**

   One of my major divisions is Web Sites, indicating the Web sites that I work on and manage. Another major division is Books, and another is Newsletters. As you can tell, these are project categories, and I've named them intuitively. You can create folders for similar categories on your system, but they should reflect the work *you* do and the way *you* do that work.

2. **With major divisions in mind, create a folder in the root directory for each division: Right-click a blank space in the folder window and choose New⇨Folder.**

   For more about the root directory, see the section "Clearing Out Your Root Directory," later in this chapter.

3. **Type a new name for the folder and press Enter.**

4. **Place files in the newly created folders and subfolders within the new folders, as necessary.**

   This is an ongoing step. These additional folders should further refine the content you plan to place within those folders.

Virtual clutter

One of the latest and greatest additions to Windows Vista is the ability to create virtual folders. These types of folders are nothing more than dynamic search results formatted to look like a traditional folder. Virtual folders allow you to bring together, in one place, all the documents or files that match whatever criteria you define.

Virtual folders are pretty cool because they allow you to slice and dice your files in new and exciting ways. (And who isn't excited by new slicing and dicing?) The problem is that virtual folders, used unwisely, present a great opportunity for a virtual mess. The organizational power of virtual folders may tempt you to believe that it no longer really matters where you put files on your system. After all, you can pull them all back into one place using a new virtual folder.

Not so fast, bucko! That type of thinking is a sure recipe for disaster. Although virtual folders may make it appear that you're organized, they only mask the underlying problem. There's no technological tool (yet) that can solve clutter that's created through neglect on your part. If you want a truly organized system (rather than one that's just virtually organized), you still need to pay attention to where you put your data. Don't allow cool virtual folders to lull you into a sense of false security.

Watch your depth

Scuba divers use a critical piece of equipment known as a depth gauge. This device allows the diver to see how far she has descended below the surface. This is important because the diver's depth can affect the use of other equipment (such as air tanks) and can indicate her susceptibility to conditions such as decompression sickness. Without a properly functioning depth gauge, a diver is at a significant disadvantage and could die.

As you organize the data on your hard drive, be careful not to run into a depth problem. You place one folder in another, and before you know it, you have traversed many, many levels into your hard drive. When you look at the path that leads to a file, each level in your hierarchy is separated by a backslash:

```
C:\projects\acme\research\rr\finished\text\chap01.doc
```

Counting the root directory, the file `chap01.doc` is seven levels deep in organization. Windows can certainly handle several folder levels, but humans have more problems with them. More levels make it easier to forget where files are located and clutter your drive with misplaced and forgotten files. If you find yourself creating folders deeper than four levels, consider a different organization. Think through how you use the files and look for ways to decrease the levels without sacrificing usability.

Moving, renaming, and deleting folders

As you organize your data, you generally do some tasks over and over again:

- Create new folders
- Rename existing folders
- Delete folders or files
- Move folders or files from place to place

If you've been using Windows for a while, you probably know how to do these tasks. If you right-click a file or a folder, you can choose to do all sorts of things, including renaming and deleting.

Classic menus

Windows provides many ways to move folders and files. Depending on how you configured your folder windows, you can use a set of menus to help with common tasks. These menus aren't available by default; you need to tell Windows you want to use them.

To make the menus visible, open a folder window and choose Organize⇨ Layout⇨Menu Bar. Windows displays a short set of menus at the top of the folder window, as shown in Figure 7-2. (The menu includes the File, Edit, View, Tools, and Help options.)

Figure 7-2:
Windows can display menus at the top of any folder window.

To use the menus to accomplish common tasks, select a file that you want to do something with and then choose either the File or Edit menu. Each of these menus provides options to perform the tasks you want.

Folders list

The menus are helpful for some tasks, but they can't hold a candle to using the navigation pane for organizing your files. Indeed, you can get a better sense of your organization by using the folders list, which is shown in Figure 7-3.

Figure 7-3:
The folders list provides a great overview of your data's organization.

The folders list isn't always visible in the folder window; it's often relegated to a single line at the bottom of the navigation pane. Look at the bottom of the navigation pane, at the left of the folder window. If you see a single line that says "Folders," click the up-arrow at the right of that line. The folders list should pop into view, as shown in Figure 7-3.

If the navigation pane isn't visible in your folder window (it should be, by default), you need to enable it. Choose Organize⇨Layout⇨Navigation Pane to make it pop into view.

Using the folders list is a quick, clean way to see what's going on with your data organization. To move files and folders around on your system, display the objects to be moved in the right side of the folder window (by selecting the folders containing those objects in the folders list) and then drag the object to where you want it to be. You can drag it to a folder in the folders list, or you can drag it to another open folder window on your desktop. (See — who said organizing couldn't be fun?)

Clearing Out Your Root Directory

The other day, I was sitting in my root cellar, drinking root beer, and thinking about my root directory. (Things are often quiet — and weird — around the Wyatt household.) Why would I be thinking about my root directory? Because it's such a special and magical place. So special, in fact, that you should think about it, as well. Pull up a dusty trunk, grab yourself a mug of root beer, and let's talk.

Every disk drive has a *root directory,* the place at the top of the drive's file hierarchy. For instance, the root directory for the C: drive is C:\. All paths for other files and folders start with the root directory.

What makes the root directory special is that it's prime real estate. You can clutter up your root directory, sticking a lot of files and folders there, but doing so can really slow down your system and make it much less organized. Periodically clearing out your root directory helps prevent this slowdown and disorganization. Take a look at the files and folders stored there. If possible, move the files elsewhere or delete them. The only folders that should be in the root directory are those that represent major data divisions. Move folders of lesser importance further down in the hierarchy. (See the earlier section, "Creating a folder structure," where I discuss exactly that.)

Windows Vista supports FAT 16, FAT 32, and NTFS file systems. Of these three, FAT 16 is the oldest. If you upgraded to Windows Vista from an older Windows version, you may be using the FAT 16 file system on one of your drives without even knowing it. The root directory of a FAT 16 system can hold up to 512 files or folders. If you reach this limit, the drive shows as full, even if part of the drive is still empty. To overcome this problem, clean out your root directory and convert to the NTFS file system, which I discuss in Chapter 14.

What About the Default Folders?

When Windows Vista is installed, it creates a number of default folders with catchy names such as Contacts, Documents, Music, Pictures, and so on. These folders, by default, are created in your user account path. For instance, if your account name is Jessica Simpson, then the Documents folder is created here:

```
C:\Users\Jessica Simpson\Documents
```

When you install Microsoft applications (such as Word or Excel), they assume you want to store your files in the Documents folder. Many other applications from other publishers make the same assumption.

I suspect that Microsoft came up with these default folders after handling one too many support calls. I remember one caller who was concerned because his computer was acting sluggish. I talked him through a few things to check before deciding that I needed to see his machine. After traipsing over to his office and looking at the root directory on the C: drive, I discovered that this guy had installed everything — and I mean everything — into the root directory, which contained literally thousands of files. Cluttering up the root directory in this manner can cause problems. Microsoft's solution? "Default" folders that move the majority of the clutter out of the root directory and place it into a set of well-hidden folders.

For this reason, I'm not a big fan of the default folders. Instead of helping users organize their hard drives, the default folders merely move the clutter someplace else. The only way to permanently solve the problem is to determine how your data should be organized and implement a structure that works for you. That structure does *not* have to include the default folders.

You, being the organized person you are, don't need to use those default folders at all. My advice is to just ignore the default folders. Don't place items there; put them in the structure that *you* set up (which I show you how to do in the earlier section, "Creating a folder structure"). The default folders can remain where they are, so that Microsoft's "solution" will keep the rest of its software ignorant and happy.

After creating your own structure, you can force Windows to recognize the top of your data structure as the Documents destination. You can make this switch because the Documents option on the Start menu or desktop is nothing but a shortcut to a folder on your drive. If you change the folder that the shortcut points to, you get to decide where you store your data every time you choose Documents. For instance, suppose your data is stored on drive D:. If you want Documents to open the D: drive, follow these steps:

1. **Click Start, right-click Documents, and choose Properties.**

   Windows displays the Documents Properties dialog box. Make sure the Location tab is selected, as shown in Figure 7-4.

Figure 7-4: Windows allows you to modify the properties of the Documents shortcut.

2. **Click the Move button.**

   Windows displays the Select a Destination dialog box, shown in Figure 7-5.

3. **Select the D: drive and click OK.**

   Use the controls in the dialog box to locate and select the D: drive. (If you want to use some other folder or drive as the target, you can select it instead.)

   The D: drive (or the path to the folder or drive you selected) shows up as the target in the Documents Properties dialog box.

Figure 7-5:
You can pick
any drive or
folder as a
target for
Documents.

4. **Click OK to exit the Documents Properties dialog box.**

   Now when you choose My Documents from the Start menu, you're taken
   to the drive or folder you specify in Step 3. You've just made Windows
   match the way you want to work, instead of conforming to what you
   think Microsoft expects of you.

Archiving and Backing Up Data

Archives and backups are two essential parts of any data-management plan.
Regular archiving translates to a cleaner hard drive and can make backups
easier. Routine backups — an absolute must for people who rely on computer
data for their jobs — decrease the chance of losing data because of unforeseen
problems such as power outages or tornados. (Check out the "Backups save
lives . . . er, I mean, your data" sidebar to see what I mean about tornados.)

Archiving what you don't need

Some people simply delete files they think they won't need anymore. Other
people — in far worse shape — don't delete anything, afraid that deleting any
files will be a mistake. The result is that their hard drive fills up with old data
that does nothing for them. They also greatly increase the complexity of managing their data.

Archiving — not just for geeks

I went on a behind-the-scenes tour at the rare books archive at a major university. The archivist showing me around was very matter-of-fact about the work they do. As he showed me through vault after underground vault, I was agog and agape at the materials archived. (These weren't small vaults, either. They were probably 5,000+ square feet each, with 16-foot ceilings.) It was so cool!

I immediately went home and told my wife that I wanted to build a few archive vaults in the back yard. She, in a jaded voice honed from years of being married to a geek, said, "Whatever you want, dear."

Since that time, I've thought better of digging up the back yard. Despite that, I'm still impressed with the experience and more determined than ever to archive the materials on my computer — when they're ready for archiving. I urge you to do the same.

If you use your computer for any type of work, archive your old data. You never know when you might need your financial records from last year or your project files from last month. The answer isn't to leave the data on your system. If you archive the data, you can store it in a place that you can refer to later. Plus, you can leave all that data for posterity so they, too, can understand what a geek you are.

Archiving data simply means that you copy it to some sort of long-term storage media and delete it from your computer. (If you leave the data on your computer, the copy isn't an archive but a backup. I discuss backups in the following section.) The general way to store archives these days is on CD-ROM or DVD, although other storage media are also appropriate:

- ✔ **CD-ROM:** CDs are cheap and easy to create, with CD-ROM burners being very inexpensive. CDs are also durable and easily transportable to other systems.

- ✔ **DVD:** If you have a lot of data to archive, DVDs make sense. They're not as inexpensive as CDs (yet), but they're every bit as durable and transportable. Some confusion still exists as to which data format should be used to store information on DVDs, so do a bit of studying to see which way the winds of standardization are blowing.

- ✔ **Tape:** A lot of data has historically been stored on tape, using any number of tape and recording formats. The wide variety of options means that tape archives aren't as transportable as other media options. If you settle on one you like, make sure you keep your drivers and archive software up to date so you can always access the data.

> ✔ **Hard drive:** External hard drives that you connect to your computer through a USB or FireWire connection are the rage these days. You can use these handy devices to store all sorts of backups. But remember — it's still a mechanical hard drive and could, itself, be subject to failure at some time.

> ✔ **Zip disk:** For small archiving needs, Zip disks provide a convenient alternative. Many computer systems come with Zip drives, and storage on this media is quite reliable.

Pick the archive media that's right for you and start moving old data off your system. It's a good idea to make data archiving part of your routine system maintenance tasks, doing it either monthly or annually.

Periodically check your archive media to make sure you can still read it. This is particularly true as newer hardware and storage methods become available. New storage methods replace old ones, and older archives therefore become inaccessible as the hardware to read those archives becomes unavailable. (Ask anyone who still has very old archives stored on 5.25-inch floppy disks.)

Backing up what you still need

Humor me for a moment while I tell you what you've probably heard a thousand times before: You need to make backups. Backups are cheap insurance. They protect you from glitches and catastrophes that do happen when you're using computers. If you don't make backups, you run the risk of losing data that's difficult (if not impossible) to replace. If you thoughtfully organize your data, as I discuss in the section "Organizing Your Data," earlier in this chapter, your backup tasks should be easier than ever before. If your data is in a single place (perhaps one drive on your system) or a limited number of folders, you can easily identify what needs to be backed up and then do it.

In order to create backups, use the same media that you use to create archives. (See the preceding section.) The difference between backups and archives, of course, is that *backups* are snapshots of your data, as it exists today. If you're archiving your old data to get it off your system, making backups is a relatively quick and easy task.

As you develop your backup routine, consider the following:

> ✔ **Choose your backup medium: CD-ROM, DVD, tape, hard drive, or Zip disk.** If you decide to use CDs for your backup media, you can use a CD-RW drive. With this type of drive, you can both write data to and erase data from the CD. This makes it quite useful for backup purposes.

✔ **Decide how often to make backups.** This is, essentially, a business deci-sion. (Even if you don't consider your computer a business computer, the decision is still a business decision.) Remember that backups are insurance against catastrophe. If you want your "insurance" to protect you so that you have to merely re-enter a week's worth of data, then you should make your backups weekly. If you want to lose only a day's worth of data, then you need to make them daily.

✔ **Get enough media so that you can "cycle through" your backup disks.** For instance, if you decide to use Zip disks and want to make backups daily, get a week's worth of disks. That way, you have backups for each day of the week. If you run into a problem with today's backup, you'll always have yesterday's backup. (Redundancy is a good thing, at times.)

✔ **Consider any number of specialized software programs for backing up your data.** If you like one of them, use one of them — but note there's nothing magical about such software. In fact, you don't need to use a spe-cial program to make backups. If your backup media is large enough, you can simply copy files to the medium. The important thing isn't *how* you make the backup; the important thing is that you *do* make the backup.

Storing backups and archives

You need to be concerned with only two words when it comes to storage: off site. You need to get your backups out of your office or home and stored somewhere else. The reason is quite simple: The catastrophe that befalls your computer could be related to physical damage. If your backups or archives are off site, you won't lose them in the damage.

Backups save lives . . . er, I mean, your data

A company I worked for about 20 years ago was large, and my department was in the corner of the top floor of our building. One morning, we came to work to find that a tornado had caught our corner of the building and peeled the roof back. Nobody was hurt, but the damage to our department was extensive. With the roof peeled back, the rain poured in. All the acoustical tile was soaked, and it dropped from the ceiling onto the desks. (Did you know that if you get acoustical tile wet enough, it resembles wet, gritty toilet paper? Very messy.) The computers were ruined, as was our work.

Fortunately, our department had a policy of daily backups. Employees were responsible for back-ing up their own PCs, and each employee would take the backup home at night. We were down for a couple of days while the building was fixed, but we were able to get right back to work as soon as we had access to working computers.

You can put your backups and archives in many good off-site storage places. Some people place them in their safety deposit box. Others just put the backups in their car. Still others take them to a neighbor's house. The idea is to just get them elsewhere.

Part of the location decision depends on your data's sensitivity. If you work with sensitive data, store your backups and archives in an off-site location that's secure. For sensitive data, a bank safety deposit box may be the best solution.

Part III
E-Mail and the Internet

By Rich Tennant

" Ms. Gretsky, tell the employees they can have internet games on their computers again."

In this part . . .

In addition to helping you manage information you might receive when using the Internet, this part zeroes in on dealing with spam, organizing your e-mail, and identifying virus and spyware infections.

Chapter 8

Tackling E-Mail Overload

In This Chapter

▶ Establishing different e-mail accounts

▶ Hiding from spam

▶ Limiting spam

▶ Understanding a challenge/response system

Ahhh! Modern conveniences — what did we ever do without them? Can you imagine life without a copy machine? How about life without telephones, computers, or air conditioning? How about without electricity, running water, or indoor plumbing? (Don't laugh — when I was a kid about 35 years ago, I remember visiting relatives in Tennessee who had no running water and no indoor plumbing. It made for interesting visits for this city boy.)

We take many modern conveniences for granted; we just figure they've always been there and always will be. In another few years, e-mail will fall into that category. Even today, it's hard to believe how much e-mail has changed the tempo and tenor of business life (and personal life, as well).

E-mail is the convenience we love to hate. We complain when it's slow, we complain when it flakes out, and we complain when we get too much. This is a sure sign that e-mail tends to be a focus of much of our daily routine. Because of that focus, it often contributes to the clutter and the general disarray in which you find your computer systems. E-mail pours in, sometimes messing up your filing system or even bringing your operating system to its knees.

This chapter focuses on ways you can tackle the huge influx of e-mail (including spam) that you undoubtedly receive every day. If you're one of those fortunate few who only get a dozen (or fewer) e-mails a day, you probably don't need to read this chapter — your management issues are so light that there's little chance e-mail is cluttering your system. If you're like me, however, you need all the help you can get dealing with the hundreds of messages you receive each day. If you're in this camp, read on! You're bound to find something to help in your quest to become clutter free.

Using Different Accounts to Manage and Reduce E-Mail

E-mail accounts are a dime a dozen these days — or cheaper! You're not limited to a single account, as you probably used to be. You can set up accounts with your ISP, your company, your business associates, your relatives (if they run their own mail server), and the eternally springing free-account companies.

Even with all the flexibility, you may wonder whether you really need all these accounts. The answer is a resounding maybe: Maybe you should set up multiple accounts — if having multiple accounts will help you manage the load better. The following sections examine some of the issues involved in making the decision.

Managing incoming mail

I work from my home office. (The surroundings are comfortable, but the commute is a killer.) Rather than have my business mail sent to my home, I have a post office box. This allows me to segregate my incoming mail: business goes to one place and personal goes to another.

I encourage you to consider getting different e-mail addresses for the same reason. By using different accounts, you can use one for business purposes and another for personal purposes. You don't have to stop there: You can get as many e-mail addresses for as many purposes as you want. Your e-mail client can then be set up to check all your accounts and deliver your mail to appropriate folders in your client.

For instance, you could have separate accounts for general business mail, incoming orders, family correspondence, mailing lists, and e-mail publications. If you provide support for other people, you can set up accounts for your various support tasks. The management benefits are obvious:

- ✔ You can tailor your addresses to the purpose of the account, such as orders@widgeco.com.

- ✔ You can delegate order processing to someone else and set up that person to access the orders account. (You don't even have to let people know not to send their orders to your general business account. The public senses no interruption in service because they continue to use the same address.)

Although multiple accounts make it great to divvy your incoming mail by purpose, they can also increase your spam load. Each account can receive its own full measure of spam, and obvious business addresses, such as orders@widgeco.com, are easy for spammers to target. Make sure you think through the consequences of adding e-mail accounts before doing so.

Reducing unwanted mail

If you creatively use multiple e-mail accounts, you can actually decrease unwanted mail drastically. As you can find out in the section "Why You Get Spam," later in this chapter, any e-mail account is vulnerable to receiving spam. With multiple accounts, you can turn the table on the spammers — at least for a while.

Consider a scenario where you have three e-mail accounts: primary, secondary, and disposable. Here's how you use these accounts:

- ✔ **Use a *primary account* that you publicize to your friends and business acquaintances.** Because you publicize it, this account is the one where you fight most of your spam-related battles.

- ✔ **Set up a *secondary account* to use only when your primary account is unavailable.** Don't publicize this one. Give it out only if someone needs to send you something and your primary account is disabled or unreachable for some reason.

- ✔ **Create a *disposable account* for online commerce or for participating in public forums or mailing lists.** It doesn't matter if you start getting spam on this account because you can always close it and get another.

Primary accounts are typically business related, but they can be personal. You get them through your office, your ISP, or your Web hosting company. Your secondary account should be one you get through a different ISP. For instance, if your primary account is through your office, your secondary account could be through your ISP. The idea is for the account to be on a different network than the primary account. That way, if the primary goes down, chances are good that the secondary is still available.

A good place to get disposable accounts is through the free e-mail account services on the Web, such as Hotmail, GMail, or Yahoo! You can set up a free account quickly and disconnect it just as quickly.

When you decide to no longer use a disposable account, go through the process of shutting it down. If you just abandon the account, spam continues to accumulate in the inbox, which means that the ISP needs to store the messages on its hard drives. For your one account, that may not be much of a problem. Multiply it by 100,000 or so abandoned accounts, and storage needs become large. Help conserve resources by shutting down rather than abandoning the account.

Psychology 101: Don't Answer That Phone . . . er, E-Mail

I love the commercial that a well-known pizza company used to broadcast a few years ago. The scene opens with a bunch of guys sitting in a living room. One guy says "Watch this," and then rings a little bell. A dog, in the other room, jumps up and runs in to answer the bell. The guy makes a comment about the stupid dog. Then, the doorbell rings, and all five guys run to answer the door. The parallel with the dog's behavior is purposely pointed out.

Pavlovian responses are elicited by many things in life: Provide the right stimulus, and people behave in a predictable way. If the doorbell rings, we hurry to open the door. If the telephone rings, we drop everything to answer it. If new e-mail is announced, we drop everything to read and respond.

If you want to be more productive with your computer, break this conditioned response. With full-time high-speed access to the Internet, users routinely leave their e-mail clients running all the time, automatically checking at regular intervals. When the mail arrives, they look it over to see if something needs their immediate attention.

I'll bet you'd be upset if someone kept calling you on the phone every 10 minutes, trying to sell you something or get your opinion or tell you a joke. At the end of the day, you'd complain that you were frustrated and got nothing done because of all the interruptions. Yet, users allow the same thing to happen with their e-mail. Every 30 minutes, 15 minutes, 10 minutes, or 3 minutes, they check for new e-mail. Every check is an interruption, as surely as if someone had knocked on the door or called on the phone. Focus is lost, attention is demanded, and productivity goes down.

If you want to reclaim your workday, turn off your e-mail client and keep it off until you're ready to focus on addressing your e-mail. If you schedule your e-mail activities, you give yourself larger blocks of time for other work, where you won't be interrupted.

If you prefer not to turn off your e-mail client, at least configure it so that it doesn't automatically check for e-mail or it checks for e-mail only every hour or so. How you configure automatic checking depends on the e-mail client. To make the change in Outlook 2003, follow these steps:

1. **Choose Tools⇨Options.**

   Outlook displays the Options dialog box.

2. **On the Mail Setup tab, click the Send/Receive button.**

   Outlook displays the Send/Receive Groups dialog box, shown in Figure 8-1.

Figure 8-1:
The Send/ Receive Groups dialog box is where you configure automatic mail checking.

3. **Make sure the Schedule an Automatic Send/Receive Every *N* Minutes check box is selected.**

4. **Specify a time length in the Minutes control.**

   Set the Minutes control to something like 60 minutes or more. If you prefer, clear the Schedule an Automatic Send/Receive Every *N* Minutes check box. Mail is then checked only when you click the Send/Receive button in Outlook.

5. **Close all the dialog boxes.**

You can use the controls in the Send/Receive Groups dialog box to configure Outlook to check different e-mail accounts at different intervals. For instance, you might have it check your personal account every three hours but check your orders account hourly. Just use the New button to create a new group, assign accounts to that group, and then configure how often that group's e-mail accounts should be checked.

Why You Get Spam

Everyone knows what *spam* is — unsolicited e-mail that usually tries to sell you something. If you purchased something from Amazon.com and Amazon sends you an advertisement, the message is probably not spam (unless you've opted out of receiving such e-mails — I further discuss opting out in the section "Purchasing addresses," later in this chapter). If you get an advertisement from someone you've never heard of, that message probably is spam.

I've had the same e-mail address since January 1997. I get more than 700 spam messages per day on that account. I'm not alone. Many people get hundreds of unsolicited e-mail messages every day. Dealing with the literal deluge of spam can be a challenge for any computer user.

Spam gets sent to an e-mail address for any number of reasons. The simplest reason is because a spammer has your e-mail address. (That seems sort of obvious, doesn't it?) You may wonder how that spammer ever got your e-mail address in the first place. They get addresses in three main ways: harvesting, guessing, and purchasing.

Harvesting addresses

Harvesting is done automatically by software. Computer programs used by spammers look through Web pages with the express purpose of garnering e-mail addresses. If an address is found, the program "harvests" the address by adding it to a database. This database then sends messages to that address.

Spammers harvest e-mail addresses not only from Web pages but also from other public sources. Your address could be used in a message forum, on a newsgroup, or on a friend's Web site. If you doubt your e-mail address can be harvested, just do a Google search for it. Put your address in quotation marks and search for it at www.google.com. When I did that with my e-mail address, Google returned dozens of matches for awyatt@dcomp.com. Take a look at Figure 8-2. If Google is able to find and index your e-mail address, spammers are able to do it, as well.

Figure 8-2:
Searching
for your
address on
Google is a
good way to
determine
your
harvesting
vulnerability.

You may also instigate another method of harvesting. If you send a funny story, via e-mail, to 20 friends and put all their addresses in the To: or Cc: message lines, some of those friends may forward the story to a bunch of their friends. The addresses that you sent the message to now show up in the body of the forwarded message. The message continues to be forwarded, and after about five forwards, there could be a hundred or so e-mail addresses in the forwarded e-mail. These addresses are very easy to harvest. You may trust your friend to not send you unsolicited e-mail, but do you trust your friend's friend's friend's friend's friend? (Probably not.)

Guessing addresses

Some spam-sending software is very good at guessing correct e-mail addresses. Sometimes called a *dictionary attack,* the guessing works like this:

1. A spammer creates a list of words that serve as a dictionary. The dictionary may contain common words, such as *webmaster, info, sales, retail, customerservice, manager, admin, help,* and so on.

2. The spammer's software then connects with your mail server and uses the words as potential e-mail accounts. When the software connects to the Widgeco.com mail server, it tries these addresses: `webmaster@ widgeco.com`, `info@widgeco.com`, and so on.

3. The mail server at Widgeco.com tells the spammer's software whether the address is valid. If the address is valid, the spammer adds the address to its database of known good addresses.

Obviously, the dictionaries used by a spammer's software are much more complex and comprehensive, but you get the idea — the software tries different addresses until it finds those that are good.

Closely related to the dictionary attack is a different method of guessing addresses. If your name is John Smith and your name appears on your company's Web site, the spammer's software can try to put together probable e-mail addresses for you. Based on your name, the software could try jsmith, johnsmith, john.smith, johns, john, smith, j.smith, or any other permutation of your name. When the software tries these addresses, your mail server politely responds whether each guess is good or bad. If the guess is correct, the address ends up in a spammer's database.

Purchasing addresses

The third method that spammers use to get your address is by purchasing it. In my daily serving of spam, I routinely see advertisements offering "39 million Internet e-mail addresses on a single CD." These addresses have been collected in other ways, but if I was a spammer, I could purchase the addresses and use them for my own messages.

Call me odd, but purchasing a list of e-mail addresses through spam sent to me seems sleazy. Legitimate e-mail address purchasing exists. Many direct marketing companies sell e-mail addresses that are gathered quite legitimately.

Consider this scenario: You purchase a product from Company A, and your e-mail address is added to its database. You don't notice that Company A's privacy policy states that you may receive notices (advertisements) from it "and its affiliates." This policy means that Company A may send you messages, but also that Company A may sell your address to other companies. Those companies can then send you messages and sell your address to still other companies. Before you know it, you're on the list of "39 million Internet e-mail addresses" and receiving spam on a regular basis.

When you visit a commercial Web site, you may see a check box that allows you to "opt out" of receiving e-mail from the company or its affiliates. Unchecking the affiliate-related check box is always a good idea. You should also uncheck the primary check box, unless you really do want e-mail from the company.

Spam isn't a treat

"Have you got anything without Spam?"

"Well, there's Spam, egg, sausage, and Spam. That's not got much Spam in it."

"I don't want ANY Spam!"

Most people feel like the Graham Chapman character in the original Monty Python Spam skit: We don't want ANY spam. And still we get it. Morning, noon, and night, you get spam, undoubtedly served up by a cadre of brainless, horn-helmeted Vikings, singing the virtues of Spam as they shovel yet another helping your way.

Dealing with spam has developed into its own area. This chapter provides an introduction to some things you can do to combat the problem, but it isn't an exhaustive treatment of the topic. For more detailed information on the topic, see *Fighting Spam For Dummies,* by John R. Levine, Margaret Levine Young, and Ray Everett-Church (published by Wiley).

Tactics for Limiting Spam

In the real world of the Internet, there's nothing you can do to make sure you never get spam. Such thinking is unrealistic. If you have an e-mail address, you *will* receive spam sooner or later. However, a few guidelines can help limit the amount of spam you receive:

✔ **Use an address that isn't easily guessed.** The addresses `jsmith@ widgeco.com` or `jsmithb@widgeco.com` are much easier to guess than `josmi27th@widgeco.com`. If you place a few numbers in the middle of your e-mail address, it can't be guessed nearly as easily. (Don't place the numbers at the end or beginning; place them in the middle. Numbers at the beginning or end are too easy for spammers to guess.)

✔ **Don't give out your address.** The more places you use your e-mail address, the more likely your address will end up on someone's list. If you don't want your address to get around, be very, very selective about whom you give it to.

✔ **Don't use electronic greeting cards.** Chances are good that you've received electronic greeting cards before. Everyone seems to like them, and they're much easier to send than the paper-and-stamp variety. Unfortunately, many greeting card companies (but not all) are spammer collection points. If you enter your e-mail address (or that of a friend) into a greeting card form, it ends up in a database. That address is then often sold. Before you know it, you (and your friend) start getting spam like crazy.

✔ **Use throwaway addresses for online commerce.** In the section "Using Different Accounts to Manage and Reduce E-Mail," earlier in this chapter, you can discover how to use multiple e-mail addresses as a tactic for dealing with a flood of e-mail. Come up with a throwaway address to use for your online commerce needs for a while; never use your primary address for e-commerce. When the throwaway address starts to be overrun by spam, throw it away and get another address for that purpose.

✔ **Don't use autoresponders.** When it comes to business e-mail accounts, many people use a "gone on vacation" autoresponder for those times they're out of the office. If you send them an e-mail, you get a message back stating that Sue is on vacation and can't answer your message right now. Sue not only lets you know she's gone, but also lets spammers know they have a live, valid address. If Sue gets spam, the spammer (or an unwitting victim, if the reply-to address is forged) gets a message indicating Sue's mailbox is open for business, even if Sue is on vacation.

✔ **Don't click Remove My Name links.** This has been one of the general rules for dealing with spam for a long time. You may think that it's okay to click such links now that the highly publicized CAN SPAM legislation is in place. Wrong! There's no guarantee that the spammer feels he's subject to U.S. laws in the first place or that he's acting on the up-and-up. Only click such links for mailing lists you specifically signed up for or for companies with which you have a longstanding relationship.

✔ **Don't reply to spam.** You never know if the e-mail's return address really belongs to the spammer. (Many spam messages have forged e-mail addresses as return addresses.) If you do get through to a spammer, they often view your address as proof of a live e-mail account. If they're unscrupulous enough to send you spam, what makes you think they'll take your return response seriously?

Implementing Spam Filters

The proliferation of spam has lead to a proliferation of spam filters. An entire industry has built up around the idea of preventing unwanted e-mail from getting to your inbox. The following sections examine the types of filters available, as well as the technology those filters use.

Types of filters

Let's see . . . there's a HEPA filter, a reverse-osmosis filter, an activated charcoal filter, and an infrared spectrum filter. Yup. That should just about cover it. Implement all these filters, and you'll have cleaner air, cleaner water, cleaner charcoal, and a cleaner spectrum. (Who doesn't need a cleaner spectrum?) But you won't have a cleaner e-mail inbox.

When looking for an e-mail filter, consider the following:

- ✔ **ISP-provided spam filters:** Some ISPs provide spam filtering as part of their e-mail service. This is common practice from providers such as Google, AOL, Hotmail, MSN, Juno, and Yahoo! Typically, these providers provide filtering by default, without you needing to do anything. Their programs provide a junk mail folder, where e-mail suspected of being spam is automatically quarantined.

- ✔ **Integrated client spam filters:** More and more e-mail programs are including their own filtering methods. Some are very good, but others have a way to go. For instance, Microsoft's Outlook 2003 includes a good built-in junk filter. If you don't have the latest version of your e-mail client, you may want to check with the publisher to get it.

- ✔ **External client spam filters:** A wide range of third-party software packages filter spam. These packages generally act as an intermediary between your mail server and mail client. The program isn't a part of either, but instead weeds out suspected spam before delivering e-mail to your client.

- ✔ **Server-based filters:** Many companies — large and small — maintain their own mail servers. These companies may also implement server-based filters to try to stop both inbound and outbound spam. These filters are different than those you may use on your desktop; it filters all mail, for all mail server users.

Each type of filter has its pros and cons. You get the most control with spam solutions installed on your local computer, whether those solutions are integrated into your e-mail client or implemented through a third-party solution. On the other end of the spectrum, you have very little control over filters used by your ISP or implemented on your mail server.

No rule says you can't use more than one filter at a time. For instance, your company could have a server-based filter installed, and you could supplement that with a desktop filter. You should intelligently choose the solution right for your needs.

If you choose a filter that runs on your desktop computer, make sure you pick something that has been well-reviewed by other users. (Don't rely on the publisher's hype.) Some scum-sucking lowlifes hawk e-mail filters that are nothing but spyware. You think you got it bad with e-mail? Wait until you get a good dose of spyware on your system. (You find out more about spyware in Chapter 10.)

Types of filter technology

Regardless of where the filter is installed (on your machine, by the ISP, or on your mail server), all filters use the same general approach. Four predominant filtering technologies exist:

- **Rules-based:** The most prevalent type of anti-spam technology is *rules-based filtering*. Each incoming message is examined to see if it meets specific conditions. The rules are used to determine whether a message has a certain set of phrases, a certain quantity of keywords, or other identifiers commonly associated with spam.

    For instance, a rules-based system may be programmed to identify a message as spam if it contains a lot of uppercase words, sexually explicit words, or wording normally associated with advertisements (such as *free, discount, buy now,* or *money back*). If the rules are met, the message is either refused, deleted, or quarantined, depending on how the filter is designed.

- **Bayesian:** Another type of technology is called *Bayesian filtering*. This type relies on complex statistical analysis. You essentially "train" the filter to know what you consider spam. The more training you give it, the greater its accuracy. Well trained, these filters do an amazing job of identifying spam and have a low incidence of false positives.

- **Blacklists:** *Blacklists* identify known spam sources. Some spam filters allow you to create your own blacklist or use one created by other people or companies. Incoming e-mail is compared against the list. If there's a match, the e-mail is quarantined or deleted — you never see it.

- **Whitelists:** The opposite side of the coin is a *whitelist*. These lists identify e-mail sources that you consider legitimate. If you place a source on the whitelist, e-mail from that source is automatically passed through to you.

Unfortunately, blacklists and whitelists sometimes work against each other. This is particularly true if a blacklist is maintained by your ISP or network administrator. The list could be used by the ISP's spam filters or by those implemented on your local network. If you're also using your own spam filter, placing something on your whitelist doesn't guarantee you'll get e-mail originating from that source. Instead, the e-mail could be filtered out by those lists further up the line. Your filter never gets a chance to say the message is okay. If you get into a situation of dueling lists, contact your ISP or network administrator and let her know to whitelist the same sources you have. That way, you get the e-mail you expect with no problems.

I'm positive — it's false!

One of the problems with filtering technologies is the concept of false positives. A *false positive* happens when a message is incorrectly identified as spam. If your spam filter ever had an e-mail newsletter or sales receipt quarantined (or deleted), you've experienced a false positive.

Makers are constantly trying to improve their filters because false positives destroy confidence in the program. If you have to examine your quarantine folder to see whether it contains mail it shouldn't, you may question the filter's value. After all, examining your quarantine folder all the time isn't much different from wading through all the spam in your inbox.

Blacklists and whitelists can be based on the message sender, the sender's domain, or the sender's IP address. The most accurate lists are created via IP addresses. An *IP address* is the unique numerical Internet address of the sending server. If you identify the IP address, you can blacklist or whitelist all e-mail that originates with that server, regardless of who sends it.

Combating Spam with a Challenge/ Response System

Besides run-of-the mill filters, another spam-fighting tool is known as a *challenge/response (C/R) system*. C/R systems aren't technically filters; they're blocking systems. No analysis is done on the message to see if it meets a set of criteria. Instead, a C/R system is analogous to one huge list system. Everyone in the world is assumed to be on a blacklist, so everyone must respond to a "challenge" in order to be removed from the blacklist.

Because most spam is generated by machine and the return addresses on most spam are forged, C/R systems are very attractive. They ensure that the person sending the e-mail is real. A C/R system works like this:

1. John Doe sends you an e-mail.

2. The C/R system intercepts the e-mail.

3. The C/R system returns a message to John, asking him to visit a Web page.

4. When John gets to the Web page, he's asked to enter a password or type in something he sees onscreen.

5. John provides the requested information and clicks a Submit button.

6. The C/R system ensures the proper information was provided. If so, John's address is marked as a verified sender and his e-mail is passed on to you.

John's e-mail never makes it through if he never correctly answers the C/R system's challenge; the message is deleted after a specified period of time has elapsed.

A wide variety of C/R systems are available. Some run on your desktop, others are available as Internet resources. One popular Internet-based C/R system is Spam Arrest, which you can find at www.spamarrest.com (see Figure 8-3).

Figure 8-3:
One of the most popular challenge/ response systems is Spam Arrest.

Chapter 9

Organizing Your E-Mail

In This Chapter

▶ Organizing e-mail with folders

▶ Creating and using message rules

▶ Focusing on message attachments

▶ Archiving important messages

*Y*ou're unique. (Some would say that's a good thing.) It follows that unique people receive unique e-mail. It also follows that unique people use e-mail for unique purposes. One person uses it to conduct business, and another keeps in touch with Aunt Mildred and Uncle Buck. Still another uses e-mail to keep tabs on far-flung members of her Purple Iguana Lovers' Club.

Fortunately, e-mail is flexible, and most e-mail clients are quite adaptable when it comes to organizing all your business, personal, and extracurricular social messages. Figuring out how to use those tools can be a bit taxing — just *one more thing* to add to the repertoire (sigh) — but well worth the effort.

This chapter focuses on the ways you can use your e-mail client to help organize your e-mail load. E-mail is such a big part of most people's lives that establishing good habits and tackling remedial organizational chores can reap immediate benefits.

A wide variety of e-mail clients are available. Most clients accomplish the same basic tasks: checking your e-mail, allowing you to download it, and providing ways to manage what you receive. Different clients accomplish these tasks in different ways, however. The examples in this chapter cover how to do specific tasks using Outlook. These examples are just that — examples. If you use a different e-mail client, you can probably accomplish the same task, although you may need to search around a bit to find out exactly how. (This book's use of Outlook shouldn't be considered a rebuff of the client you use. Outlook is used in the examples for the sake of example only.)

Using Folders Effectively

In Chapter 7, you can discover how to use folders to help organize the data on your hard drive. I don't know of a single e-mail client that doesn't allow you to use folders to organize your e-mail. In fact, folders are a great boon to keeping your incoming e-mail uncluttered and under control.

Don't confuse e-mail folders with file folders on your disk drive. Conceptually, they're similar to each other only in that each allows you to organize information. Although some e-mail clients may use file folders to store your e-mail, many don't. The folders are maintained within the client as a logical structure, with no relation to file folders on the hard drive.

Instead of leaving all your e-mail in your inbox, give some thought to how you can organize it by using folders. For instance, you could have a folder for your work-related e-mail or a folder for each project you're working on. You could also create folders for family e-mail, hobbies, and other categories.

You can configure most (if not all) e-mail clients to display available folders onscreen. The folders in Outlook are part of the Navigation pane. When displayed, the pane is at the left side of the program window, as shown in Figure 9-1.

Figure 9-1:
The Navigation pane in Outlook is handy for working with folders.

The Navigation pane (or its equivalent) is helpful when working with folders. You can easily drag messages from one folder and drop them in another, or move entire folders. To create an e-mail folder, simply right-click an existing folder and choose New Folder. Name the folder and start using it to store messages.

Smart Move: Using Mail Rules

One of the most helpful things I found in Outlook is the ability to establish rules related to incoming message processing. For instance, I'm on a couple of mailing lists for right-handed computer geeks who happen to be Geminis. (Don't ask. These are very select groups, and you can't join — so there!) I get a couple dozen e-mails per day from the lists, but I don't need to review them all the time. To deal with this influx, I create a *mail rule* that causes Outlook to move all of those specialized e-mails into their own folder. The benefit is that I can then pay attention to that e-mail when I have the time and inclination, instead of dealing with it every day.

You can create similar mail rules for any number of purposes. If you can define how a particular piece of e-mail should be treated based on any number of characteristics, you can set up a rule for Outlook to process it.

Several e-mail clients allow you to create mail rules. The concepts presented in the following sections can help you understand what mail rules do, but if you use something other than Outlook, you must look at your own e-mail client to see how to define and use rules.

Creating a rule

Creating a mail rule can be quite easy. Suppose you receive e-mail through two accounts: jsmith@widgeco.com and orders@widgeco.com. You want the e-mail that comes to the orders account to automatically be moved to a folder named (appropriately enough) Orders. Follow these steps to set up the appropriate rule:

1. **Choose Tools⇨Rules and Alerts.**

   Outlook displays the Rules and Alerts dialog box, with the E-mail Rules tab selected.

2. **Click New Rule.**

   The Rules Wizard dialog box appears, as shown in Figure 9-2. From here, you can pick one of the more common types of rules (those generated by templates), or you can select the Start from a Blank Rule radio button (which gives you the most versatility).

Figure 9-2:
Use the
Rules
Wizard to
design a
rule.

3. **None of the predefined templates describe moving mail from a particular account to another folder, so select the Start from a Blank Rule radio button.**

   The dialog box changes, and the choice Check Messages When They Arrive is selected.

4. **Click Next.**

   The Rules Wizard asks you to specify what conditions make the rule applicable to the incoming mail. See Figure 9-3.

5. **Because you want to move e-mail that comes through a specified account (such as orders@widgeco.com), select the Through the Specified Account option.**

   The area at the bottom of the dialog box changes to reflect the selected condition.

6. **At the bottom of the dialog box (under Step 2: Edit the Rule Description), click Specified (the underlined word).**

   Outlook displays a dialog box that shows all the accounts you've set up in Outlook.

Figure 9-3:
Pick criteria
for incoming
e-mail.

7. **Using the drop-down list in the dialog box, choose the account that uses the appropriate address (such as orders@widgeco.com). Then click OK.**

   The word Specified (which you click in Step 6) is replaced with the account name you select in this step.

8. **Click Next.**

   The Rules Wizard asks you to specify what you want done with a message that meets your criteria. See Figure 9-4.

Figure 9-4:
Decide
what to do
with e-mail
meeting
your
criteria.

9. **You want Outlook to move messages, so select the Move a Copy to the Specified Folder option.**

   The area at the bottom of the dialog box changes to reflect the desired action.

10. **At the bottom of the dialog box (under Step 2: Edit the Rule Description), click Specified.**

    Outlook displays a dialog box that shows all the folders available.

11. **Choose a folder, as desired, and click OK.**

    The word Specified (which you select in Step 10) changes to reflect the name of the folder you select in this step.

12. **Click Next.**

    The Rules Wizard asks you to specify any exceptions to this particular rule.

13. **If you can think of any exceptions, click the check box next to the exception's description.**

    The bottom of the dialog box changes to reflect the exception you choose.

14. **If you specify an exception in Step 13, click the link at the bottom of the dialog box.**

    Outlook displays a dialog box where you can select the exception details.

15. **Pick a check box and click OK.**

    The wording in the dialog box updates to reflect the completed exception.

16. **Click Next.**

    The last step of the Rules Wizard appears, as shown in Figure 9-5.

17. **Specify a descriptive name for your rule and click Finish.**

    If desired, you can run the rule on the current folder. In most cases, you don't need to select this option; just finish out the Rules Wizard.

With your rule completed, it runs automatically every time e-mail is received. If anything comes through the orders@widgeco.com account, the rule moves the message automatically to the Orders folder.

Figure 9-5:
Wrapping
up the Rules
Wizard.

Rearranging the rules

After you get the hang of creating rules, you may get a whole passel of them.
(I think *passel* is the proper group nomenclature for rules; it certainly sounds
better than "a gaggle of rules" or "a pride of rules.") When you have your
passel defined, they show up in the list of rules when you choose
Tools➪Rules and Alerts; see Figure 9-6.

Figure 9-6:
You can
define quite
a number of
rules in
Outlook.

Notice the wording at the top of the list of rules: Rule (Applied in the Order Shown). Normally, this hierarchy isn't a problem. But say you have two rules that could apply to the same message. Perhaps you have a rule that moves orders to one folder and another that moves anything containing the word *sample* to a different folder.

What happens if a message through the orders account contains the word *sample?* Do you want it moved to the `Sample` folder or to the `Order` folder? Exactly what happens depends on the order in which your rules occur in the rules list. You need to make sure that the rules occur in the order you want them processed.

To move a rule up or down the list of rules, click the rule and use the up and down arrow buttons on the toolbar.

Sometimes, rules conflict with each other. If you have an order that deletes a message, and the subsequent order would have moved the same message to a folder, Outlook may generate an error when it processes the rules. The only solution is to think through your rules and make sure you remove any that obviously conflict with each other.

Deleting a rule

Anarchy rules! (Oops, another oxymoron.) If you decide you no longer need to follow rules, and you don't want Outlook to suffer under the tyranny of rules (even if you created them), you can delete rules.

Follows these steps to delete a rule:

1. **Display the Rules and Alerts dialog box by choosing Tools⇨Rules and Alerts.**

2. **Select the rule you want to delete.**

3. **Click the Delete button or press the Delete key.**

   The rule is removed from your system.

Deleting E-Mail Regularly

I just checked — I officially have a gazillion old e-mails in my e-mail client. (Lest you doubt my veracity, the e-mail database is currently 315MB.) The sad thing is that most of that e-mail isn't in my Deleted Items folder, but in other organizational folders I set up to help manage my e-mail over time.

I think it's time to do some housekeeping.

I suspect I'm not alone in needing to clean out e-mail. Over time, it tends to accumulate like barnacles on the hull of a ship. Individually, each barnacle doesn't slow down the ship much, but in aggregate, they can seriously degrade the performance of the vessel. Old, collected e-mail messages can similarly burden your system almost imperceptibly, decreasing response time and increasing system overhead.

The primary reason e-mails accumulate is phobias. Phobias about throwing them away. The following sections cover a few points you may want to consider concerning deleting messages.

Determine a cutoff point for e-mails

Fine wines and some actors get better with age. E-mail doesn't. Its primary purpose is immediacy. As your messages get older, they lose immediacy and their associated value. You may determine a cutoff point of 30, 60, or 90 days. When an e-mail reaches that age, just delete it. (Or archive and then delete it, as I discuss in the section "Archiving Valuable E-Mail," later in this chapter.)

Empty the deleted items folder

When you press the Delete key, you may think the message is gone and you don't need to worry about it again. You'd be wrong. On most clients, the message is simply moved to a Deleted Items folder, where it awaits a specific command to be permanently removed.

You unclutter your system and improve its responsiveness by simply emptying the deleted items folder on a regular basis. If you're using Outlook or Outlook Express, just right-click the folder and choose Empty Deleted Items Folder. (If you prefer, choose Tools⇨Empty Deleted Items Folder.)

You can also set up Outlook to automatically clear the folder for you. Follow these steps:

1. **Choose Tools⇨Options.**

   Outlook displays the Options dialog box.

2. **On the Other tab (shown in Figure 9-7), select the Empty the Deleted Items Folder Upon Exiting check box.**

Figure 9-7:
You can configure Outlook to automatically empty the Deleted Items folder for you.

When this option is selected, the Deleted Items folder is automatically emptied whenever you exit Outlook.

3. **Click OK.**

Empty the junk mail folder

Many e-mail clients (and many online e-mail systems) have a folder where suspected spam is automatically stored. If you have a high volume of spam, delete that folder's contents often. Depending on your spam filter, you may also have a quarantine folder, which I also recommend that you check and empty often.

Many e-mail clients (and spam-filtering software) can be configured to automatically empty your junk mail or quarantine folder. For instance, the junk e-mail filter in Outlook 2003 allows you to permanently delete junk e-mail as it's detected. To enable Outlook's junk e-mail filter, follow these steps:

1. **Choose Tools⇨Options.**

   Outlook displays the Options dialog box.

2. On the Preferences tab, click the Junk E-mail button.

Outlook displays the Junk E-mail Options dialog box, shown in Figure 9-8.

Figure 9-8:
Outlook can, if directed, automatically delete junk e-mail.

3. Select the Permanently Delete Suspected Junk E-mail Instead of Moving It to the Junk E-mail Folder option.

Don't you love check boxes that have paragraph-size descriptions of what they do? With this option selected, an incoming suspect message is deleted on the spot.

4. Click OK.

If you configure your client or spam filter to automatically delete suspected spam, those messages are gone. If someone calls you and says they sent you something, you have nowhere to look if it was trashed. Unless you're very confident in your filter's work, you may want to let the spam pile up in the junk folder or quarantine area until you explicitly review and delete it.

Watching Out for Attachments

E-mail messages aren't just for sending text anymore. People attach all sorts of things to their messages. Many of the messages I get every day have attachments. As I'm writing this book, I send the manuscript to my editor as an attachment. The edited manuscript comes back to me as an attachment.

Attachments make transporting information easy and convenient, but they're problematic for two reasons.

The first reason is that there are good attachments, not-so-good attachments, and downright bad attachments. Everyone gets attachments that fall in these three categories:

- ✔ **Good attachments:** Manuscripts flying back and forth through the ether fall in the good attachment category.

- ✔ **Not-so-good attachments:** Funny pictures (visual jokes) that get sent around the Internet like chaff in the wind probably are in the not-so-good attachment category.

- ✔ **Bad attachments:** The viruses, worms, and Trojan horse programs that are often sent as attachments to innocent-looking messages are definitely bad attachments and something you need to look out for.

You need to carefully review messages with attachments as you receive them so that you don't open a bad attachment. I discuss viruses, worms, and Trojan horses — and how to protect yourself from them — in Chapter 10.

The second reason attachments are problematic is that they take up a lot of space and can quickly clutter up your system. Plain text e-mail messages don't take up much space at all, but messages that include attachments are larger, require more time to transmit, and need more room to be stored. Some e-mail clients store attachments as part of the actual e-mail, in a specialized database. Other clients store the attachments in a temporary folder, waiting for you to determine what you want done with them. I recommend that you determine the fate of messages with attachments as quickly as possible. If you don't need the message (or its attachment), delete it right away.

If you send attachments, chances are good that those attachments are taking up double the space on your hard drive. When you attach a file to a message, the file is copied by the e-mail client, along with your message, to the Sent Items folder. The upshot is that you have one copy (the original) where you expect it and another copy (the attachment) in your e-mail client. Check and delete messages in your Sent Items folder on a regular basis.

Archiving Valuable E-Mail

The concept of archiving should be part of any e-mail organization campaign. Most e-mail is of no value after a short time. (Some e-mail is of no value before you even get it.) You may need to keep other e-mail, however, for historical purposes. Archiving comes in handy here.

In Chapter 7, you can find out how to archive files on your computer system. Archiving e-mail messages is very similar. The idea is to move the old-but-I-need-to-keep messages out of your primary mailbox into some other area where you can access them.

Several approaches exist for generating archives from your e-mail, ranging from using the e-mail program's own archiving capabilities to creating your own solution. I cover these approaches in the following sections.

Enabling built-in archives

Most e-mail clients include some facility for archiving your messages. Archiving capabilities are typically date based, which means you can automatically archive messages that are older than a particular date. For example, Outlook allows you to configure its AutoArchive capabilities in the following manner:

1. **Choose Tools⇨Options.**

   Outlook displays the Options dialog box.

2. **On the Other tab (refer to Figure 9-7), click the AutoArchive button.**

   Outlook displays the AutoArchive dialog box, shown in Figure 9-9.

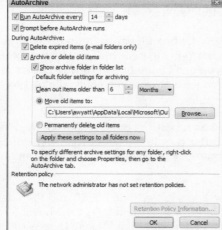

Figure 9-9:
You control what Outlook does when it archives older messages.

3. **Use the controls in the dialog box to specify how you want archiving performed by Outlook.**

   If you get an average amount of e-mail, archiving every two weeks (the default) should be sufficient. You should make sure the other settings result in moving older items to the archive folders and deleting them from your regular inbox area.

4. **Click OK twice to close all the dialog boxes.**

Outlook (and some other e-mail clients) allow you to specify archiving on a folder-by-folder basis. In Outlook, just right-click a folder and choose Properties. In the dialog box, use the AutoArchive tab to configure archiving for the specified folder.

Some online e-mail systems also include ways to archive messages. Normally, this involves simply moving your older messages out of your regular folders and placing them in some archive folder.

Some online e-mail systems limit the amount of e-mail you can archive. If you try to surpass the storage limit, the system may either delete your oldest messages or start refusing to accept new e-mail. The upshot is to not allow your archive folder to become a catch-all. Make sure you periodically clean it out.

Using the Mailbox Cleanup tool in Outlook

Outlook 2003 includes a helpful tool. Appropriately titled Mailbox Cleanup, the tool allows you to see the size of your mailbox, archive or delete old items, and get rid of your deleted items.

To start the tool, choose Tools⇨Mailbox Cleanup. Outlook displays the Mailbox Cleanup dialog box, shown in Figure 9-10. The Mailbox Cleanup tool doesn't provide any features you can't accomplish through other menu selections — all it does is put those features on a single dialog box so you can easily access them.

On the Mailbox Cleanup dialog box, I get the most help from the Find button. You can easily search for older items or items larger than a specific size. When you click Find, Outlook runs the Advanced Find feature and uses the parameters you specified.

For instance, I often search for items larger than 500KB and then delete them. In the Advanced Find dialog box — where the results are shown — simply right-click an item you no longer want and then choose Delete.

Figure 9-10:
Use the
Mailbox
Cleanup tool
to perform
routine
house-
keeping
chores.

Rolling your own archive process

One good way to create archives is to get the messages completely out of
your e-mail client and into a standard file format. Most e-mail clients allow
you to export messages to a text file. You can archive a message by exporting
it to a text file and deleting the original message. You can archive the text file
as you would any other file on your hard drive.

Some e-mail clients allow you to create macros to automate regular tasks.
Outlook is one such client. (If the thought of macros gives you the heebie-
jeebies, you may want to skip the rest of this section.) To help with my archival
needs, I wrote a macro that archives and then deletes selected messages:

```
Sub SaveStuff()
    Dim oMailItem As MailItem
    Dim iMsgCnt As Integer
    Dim J As Integer
    Dim sFileName As String
    Dim dSent As Date
    Dim sBase As String

    sBase = "f:\archives\"
    'Save and delete each of the selected e-mail messages
    iMsgCnt = Application.ActiveExplorer.Selection.Count
    For J = iMsgCnt To 1 Step -1
        Set oMailItem =
            Application.ActiveExplorer.Selection.Item(J)

        If oMailItem.Attachments.Count = 0 Then
```

```
            dSent = oMailItem.SentOn
            sFileName = sBase & Format(dSent, "yyyymmdd-
        HhNnSs") & ".txt"
            oMailItem.SaveAs sFileName, olTXT
            oMailItem.Delete
        End If
        Set oMailItem = Nothing
    Next J
End Sub
```

To use the macro, select a group of messages that you want archived and run the macro. It steps through all of those selected messages and then saves them, in text format, in the designated folder. The sBase variable designates the target folder for the archives. If the message has an attachment, the macro doesn't archive or delete the message.

Chapter 10

Banishing Internet Villains

. . . .

In This Chapter

▶ Detecting and removing viruses

▶ Understanding and eliminating spyware

▶ Dealing with pop-up advertisements

▶ Keeping your system free of potential problem programs

. . . .

As Sarah, little Timmy, and Crusty Bob hunkered down beneath their wagon, the marauding outlaws circled the camp and looked for the right moment to attack. Sarah and little Timmy cowered in fear, waiting for the attack to begin (and hoping for a rescue). Little did the outlaws suspect that Crusty Bob was well protected, holding his Acme ZX-31 rocket launcher at the ready but always out of sight.

When you fight the good fight to keep your system free from viruses, spyware, and pop-ups, you may feel like Sarah and little Timmy. With the right information and tools, you can begin to feel more crusty, just like old Bob, lying in wait for the unsuspecting bad guys.

This chapter addresses some of the bad things that can infect and affect your system by virtue of your connection to the Internet. If your system has ever been infected with a villainous virus, suspicious spyware programs, or a plethora of pop-ups, you know that not only can your system get cluttered up quickly, but it can also become downright unusable in a hurry.

Applying the information in this chapter helps you reclaim your system and productivity while maintaining your sanity.

This chapter provides some good guidance on how to begin cleaning your system of the bad stuff. Please don't consider this chapter the end-all and be-all on this topic, however. If you need to deal extensively with viruses, spyware, and pop-ups, consider reading books that focus just on those topics. *Computer Viruses For Dummies,* by Peter Gregory, and *Fighting Spam For Dummies,* by John R. Levine, Margaret Levine Young, and Ray Everett-Church (both published by Wiley) are a couple good places to start.

Uh-Oh! Do I Have a Virus?

Thousands of viruses are out in the wild. The phrase *in the wild* means that the virus isn't in a lab or on a single computer, but loose and propagating around the Internet. Each of these *viruses* is a program designed to do different things to computers. Some viruses are a nuisance, with annoying but otherwise harmless messages. Others are programmed to destroy data or attack specific computer networks across the Internet.

Just like people develop symptoms that indicate when they're sick, computers do, as well. ("Quick! Call the doctor; Junior seems to have some sort of a bug!" When my kids got sick, some sort of telltale sign always appeared. Lethargy, achy pains, fever, sweating, and nausea were sure signs that Junior was coming down with something that wouldn't be fun for a few days.) The broadest possible sign of a virus-infected computer is that the computer just doesn't behave like it used to. Perhaps it reboots all the time, or its files disappear, or strange messages pop up — all these (and more) are signs that you may have a virus.

Essentially, you have two ways of handling viruses:

- ✔ Search for and eliminate a virus after it's already on your computer by downloading and running a virus checker.
- ✔ Prevent a virus from getting onto your computer in the first place by installing antivirus software.

I explore each option in the following sections.

Finding viruses on your computer

The best way to find out whether you have a virus is to use one of the free virus checkers available on the Web. Most of these are programs that you download and install on your system, and there are many good ones available.

You can find lots of "free" virus checkers that aren't really free. Some of them are only free for a short period, and then you will need to sign up for a paid subscription service. Make sure you read the fine print to ensure that you are actually getting a free product.

As an example of a free virus checker, consider avast! 4 Home Edition, which is entirely free for Vista users:

```
http://www.avast.com/eng/avast_4_home.html
```

Download the software (available in a variety of languages) and run the install program. The software can check for viruses and protect your system against any that may come your way in the future.

Not all virus checkers catch all viruses — too many are out there to catch! For that reason, you may want to seek out some other online sites to see what they have to offer. Another good one to try is AVG from Grisoft (`www.grisoft.com/doc/40/lng/ww`). The process is generally the same: You go to the virus checker's Web site, where you may have to provide some basic information before downloading and running the checker. Easy as pie.

Blocking viruses

The best way to avoid virus infection is to catch them as they arrive at your computer. This means you should use antivirus software to protect your system. Although you can use online scanners (covered in the preceding section) to check your system, *antivirus software* provides better coverage. It hooks into your operating system and checks everything coming to and (in some cases) everything leaving your computer. Online scanning systems can't do that.

A wide variety of antivirus programs are on the market. Some of the most popular follow:

- **McAfee VirusScan Professional:** This is the home version of the same technology used in many corporate networks. You can find more information at `http://us.mcafee.com/root/package.asp?pkgid=276`.

- **Norton AntiVirus:** This product is one of the true old timers. (Is Peter Norton even still around?) You can find out more information at `www.symantec.com/home_homeoffice/products/overview.jsp?pcid=is&pvid=nav2006`.

- **eTrust Antivirus:** You can find more information about this well-designed solution from the folks at Computer Associates at `www3.ca.com/Solutions/Product.asp?ID=156`.

- **F-Secure:** An award-winning antivirus provider, this product includes solutions for home, small business, and network users. This isn't the least expensive antivirus software, but many consider it the best. Info is available at `www.f-secure.com`.

- **Panda Software:** This relative newcomer is making a splash and offers three solutions. You can find more information at `www.pandasoftware.com`.

Literally scores of other vendors are selling antivirus solutions. Before you settle on one, spend some time looking around, checking features, and reading reviews. Make sure to purchase from a reputable vendor — viruses and spyware have been known to masquerade as antivirus solutions.

After you purchase or download your selected antivirus software, follow the publisher's instructions on how to install it on your system. Most programs are fairly similar in this area — you run an installation program or insert the program's CD-ROM in your system, follow the on-screen instructions, and are protected before you know it.

Virus software is only as good as your latest signature upgrade. All virus software depends on signature files, which help the software identify a virus. If the signature files are out of date, the virus software offers no protection from the latest viruses. Most vendors provide an annual subscription service that allows you to automatically download the latest and greatest signature files so you're protected at all times.

Sizing Up Spyware

Spyware is a particularly pernicious "innovation" in malicious software. *Spyware* is a broad term that includes software that tracks what you do on your computer, information that may be delivered to someone else or to a company that collects such information (normally the spyware's developer). Spyware can use this information to display advertisements on your system (harmless but annoying) or to get unauthorized access to your computer or its data (a serious security issue).

Technically, spyware is a subset of a larger category of software called *malware,* which is a contraction of the phrase *malicious software.* Many people use spyware as a synonym of malware, as I've chosen to do in this book. Malware is often broken down into other categories, such as *adware* (software that sends you unwanted ads or pop-ups), *browser hijackers* (software that takes over your browser), *dialers* (software that reroutes your dial-up Internet account), and many other categories.

In this book, I use the term *spyware* to refer to any malicious software that doesn't include viruses, worms, or Trojan horse software.

Identifying spyware

Not all spyware displays advertisements, so it's not always evident that you have spyware on your system. Some types of spyware quietly and secretly track what you do on your computer — gathering information including your passwords, credit card number(s), personal data, and online behavior.

Obviously, spyware compromises your system's security. It can also adversely affect Windows and make your legitimate software less stable. Literally hundreds of spyware programs are identified on the market. Some are sold as commercial PC surveillance programs, system recorders, parental control software, or spouse monitors. If you see an advertisement for software that lets you know what your employees, children, or spouse are doing on the Internet, you're viewing an advertisement for spyware.

Many other spyware programs are out there; most are installed without people even knowing it. You could have spyware installed on your system if you notice any of the following symptoms:

- ✔ **Flickering screen:** If your computer screen flickers periodically without apparent reason, it could be due to spyware. Many spyware programs — particularly those used in office environments — periodically take screenshots and store them. While the screenshot's being made and stored, the screen can flicker.

- ✔ **New browser toolbars:** Some spyware installs its own toolbars in your browser. If you don't know where the toolbar came from, chances are good that it came from spyware.

- ✔ **Unexplained disk activity:** Information gathered by spyware is often stored in log files on the local computer. These files are periodically sent to a remote system. While the files are accessed, the drive activity light may remain on for extended periods. (If you don't have a lot of memory on your system, Windows could do a lot of disk access on its own.)

- ✔ **Sluggish system:** If your system starts responding slower than you remember, it could be due to spyware. Running spyware (it is, after all, a program) takes time normally spent running your other programs.

- ✔ **Low system resources:** Windows lets you know when it detects that your system resources (typically memory and disk space) are getting low. If you start seeing warnings about your system resources, it could be due to poorly written spyware consuming the resources normally allocated to other programs.

- ✔ **Inability to change home page:** If your browser's home page suddenly changes to a different page than what you chose, you could have a browser hijacker on your system. If you can't change the home page to one you want and have the change remain, you're infected.

- ✔ **Unwanted advertisements:** If you see pop-up or banner ads appear on your screen, you may have spyware installed. (Believe it or not, you shouldn't need a pop-up blocker if your system is free of all spyware.)

Don't think that a single symptom is a sure sign you have spyware on your system. Individual symptoms could be due to other causes. For instance, if your system doesn't have a lot of memory, Windows can spend quite a bit of time swapping memory to a disk file. This causes a lot of disk activity, which is one of the symptoms listed. In general, the more concurrent symptoms you have, the greater the chances you have spyware on your system.

If you suspect you have spyware, the first rule is to not panic. Don't start deleting files left and right, thinking you're solving the problem. You probably aren't, and you may be making matters worse. In the section "Eliminating spyware," a little later in this chapter, you can discover how to remove spyware.

Getting to know spyware

Even if you haven't experienced the telltale signs outlined in the preceding section, it's important to know about spyware. In this section I explore the following questions, the answers to which can help keep your computer safe from this Internet villain:

How does spyware get installed on my computer?

Is spyware a serious matter?

Where can I find reliable information about spyware?

How does spyware get installed on my computer?

Believe it or not, you typically install spyware yourself — you just don't realize it. The following list highlights places you may unwittingly pick up spyware:

- ✔ **Popular file-sharing utilities:** Kazaa and LimeWire, to name just two, often include spyware installed automatically when you install the utility.

- ✔ **Innocuous-looking software:** Spyware may be included with software that reports the day's weather forecast or that synchronizes your PC's clock. These programs entice you with something neat, but you also unknowingly install the spyware.

- ✔ **Less-than-scrupulous Web sites:** Visit the site, and your browser attempts to download and install a driver that's nothing but spyware. The browser lets you know what it's doing, and you can refuse to install the "driver." But every time you load a page at the Web site, you're asked over and over again if you want to load the driver. If you give in and say yes, spyware is installed on your system.

The legal side of spyware

In some instances, spyware is actually legal. For example, your employer can use spyware to monitor how employees use work computers. Courts have ruled that such monitoring is completely legal. You may be tempted to think that your company doesn't trust you if it utilizes spyware. Your employer, on the other hand, has a huge liability for whatever happens on the company computer systems. If the company is liable, it has a right to monitor and protect the system that carries the liability.

The bottom line is that you should be aware that spyware may be installed on your work computer and that it's perfectly legal. Check with your IT department to determine whether your company uses spyware and how you can detect and remove other spyware without damaging the monitoring software that IT has in place.

Many spyware companies claim their software is installed legitimately because they include information in the software license agreement that indicates their intent to collect and use information. Reading the license agreements of all downloaded software is very important — *before* you install it on your system.

Is spyware a serious matter?

Many people view spyware as nothing more than an annoyance. Granted, it is annoying — but there's more to the story. Imagine, for a moment, that spyware monitors your browsing, detects when you're shopping online, and then transmits your credit card information to a hacker. From there the hacker can use your credit card without your knowledge or steal your identity.

Reports are starting to emerge concerning people who have lost jobs or spent time in jail due to spyware. If you have spyware on your computer system at work and it brings up pornographic ads, you could easily lose your job — if your boss assumes you've been visiting those sites.

In May 2004, *Wired* magazine ran an online news story about Jack (not his real name) and how he spent time in jail because of spyware that loaded child pornography onto his computer. Someone saw the never-ending pop-ups on his system and reported him to the police. When they raided his home and found the pornographic images on his system — put there, according to Jack, by spyware — he was convicted as a sex offender and sentenced to jail. Jack's case may be extreme, but spyware on your system is a serious matter that you need to address as soon as possible.

Where can I find reliable information about spyware?

The number of spyware programs is increasing, as is the number of sneaky ways for spyware to get on your system. Because the battlefield is changing so rapidly, you need a reliable source of information regarding spyware.

I routinely recommend the following two sites:

- ✔ **SpywareGuide** (`www.spywareguide.com`): This site has some great educational tools, along with descriptions of all the identified spyware programs.
- ✔ **SpywareInfo** (`www.spywareinfo.com`): This site features a weekly newsletter about spyware, along with helpful forums and software.

Eliminating spyware

Spyware is notoriously hard to remove. In that respect, spyware is very similar to a virus — both can actively thwart your efforts. Spyware programs often install themselves in several places on your system and include methods for "healing" themselves. In other words, if you don't get rid of all the spyware, it reinstalls itself from the pieces and parts you missed.

You could seriously cripple your system if you start deleting files willy-nilly. Spyware often hooks itself deeply into your operating system. Deleting the wrong files could make the system unusable. My son's system became infected with spyware when he put a file-sharing program on his computer. I started deleting the spyware and then could no longer boot the computer. Ultimately, I needed to do a complete operating system reinstallation.

If you have functioning antivirus software on your system, it may detect many of the spyware programs that vex you. Some spyware programs use the same tactics Trojan horse software uses, and therefore are vulnerable to detection and removal by antivirus software. If you suspect undetected spyware on your system, a number of detection utilities are available. The best free program I have seen is Spybot Search & Destroy, available at `www.spybot.info`.

To run Spybot Search & Destroy, follow these steps:

1. **Go to** `www.spybot.info` **and download Spybot Search & Destroy.**

    The latest version as of this writing is 1.4, and it's approximately 4.9MB.

2. **Double-click the icon to install the software.**

    You may need to answer a few run-of-the-mill questions during the install. That's okay; take your time and install it fully.

3. Run the program by choosing Start⇨All Programs⇨Spybot - Search & Destroy⇨Spybot - Search and Destroy.

The main program window, shown in Figure 10-1, appears shortly. The interface for Spybot S&D is very easy to understand and use.

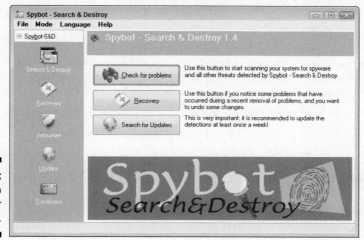

Figure 10-1: Get ready to check for spyware.

4. Click Check for Problems.

The program runs through thousands of permutations of spyware programs that could be on your system.

Don't get hijacked!

An annoying variation on spyware is the browser hijacker. This type of pest loads into your system and constantly modifies your browser so you can't change your home page. Every so often, it may even switch the page you're viewing to someplace you don't want — such as a porn site.

Some browser hijacking can be taken care of by following the steps to get rid of spyware. Other hijackers are particularly nasty and need special attention. One tool that's particularly good at removing hijackers is CWShredder. You can find more information on this tool at `www.intermute.com`. You can also find a very good tool called HijackThis at `www.spywareinfo.com/~merijn/downloads.html`.

Depending on your number of files and hard drive sizes, letting Spybot S&D run its course can take a good amount of time. On my system, it ran for almost 12 minutes. When it was finished, the program had discovered traces of spyware in a couple of places on my computer; you can see them in Figure 10-2.

5. **Select which things you want the program to correct (by choosing the check box beside each item) and click Fix Selected Problems.**

   Most problems are solved through deletion, but Spybot S&D automatically creates a Windows Vista system restore point before doing anything else. This restore point helps in case the spyware deletion causes problems; you can then use Windows to restore the system to its condition just before the restore point was set.

6. **When Spybot S&D is done, exit the program and restart your system.**

   You should notice a difference in performance right away.

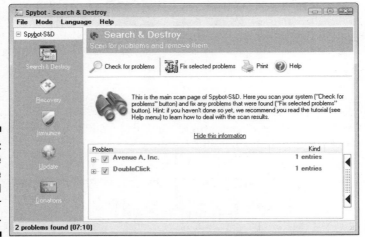

Figure 10-2:
Any trace
of spyware
is called
to your
attention.

Blocking Pop-ups

Everyone has seen *pop-up ads* — small advertising windows that appear onscreen seemingly out of nowhere. One or two popping up now and again is an annoyance; several constantly popping up cripples your system. Where do these pop-ups come from? It's been my experience that most are the result of installed adware (a type of spyware). The software delivers ads with the hope you click a link and purchase something. Trouble is, if you get five, six, or more adware programs, each delivering pop-ups, getting anything done is hard.

Google toolbar = spyware?

Some people consider Google's toolbar slick spyware, and with good cause. The Google toolbar has a tight integration not just with your system, but also with the folks back home in Googleland. With its advanced features enabled, the toolbar sends information to Google computers about every page you visit in your browser. (Google states this in its privacy policy.) The biggest difference between regular spyware and Google's toolbar is that you can uninstall the Google toolbar much easier than you can regular spyware.

In the following sections, I discuss pop-up blockers (which can eliminate most pop-up problems) and a newer type of pop-up ad that appears directly within your browser's window — the Flash pop-up ad. Knowing that many people block pop-ups, advertisers with larger budgets are turning to TV-type commercials, written in Flash.

Employing pop-up blockers

If you have a lot of pop-ups on your system, first get rid of the spyware on your system. (See the earlier section, "Eliminating spyware.") After the spyware is gone, see if your pop-ups go away. If they do, you have no problems — just keep your system clean. If they don't go away or if pop-ups at some Web sites just bug you, I recommend investigating pop-up blockers.

Pop-up blockers do just that — they block pop-ups. Recently, other products have integrated pop-up blockers. For instance, it's not unusual for Web browsers and antivirus software to include pop-up blockers. Google even includes a pop-up blocker in its popular toolbar.

If you want to use a pop-up blocker, first check to see if one is included in your Web browser. Internet Explorer 7 (the version shipped with Windows Vista) includes a pop-up blocker, and it's turned on by default. You can configure the pop-up blocker by following these steps:

1. **Start Internet Explorer and choose Tools⇨Internet Options.**

   You'll see the Internet Options dialog box fade into view.

2. **Click the Privacy tab.**

   Note the Turn on Pop-Up Blocker check box at the bottom of the tab. This is the control that turns pop-up blocking on and off; it's turned on by default.

3. **Click the Settings button.**

   The Pop-Up Blocker Settings dialog box appears, as shown in Figure 10-3.

Figure 10-3:
You can
control
which pop-
ups are
blocked by
Internet
Explorer.

4. **In the top portion of the dialog box, enter any sites for which you want pop-ups allowed.**

   Believe it or not, there are some sites where you may want pop-ups to be permissible. For instance, if your bank uses pop-ups to prompt you for security information, you don't want these pop-ups blocked.

5. **Select how you want the pop-up blocker to work by using the controls at the bottom of the dialog box.**

6. **Click Close.**

   Your settings are saved and implemented immediately. You can then close the Internet Options dialog box.

If you prefer to use a different pop-up blocker (or if you're using a different browser that doesn't include one), check your antivirus software to see if it includes a blocker. If not, others are out there. I've heard good reports about Popup Ad Filter from Meaya Software (www.meaya.com). This low-priced product is very capable of filtering out even the toughest pop-ups.

Be careful not to download and use just any pop-up blocker. Some of them are nothing more than adware disguised as pop-up blockers. Make sure your blocker is from a reputable company and that the product receives good reviews.

We always did like that boy

Every once in a while, I go visit my in-laws, who live about 700 miles away from us. One of my regular duties (as the resident computer geek in the family) is to "fix" their computer from all the ills it has garnered since my last visit. On a recent visit, my mom-in-law told me that the computer has a few advertisements that pop up and that they bother her. I told her I would take a look.

When I started the computer, everything looked normal. Within 45 seconds, though, all heck broke loose. (Things are really, really bad when heck breaks loose.) There were pop-ups appearing about every 15 to 20 seconds. Even with good hand-eye coordination, they made the system almost unusable. I was closing windows so often that I thought I discovered a new video game.

My first tack was to disconnect the computer's connection to the Internet. That did away with the ads because they couldn't download, but the computer slowed to a crawl as the system went searching for ads (through the missing Internet connection) and then timed out.

The solution was to run Spybot Search & Destroy (see "Eliminating spyware" section), which identified about a dozen spyware programs on her system. After I deleted those and restarted the system, all the pop-up ads disappeared.

Blocking Flash ads

Flash is a content-presentation system developed by Macromedia. It's pretty slick, easily allowing developers to create animations and video presentations. If you prefer to leave your commercials on the TV, you can configure your browser so your computer doesn't display any ActiveX content at all. (ActiveX is a technology that includes, among other things, Flash files.)

Several programs are designed to block Flash advertisements. In fact, some commercial pop-up blockers also stop Flash ads. If you don't use a blocker but are looking for a freeware solution for Flash ads, consider using No! Flash (www.bbshare.com), written by Barry Lee. It has received good reviews for some time now.

Resisting the Lure of Trinkets

I remember the amazement I felt when I first hopped on the Internet in early 1995. With a background in computers, publishing, and information systems, I was agog at what I saw. I was, to borrow a well-worn phrase, like a kid in a candy store. Many people have this same reaction to the World Wide Web.

They spend hours browsing around, looking at this thing or that thing, peering into far-flung places that were previously inaccessible. Like a kid in a candy store, new Internet users want to pick up and try every new thing they see, ohhing and ahhing all the while.

It's a fairly safe bet that the neighborhood candy store is a safe place. Unfortunately, the World Wide Web isn't a safe candy store. People are out there who want, for no discernable reason, to feed you things that harm your computer.

You need to resist the urge to download, install, and try out every new trinket that you find on the Internet. Some trinkets may include spyware; others may include things that damage your system.

I make it a personal rule to never download a program unless:

> (a) I know the developer to be reputable.
>
> -or-
>
> (b) The program received good reviews from others, without charges of being harmful.

If I don't know the developer, I also do one other thing — I read the vendor's privacy policy and license agreement. The privacy policy is important because it governs what the vendor does with information about me. The license agreement is important because it often gives hints regarding whether its software does things on my system that I don't want.

This last point — about the license agreement — is particularly important. License agreements may include important tidbits that indicate what you're agreeing to do if you allow a vendor's software on your system. Look for phrases that indicate the vendor's right to collect data from your system, share your information with their partners, or display advertisements. Unless you like spyware, this type of phrasing is a dead giveaway that you don't want the software installed.

Chapter 11

Managing Internet Information

In This Chapter

▶ Getting your knickers in a knot over cookies

▶ Managing newsgroups and newsgroup data

▶ Organizing Web favorites

▶ Making sense of cache files

*T*he phrase *information superhighway* is synonymous with the Internet. With every passing month, the Internet handles more and more information, speeding that information to all corners of the globe — even to your corner.

Yes, your little corner of the globe receives its fair share of Internet information. The Internet applications you use invariably clutter your computer with different files — sometimes hundreds or thousands of files. Knowing what these files are and how to manage them can be a big help toward keeping your system in top form.

In Chapters 8 through 10, I show you how to manage e-mail and keep your system safe from the harmful effects of the Internet. This chapter addresses some of the ways you can manage the information your little corner receives, without ending up cluttered.

Are Cookies a Reason for Worry?

Seasoned Web mavens often refer to *cookies* when discussing the Internet. To those less seasoned, the term *cookies* conjures up thoughts of tasty chocolate chip or (my favorite) snickerdoodles. Those mavens you're eavesdropping on aren't talking about their favorite recipes, though; they're discussing something much less flavorful and much more controversial. Many Web sites include programming code that writes small files on your computer when you visit. Before you run off screaming "How dare they do that!" it's helpful to understand what cookies do and what they don't.

First of all, cookies aren't insidious programs destined to suck the life out of your computer. In fact, *cookies* aren't programs at all — they're data. (Viruses and other life-sucking things aren't related to cookies. See Chapter 10 for more information.) Cookies store data necessary for the Web site you're visiting to customize your experience in some way.

For instance, I run a couple of e-commerce sites that use shopping carts. As people browse my sites, they can add items to their shopping carts prior to checking out. The items added to a shopping cart are actually stored in a cookie on the user's system. After the shopper pays for the items, the cookie is left behind on the user's system.

Another example is when you visit sites like Amazon.com. When you visit the site after purchasing something, you see recommendations for different products that may be of interest to you. Amazon recognized you because the last time you visited, it wrote a cookie on your system that contained information about your purchases and interests. When you visit again, that information is accessed and used to generate the new recommendations.

Cookies are, without exception, harmless. Some people consider them controversial because they think cookies are used to gather personal information. That's not entirely true — cookies don't gather information on some far-away site; they remain right on your system. In fact, if any information gathering happens at all, it's done when you first provide your personal information at a site.

Still, some people don't like the idea of cookies being on their systems. Recognizing this, Internet Explorer provides ways to delete and block cookies. In addition, you can use third-party software to more effectively manage any cookies you allow on your system. The following sections describe different ways you can slice, dice, and otherwise deal with cookies, all with the goal of de-cluttering your system.

Blocking cookies

If the idea of anyone storing anything, of any nature, on your computer drives you absolutely nuts, you may want to block cookies completely. Using Internet Explorer, you can both block and minimize the cookies stored. Follow these steps:

1. **In Internet Explorer, click Tools⇨Internet Options.**

   IE displays the Internet Options dialog box, probably with the General tab selected.

2. **On the Privacy tab (see Figure 11-1), use the slider control at the left side of the dialog box to specify the way you want to limit cookies on your system.**

Figure 11-1:
Internet
Explorer
allows you
to specify
how
cookies
should be
accepted.

IE allows you to set any of six different acceptance levels:

- **Block All Cookies:** Blocks all cookies from being written, and existing cookies can't be read.

- **High:** Allows only a tightly controlled set of cookies.

- **Medium High:** Blocks some first-party cookies and most third-party cookies.

- **Medium:** Restricts some first-party cookies and most third-party cookies. (Differs from Medium High by restricting, not outright blocking, some first-party cookies.)

- **Low:** Accepts all first-party cookies and only a tightly controlled set of third-party cookies.

- **Accept All Cookies:** The door is wide open — any and all cookies are free to jump in your jar.

If you don't mind cookies, use the Accept All Cookies setting. If you're more persnickety, choose Medium (the default) or Medium High. As you tighten the restrictions on cookies, you increase the likelihood that you might not be able to use some Web sites; some sites rely on cookies to work properly.

3. Click OK to apply your choice.

When setting your privacy level, the slider you use in Step 2 can specify a full range of settings. Most of the nuances between different settings have to do with how Internet Explorer handles first-party versus third-party cookies.

First-party cookies are those cookies that are written on your system (or read from your system) by the actual page you're visiting. A *third-party cookie* is one that's read or written by a site other than the one you're visiting — for instance, by a pop-up advertisement.

Other programs on the market can block cookies. A popular one is ZoneAlarm, a personal firewall program. One of its features is alerting you if someone tries to save a cookie on your system; you can block it so it isn't saved.

Managing your cookies

Unfortunately, Windows Vista (and Internet Explorer) don't provide much versatility when it comes to managing cookies. Sure, you can do these things:

- ✔ **List cookie files.** Browse to the folder on your system where the cookies are stored.
- ✔ **Limit what cookies are accepted.** See the preceding section.
- ✔ **Delete all the cookies on your system.** See the following section.

But these options don't really count as management except by the most liberal of definitions. Good management practice dictates that you can do cool things, such as examine individual cookies and make deletion decisions on a case-by-case basis. Any number of cookie managers is available, and most are *freeware* (available at no cost) or *shareware* (available at a low cost after a short trial period).

One tool I find particularly useful is Cookie Pal, from Kookaburra Software (www.kburra.com). The software allows you to block a variety of cookies but uses a more intuitive interface than what's provided in Internet Explorer. In addition, it works seamlessly with a wide variety of browsers, not just IE.

I typically have no beef if sites want to deposit cookies on my system; the vast majority are no problem at all. Periodically, however, I like to look through what's already there and perhaps clean up the clutter by removing cookies from sites I either don't recognize or don't plan on visiting again in the near future. Cookie Pal works great for that purpose, allowing me to see who put what on my system and delete it if desired.

Deleting all cookies

Cookies tend to collect and collect and collect over time. I checked one of my systems and it has over 600 cookies — and I had deleted all cookies on that system only about four months ago!

Saving your cookies

Cookies are nothing but files stored on your system. After you know where the goods are stored, you can display the folder they're in and back up the files, as desired.

If you plan on deleting all of your cookies, it's a good idea to back them up first. Simply open the folder in which your temporary Internet files are located; the cookies are clearly marked. You can then copy them to another directory or to

removable media — a floppy or Zip disk — before deleting. If you back them up, you can restore one of the cookies if you find that you have unanticipated problems at one of your oft-visited Web sites.

If you need help figuring out where the temporary Internet files are stored, see the section "Finding the cache," in this chapter.

Internet Explorer provides a way to delete all the cookies on your system, all at once. Before you rush to delete them, however, remember that cookies can serve a good purpose — they make using some Web sites fast and easy. If a cookie contains a site's username and password, deleting the cookie means you need to re-enter that information the next time you visit the site.

To delete all your cookies, follow these steps:

1. **In Internet Explorer, choose Tools⇨Internet Options.**

   IE displays the Internet Options dialog box.

2. **On the General tab, click Delete in the Browsing History portion of the tab.**

   IE displays the Delete Browsing History dialog box, shown in Figure 11-2.

Figure 11-2:
Getting ready to toss your cookies.

Delete Browsing History

Temporary Internet Files
Copies of webpages, images, and media that are saved for faster viewing.   [Delete files...]

Cookies
Files stored on your computer by websites to save preferences such as login information.   [Delete cookies...]

History
List of websites you have visited.   [Delete history...]

Form data
Saved information that you have typed into forms.   [Delete forms...]

Passwords
Passwords that are automatically filled in when you log on to a website you've previously visited.   [Delete passwords...]

About deleting browsing history   [Delete all...]   [Close]

3. **Click Delete Cookies.**

   A dialog box asks if you really want to delete all your cookies. (Never can be too careful, you know.)

4. **Click OK.**

   The cookies are permanently deleted.

Negotiating Newsgroups

I've never caught the newsgroup bug, but I know people who swear by them. Through a system of bulletin board messages and replies, *newsgroups* enable people to discuss, pontificate, argue, harangue, and otherwise kvetch about anything and everything you can think of (although each newsgroup is generally restricted to one topic of interest). Newsgroups have been around longer than the Web and will be here long into the future.

Thousands of newsgroups are accessible. Most dedicated newsgroupies use special *newsreader programs* that allow users to access the newsgroups, subscribe to them, and download headlines, articles, and files. Following are just three such programs:

✔ Agent at www.forteinc.com

✔ Digibin at www.sixpencesoftware.com/Digibin.htm

✔ NewsBin Pro at www.newsbin.com

Everything downloaded by your newsreader, however, can clutter your system quite amazingly. I know people who have saved their newsgroup conversations from 1998. Think about that — people are using precious hard drive space to store conversations that occurred the better part of a decade ago. These same people have all the conversations since then, as well.

The bottom line is that newsreader files can quickly fill up megabytes of storage on your system. If you aren't discerning in what you save, you eventually run out of space. When jumping into the wild world of newsgroups, remember a few things:

✔ **Minimize the newsgroups you subscribe to.** You can't subscribe to everything; there aren't enough hours in a day. Be selective about the groups you follow, and you'll automatically reduce the clutter they produce. (You probably need to get a real life, anyway.)

✔ **Archive important conversations.** If you're impressed with the words of wisdom imparted by others (or amazed at your own eloquence), archive what you want to keep. If the conversation is older than three months, it's a prime candidate for archiving.

- ✔ **Delete uninteresting threads.** Don't let old messages, downloaded in error, continue to consume space on your drive. Get rid of them as soon as you can.

- ✔ **Clean out old binary files regularly.** Many newsgroups allow you to download binary files — pictures, videos, audio, and so on. Sometimes, the files are huge. Make sure you keep only what you really need and delete or archive the rest.

A large part of effectively managing newsgroup clutter is mastering large numbers of files. Chapter 7 presents a wealth of ideas for decreasing clutter and increasing efficiency when working with data files.

Organizing Web Favorites

I visit some Web sites over and over and over again. I check out my company's site daily. I regularly visit my bank's site to do some online banking. I go to the Discover Card site to see if my payment was applied. I pop off to Google to check the news or do a search. I check movie times at the local theaters. The list goes on and on — I visit literally dozens of sites quite regularly, sometimes a few times each day. These sites end up in my Favorites list, where I can access them quickly and easily.

When you first install Windows (which also installs Internet Explorer), a good number of different sites are deposited in your Favorites list. I consider these filler sites put there to take up space until you populate the list with your real favorites. Still, when I look at other people's systems, I find that often the pre-installed favorites are still there, taking up space unnecessarily.

In the true spirit of getting rid of clutter, I implore you to vow to delete the favorites you no longer need and organize the rest. Without the unused clutter, you can find and use your favorites quicker than ever before. In Internet Explorer, you can organize your favorites by displaying the Favorites toolbar: Choose Tools➪Toolbars➪Favorites. The toolbar appears at the left side of your IE window, as shown in Figure 11-3.

To make changes in the layout of your favorites, simply click and drag links or entire folders. You can create new folders by right-clicking anywhere in the toolbar area, and you can delete items by selecting them and pressing Delete. Right-clicking an item reveals a plethora of potentialities; you can do most anything you want with an item in the list.

Figure 11-3:
The
Favorites
toolbar is
where you
do your
organiza-
tional work.

When you're done making changes to your favorites, click the Close button at the top-right corner of the toolbar.

A quick way to display (or hide) the Favorites toolbar is to press Ctrl+I. Plop! There it is. Poof! There it goes.

Taming Web Cache Files

If I go on a road trip of any length, it's not a pretty sight. I tend to minimize my stops, trying to coordinate restroom breaks with gas fill-ups. (With 400 miles between fill-ups, my wife variously accuses me of sadism and masochism.) I get into the fast lane, stick the car on cruise control, and crank up the tunes. (I prefer classic rock for road trips.) I nibble, snack, and slurp as I drive, often tossing spent boxes, cups, and papers into the back seat. After a day's worth of driving — sometimes 1,000 miles on a long day — the back seat is pretty cluttered (and my bladder is feeling somewhat abused). It takes a concerted effort to get both areas back into the shape they should be.

When you take a road trip on the Internet, your Web browser has a lot in common with my long-distance driving habits. As you nibble, snack, and slurp up the information you find, the browser discards pieces and parts into your computer's back seat. After a while, that back seat gets pretty messy, and it needs your attention.

Web browsers maintain what is called a *cache,* an area of your hard drive where the browser stashes recently stored Web pages and, more likely, recently stored images downloaded on your Web travels. If you have a slow Internet connection, the cache is a necessity because it prevents the need for downloading graphics every time you visit a Web page. Visit once and the graphics are downloaded to the cache. Visit the site again and the graphics are loaded from the cache, eliminating the need to download them over the slower Internet connection. (The cache is less useful if you're using a high-speed connection simply because downloading graphics takes less time.)

The problem is that if you visit thirty Web pages, each with an average of 10 graphics, you end up with 300 graphic images in your cache. Multiply that times a month of browsing every day, and all of a sudden you have 9,000 graphics in your cache. (Do you see the problem with my back seat yet?)

In the following sections, you can find out how to locate the cache, clean it out, manage its size, and make sure it contains only what you want.

Cleaning the cache

If you're using Internet Explorer, cleaning out the cache is relatively easy. You can do it in a couple of different ways. If you have the browser open, follow these steps:

1. **Choose Tools⇨Internet Options.**

   IE displays the Internet Options dialog box.

2. **On the General tab, click the Delete button in the Browsing History area of the tab.**

   The Delete Browsing History dialog box appears. Refer to Figure 11-2.

3. **Click the Delete Files button.**

   A warning dialog box appears, also offering to delete all your offline content, as well. For most folks, this doesn't matter — they don't browse offline. If you're in the minority that does, select the check box.

4. **Click Yes.**

   IE deletes the cache files. Depending on how cluttered your system is, this can take a while. Sit back, relax, and don't be too worried if it appears your system is on vacation.

5. **When IE is done deleting cache files, close all the open dialog boxes.**

You now have a fresh, clean cache, ready once again to be cluttered with new pictures from your Internet road trips.

You can also clean out the cache without even opening the browser — just use the Disk Cleanup tool (which I describe in Chapter 6). In a nutshell, you follow these steps:

1. **Choose Start➪All Programs➪Accessories➪System Tools➪Disk Cleanup.**

   The Disk Cleanup tool starts running. If you have multiple user accounts on your computer, you are asked whether you want to clean up just your files or all files on the computer.

2. **Click All Files from All Users on This Computer.**

   If you have multiple hard drives on your system, you're asked to choose which hard drive to analyze.

3. **Pick a hard drive and click OK.**

   Disk Cleanup looks through your hard drive, calculating how much space it can reclaim. This process may take a while. A dialog box, shown in Figure 11-4, indicates things you can clean.

Figure 11-4:
Choose what you want Disk Cleanup to clean up.

4. **Make sure the Temporary Internet Files option is selected.**

   Temporary Internet files translates to what's stored in the cache. You can also pick other things to clean up, if desired. Chapter 6 includes additional information on your options.

5. **Click OK.**

   Disk Cleanup displays a dialog box asking if you want to proceed. (I bet you know how to answer this one.)

Depending on what you ask Disk Cleanup to do, the actual cleanup can take a few minutes to complete. Cleaning out cache files this way takes no longer than cleaning from within the browser.

Finding the cache

Most normal people never worry about where their browser stores its cache files. Microsoft recognizes this and doesn't make a big deal of advertising where the cache is located. You can locate the cache by displaying the Internet Options dialog box (in the browser, click Tools⊅Internet Options) and then clicking Settings (on the General tab, in the area under Browsing History). The resulting Temporary Internet Files and History Settings dialog box (shown in Figure 11-5) indicates where the cache is located (beneath Current Location in the middle of the dialog box).

Figure 11-5:
Find out where the cache is located.

As you examine the path name, notice that it's associated with the current user. If your computer is shared by multiple users, Windows creates a cache folder for each.

Another interesting tidbit is that Microsoft hides the cache folder. It doesn't hide it in the Temporary Internet Files and History Settings dialog box, but it does hide it if you try to get to the folder yourself.

To see how this works, open a window for the C: drive. Double-click the Users folder, then your account name. (On my system, I double-click the folder named `awyatt`.) If your system is like mine, you won't see an `AppData` folder in the account folder, even though the Temporary Internet Files and History Settings dialog box says you should. The reason for this is that the `AppData` folder is configured as a hidden folder; it doesn't show up when normally viewing folders.

To see the hidden folder, follow these steps:

1. **In the folder window, choose Organize⟹Folder Options.**

   Windows displays the Folder Options dialog box, shown in Figure 11-6.

Figure 11-6:
Changing what's displayed in a folder window.

2. **In the Advanced Settings area on the View tab, select the Show Hidden Files and Folders option.**

3. **While you're at it (and especially if you wanna be a good geek), deselect the Hide Extensions for Known File Types and also the Hide Protected Operating System Files options.**

   You might have to scroll down the list to see both of these options. These two options ensure that you see as much information as possible concerning the files on your system, and with more information, you can make better decisions in the long-run.

4. **Click OK.**

As the Folder Options dialog box disappears, the information in the account folder is updated. You can now see the `AppData` folder, but the folder icon should appear a little more washed out than other icons. The icon's appearance indicates that the folder is normally hidden. You can still double-click it and then proceed to double-click your way down the path to the Temporary Internet Files folder to see what's in your cache.

Changing the cache size

Internet Explorer makes a point of ensuring that your cache never gets too big. In some respects, the cache is similar to the Recycle Bin — when its maximum size is attained, it starts deleting the oldest files to make room for the new files.

The problem is that the cache is often set much larger than it needs to be. The Settings dialog box (refer to Figure 11-5) has a control that indicates the amount of disk space to use for the cache. By default, Internet Explorer allocates 10 percent of your disk to its cache folder. This doesn't mean the folder automatically uses that much space, just that IE keeps storing files in the cache (without deleting any of them) until that 10-percent mark is reached.

Think about that for a moment — most computers these days come with at least a 40-, 60-, or 80GB hard drive. If all that space is allocated to a single drive and IE uses that drive for its temporary files, you can easily set a maximum cache size to 4-, 6-, or 8GB. Wow. If the average image downloaded from a Web site is approximately 10KB, IE could store anywhere from 200,000 to 600,000 images on your system without deleting anything. Talk about clutter! When hard drives were smaller, the 10-percent rule made more sense.

You can lower the cache size by following these steps:

1. **In the browser, choose Tools⇨Internet Options.**

   The Internet Options dialog box appears.

2. **On the General tab, click the Settings button in the Browsing History area.**

   The Temporary Internet Files and History Settings dialog box appears. Refer to Figure 11-5.

3. **Adjust the cache size via the Disk Space to Use control.**

   Just type a value in the text box for the control. (That's the easiest way to change it.) You shouldn't hesitate to lower the cache space to 75MB. If you have a high-speed Internet connection, lower it even more — to perhaps 35MB or 40MB.

By making this simple adjustment, you can save a lot of hard drive space for better uses, and you won't hurt the overall performance of Internet Explorer.

Part IV
The Operating System

"How do you like that Aero glass interface on Vista? Nice, huh?"

In this part . . .

In Part IV, you find out how to clean up the user interface, streamline Windows, and speed up the file system. In addition, you discover when to update and when to get a new system.

Chapter 12

Cleaning Up the User Interface

● ●

In This Chapter

▶ Applying a deep cleaning to your desktop
▶ Configuring the menus to your liking
▶ Imposing order on the taskbar
▶ Getting clutter out of the Control Panel

● ●

A user interface is the way that Windows communicates with you, the user. Windows allows you to tweak, prod, cajole, and otherwise beat into submission most parts of the interface. Because the interface is almost elastic, it can become a dumping ground for clutter and crud.

Your mission, should you decide to accept it (cue the *Mission Impossible* theme), is to use the tactics of tweaking, prodding, and cajoling to beat the clutter and crud out of your user interface. This chapter shows you how — and you quickly discover it's not an impossible mission.

Master of the Desktop

In the world defined by your computer, your desktop is prime real estate. The things you place on the desktop should represent those items you work with the most. If you use the desktop properly, you won't have to resort to the Start menu that often.

Some folks' idea of prime real estate is more akin to downtown Gary, Indiana. (I don't wanna hear from any readers on the economic development council in Gary about my supposedly disparaging remarks — I used to live there!) The more icons you have on your desktop, the harder you'll find it is to use your desktop the way it was intended.

Your desktop was originally intended as a place to do work. (Imagine that!) If you clutter it up with every icon under the sun, your desktop becomes a catchall, not a place to work. The solution is to clean up your desktop and allow only the most critical icons.

The following sections describe different things you can do to remedy a cluttered desktop (and make your prime real estate worth more).

Displaying the traditional desktop icons

Older versions of Windows (a couple of versions ago) had a few icons that always appeared on the desktop:

- My Documents
- My Computer
- My Network Places
- Internet Explorer
- Recycle Bin

Windows Vista, on the other hand, only displays the Recycle Bin icon by default. There are, however, five other icons you can display on the desktop. If you want to display any of the other icons, follow these steps:

1. **Right-click anywhere on the desktop.**

   Make sure you right-click the desktop itself, not on an object lying on the desktop. Windows displays a context menu.

2. **Choose Personalize.**

   The Personalize dialog box springs into view.

3. **At the left of the dialog box, click the Change Desktop Icons link.**

   Windows displays the Desktop Icon Settings dialog box, as shown in Figure 12-1.

4. **At the top of the dialog box, select the check boxes corresponding to the icons you want displayed on the desktop.**

   Conversely, you can deselect the check boxes of any icons you don't want displayed.

5. **Click OK to close the Desktop Icon Settings dialog box.**

   Feel free to close all the other dialog boxes, while you're at it.

The icons you selected should be visible onscreen, along with all the others you have.

Figure 12-1:
Select the
traditional
icons that
Windows
should
include on
the desktop.

Renaming and deleting icons

Desktop icons can be renamed, just like any other object in Windows: Right-click the icon and choose Rename from the context menu. If you prefer, select the icon and press F2. Either way, the name of the icon is activated, and you can make any changes you desire.

To delete an icon, just select it and press the Delete key. If you prefer to use the mouse, right-click the icon and choose Delete from the context menu.

You should be careful of one thing, however: that you delete shortcuts only from the desktop. You can tell if an icon is a shortcut by looking closely at it. If a small upward-pointing arrow is in the icon's lower-left corner, it's a shortcut. You can delete these left and right without any real consequences — the program, folder, or file that the shortcut points to remains on the computer. (You're only deleting a reference to the program, folder, or file, not the actual item.)

If no small upward-pointing arrow appears in the lower-left corner of the icon, then the icon represents the real thing. Deleting the real thing may be something you want to do, but it may not — think through your action to make sure. If you do want to get rid of the item, delete away! If you don't, consider moving the icon to a different folder on your system so it's still accessible but doesn't clutter your desktop.

A word on themes and screensavers

Windows allows you to use different themes and screensavers for your system. Some people find it hard to resist the allure of a tropical background, dancing cursors, animated icons, or infinitely propagating walls. Fun stuff, but be aware of its dark side. This dark side is rooted in the fact that any processing done on a computer uses resources. That includes even the most mundane things — a blinking cursor, a wagging-tail animated dog, spinning icons, or elaborate system sounds.

Themes that rely on glitz and screensavers that rely on motion or 3D effects look great, but they also consume a lot of resources. If the computer's dedicating resources to a fancy theme or screensaver, it can't devote those resources to some other program you may be running on your system. Thus, the glitz, glitter, and wow effect can bog down your system and make your main computing tasks slower than they need to be.

This isn't to say that you should never use themes and screensavers — just know how they can affect your system. With all the information, you can make a decision that's right for your needs.

If you decide you like glitz and glitter over raw processing muscle, you gotta check out the Windows interfaces offered at www.stardock.com. Very cool!

Ordering the Menu System

I've been to some restaurants where the menu could almost be classified as a novella. Page after page describing in sumptuous detail exactly how the chef proposes to increase my weight and decrease my wealth. In fact, sometimes it takes longer to read the menu than it does to eat the meal.

Sometimes, I feel the same way when it comes to the menus in Windows. I know that my productivity is dropping when I find myself spending more time reading menus than using programs.

Fortunately, you have complete control over the way menus work in Windows. The following sections explain how you can exercise your control, assert your organizational acumen, and reclaim some of your lost productivity.

Picking a Start menu layout

The Start menu in Windows Vista is quite a bit different from the Start menu in previous versions. Fortunately, you can select the traditional form of the Start menu, if you prefer. To do so, follow these steps:

1. **Right-click the Start menu button and choose Properties from the context menu.**

   If you prefer, you can also right-click a blank area of the taskbar and choose Properties. Either way, Windows displays the Taskbar and Start Menu Properties dialog box, shown in Figure 12-2.

Figure 12-2:
You can easily choose the type of Start menu you want to view.

2. **On the Start Menu tab, select the radio button that corresponds with the type of menu you want to use.**

   The Start Menu option is the Windows Vista version and the Classic Start Menu option is the traditional version.

3. **Click OK.**

Customizing the Start menu

It's a good thing Windows allows you to customize the Start menu. Because most everything you do in Windows is funneled through the Start menu in one way or another, customizing it can help you match the menu to the way you want to work.

The Start Menu tab of the Taskbar and Start Menu Properties dialog box has two Customize buttons; refer to Figure 12-2. Which version of the Start menu you select dictates which button is active. If you select the Windows Vista version of the Start menu and click Customize, the Customize Start Menu dialog box appears, as shown in Figure 12-3.

Figure 12-3:
You can change quite a few options for the Windows Start menu.

The Customize Start Menu dialog box allows you to completely specify what appears on the Start menu and how it appears there. The list of items at the top of the dialog box controls what applications and features appear at the right side of the Start menu. The controls at the bottom of the dialog box primarily control what appears at the left side of the Start menu.

If you select the traditional (Classic) Start menu and click Customize, the Customize Classic Start Menu dialog box appears, as shown in Figure 12-4. The options in the Customize Classic Start Menu dialog box are quite a bit different from those available when customizing the Windows Vista Start menu. (This makes sense — the menus are entirely different from each other.) This dialog box provides these areas:

✔ **Start Menu:** The buttons at the top of the dialog box allow you to add or remove items from the Start menu. You can also use the Sort button to arrange the menu items. The Advanced button displays only the Start Menu folder, which contains shortcuts and other icons for the Start menu.

✔ **Advanced Start Menu Options:** Check boxes at the bottom of the dialog box control a different aspect of menu information display. You can experiment with the choices and select those that best reflect how you want to use the Start menu.

Figure 12-4:
Customize
the
traditional
version of
the Start
menu.

Moving items in the All Programs list

The Start menu is just the gateway; it's nothing but a doorway to the menu selections that lie just out of your reach. The real menu selections, of course, are visible when you choose All Programs from the Windows Vista Start menu or Programs from the Classic Start menu. Both selections (Programs or All Programs) display a menu hierarchy composed of groups and actual program selections.

The items in the All Programs list probably aren't in the order that best reflects how you work. In a perfect world, the menu items you use most often would be listed at the top of the menu, with the less popular options listed lower.

If you want to move things around on the All Programs list, feel free to do so. All you need to do is click a menu item and drag it to whatever position you want. When you drop it, the item appears at the new location and can be immediately used.

If your drag-and-drop efforts don't seem to work with the Windows Vista menu, you need to make one change to how Windows handles the Start menu. Display the Customize Start Menu dialog box (refer to Figure 12-3) and make sure the Sort All Programs Menu by Name check box is cleared. (You'll need to scroll down in the dialog box to find the check box.) When you click OK (to save the change), you can then drag and drop to your heart's content.

Creating your own program groups

A great way to organize the items in your All Programs list is to create your own program group and place menu items within it. Follow these steps to create the group:

1. **Right-click the Start button and choose Open from the context menu.**

   Windows displays the Start Menu folder window.

2. **Double-click the Programs folder.**

   The Programs folder contains many of the items visible when you click All Programs on the Start menu.

3. **Create a new folder in the Programs folder by right-clicking a blank area in the folder and choosing New⇨Folder.**

   You can name the folder anything you want.

4. **Close the folder window.**

This folder now appears as a program group in the All Programs list. You can move shortcuts, folders, and files into the new folder; they appear as options within the program group. Use the technique described in the preceding section to do the actual moving.

Effectively Using the Taskbar

The taskbar, at the bottom of your desktop, is where you keep tabs on your work. Each project you work on is considered a task, and the taskbar shows what tasks are currently active.

Windows uses the taskbar for quite a bit more information, as well. If you customize it effectively, you can use Window's user interface quicker and easier than ever before.

Birds of a feather . . .

. . . flock together (and sometimes leave a real mess on your car). One of the really cool features available in Windows is *task grouping*, which allows those birds to freely flock, without leaving their calling card behind.

When I start opening a lot of programs, folders, or files, my taskbar starts looking downright scary. Each task gets narrower and narrower, until I can no longer understand what the individual tasks represent.

Task grouping comes in handy here. You can instruct Windows to group tasks so that similar tasks use a single taskbar button. For instance, if I have eight different Word documents open at the same time, the individual tasks are collapsed to a single button, as shown in Figure 12-5, instead of displaying eight buttons. The taskbar button indicates how many individual tasks are collapsed into the single button. In Figure 12-5, I have eight Word documents active, indicated by the numeral 8 sandwiched between the Word icon and Microsoft Office on the taskbar button. Click the down arrow to see a list of the individual tasks.

Figure 12-5:
Grouping
tasks saves
space on
the taskbar.

Indicates how many tasks are grouped together

Click to see a list of the individual tasks

Task grouping won't make your system run faster, and it won't free up resources (such as memory or hard drive space). What it does is unclutter the taskbar so you can find tasks quicker and easier. After you get used to task grouping, you become more productive when you have a lot going on at the same time.

To make sure task grouping is enabled, follow these steps:

1. **Right-click any blank area of the taskbar and choose Properties.**

   The Taskbar tab of the Taskbar and Start Menu Properties dialog box appears, as shown in Figure 12-6.

Figure 12-6:
Task
grouping is
a good
productivity
tool.

2. **Make sure the Group Similar Taskbar Buttons check box is selected and click OK.**

   That's it; task grouping is immediately in play.

Cleaning the Notification area

The area at the far-right side of the taskbar is known by many names. Traditionally, it's called the *system tray,* but it's also been referred to as the *task tray* or simply the *tray.* With the release of Windows Vista, it's going by the name *Notification area.*

Sometimes, I think Microsoft has people sitting around thinking up new terminology and looking for ways to change old terminology. I guess if I had a billion dollars in the bank, I could hire people to routinely and perpetually change terminology, as well. Go figure.

Regardless of what you call it, the Notification area contains a bunch of icons representing programs running on your system right now. You can click the Show Hidden Icons button (to the left of the icons in the Notification area) and expand the Notification area so that you can see all the icons it contains.

If you don't want Windows to hide icons in the Notification area, right-click a blank area of the taskbar and choose Properties from the context menu. On the Notification Area tab of the Taskbar and Start Menu Properties dialog box (Figure 12-7), clear the Hide Inactive Icons check box.

Figure 12-7:
You can display all the Notification area icons.

You can help unclutter your system if you examine the icons in the Notification area and remove those you don't use regularly. Because each icon represents a currently running program, removing the icon represents shutting down the program and therefore freeing the resources that program was using.

If you want to close one of the programs, try right-clicking its icon. You see a context menu, and a Close or Exit option may be on the menu. Select the Exit option, and the icon should disappear from the Notification area.

To prevent the associated program from reappearing the next time you start Windows, configure things so the program doesn't automatically run. You can do this in two ways.

The first approach is to run the piece of software in question and try to make the change there. Somewhere in all the software configuration information, a control should appear that determines whether the program displays the Notification area icon. The wording used in the control could be just about anything — it could reference the system tray, the tray, the task tray, or the notification area. It could also reference automatically starting when you start Windows.

When you find the configuration setting, change it and then restart Windows. If the change worked, the icon should no longer be visible in the Notification area. If it didn't work, you have to try the second approach by following these steps:

1. **Right-click the Start button and choose Open from the context menu.**

   Windows displays the Start Menu folder window.

2. **Double-click the Programs folder.**

   The Programs folder contains many of the items visible when you click All Programs on the Start menu.

3. **Double-click the Startup folder.**

   The Startup folder contains shortcuts to some of the programs that run automatically when you start Windows. Among these shortcuts may be one for the pesky program that appears in the Notification area.

4. **Delete the shortcut for the program you don't want to automatically run.**

   Deleting the shortcut means that the associated program won't run when you next start Windows.

5. **Close the Startup folder window.**

What's really running?

Not all currently running programs have icons in the Notification area. Some have tasks on the taskbar, and others may not show any outward icon at all. (Windows can run many programs at the same time.)

If you want to see everything running in your system, right-click a blank area on the taskbar and choose Task Manager from the context menu. In the Task Manager dialog box, examine the Processes tab to see all the programs running right now.

When you see what's running, take a look at the column labeled Mem Usage. This column indicates how much memory is allocated to each item. Cluttered systems have many processes running, even if they aren't being used. If something is running, it's using resources that may best be used for something you really need.

---

6. **Repeat Steps 1 through 5 — except this time choose Open All Users in Step 1.**

7. **When you're done, restart Windows to determine if your actions fixed the problem.**

If, despite these steps, you can't stop the program from starting and depositing an icon in the Notification area, refer to the information on the System Configuration Utility in Chapter 13.

Cleaning Up the Control Panel

The Control Panel may not be the real brain of your Windows system, but it's a place where you can do some serious poking and prodding on the brain. To do the poking and prodding, it's best to view the Control Panel in Classic View, as shown in Figure 12-8. Choose Start⇨Control Panel and click Classic View at the left side of the Control Panel.

Windows doesn't hold clear title to the entire Control Panel. In fact, other programs can add applets to the Control Panel. It's particularly common for applets to be added whenever you install new hardware drivers. For instance, its not unusual to have third-party (non-Windows) applets added to the Control Panel by the installation program for a network card or an audio card.

Figure 12-8:
The Control
Panel
contains
applets that
allow you to
configure,
tweak, and
poke your
system into
submission.

Over time, your Control Panel can get quite cluttered with applets. Having too many applets can make it harder to zero in on what you need to do. If your Control Panel contains applets that you never use, consider removing them. Doing so is quite easy: Use the Windows Search feature to find all the files on your system that end with the .CPL file extension. (These files are Control Panel applets.) When you search, most of the applets are in the C:\Windows\System32 directory, but duplicates could appear in other directories. If you double-click a .CPL file in the Search Results window, the applet is opened — the same as if you double-clicked the applet in the Control Panel.

To remove an applet from the Control Panel, identify the .CPL file you want to remove and move that file to a temporary folder on a different drive or to a removable disk. That way, you can operate Windows for a while without the applet and return the .CPL file if you have problems. If you get along just swimmingly without the applet, delete or archive it, according to your mood for the day.

Chapter 13

Streamlining Windows

In This Chapter

▶ Minimizing your Windows installation

▶ Tweaking performance options

▶ Making use of the Microsoft System Configuration utility

▶ Enhancing stability with the latest drivers

▶ Getting rid of unneeded .DLLs

▶ Disabling unnecessary system services

▶ Using System Protection

*W*hen you installed Windows Vista, you probably thought it was pretty cool when compared to your older version. (Although I must admit that, at first, I wasn't too wild about many of the interface changes, but they seem to grow on you after time.) Windows Vista works faster, smoother, and more reliably than any of its predecessors.

Still, Windows Vista — out of the box — is comparable to a solidly built family sedan with a whole bunch of security features in place. (You! Stand away from the car!) That may fit your style for a while, but you may eventually want to grab a hammer, a blow torch, and a can of Bondo so you can tinker with the car to make it more sporty.

Likewise, you can streamline Windows in a zillion ways to improve its performance. This chapter focuses on some of the performance tweaks you can apply and tools you can use to de-clutter your system and make it perform better. This approach isn't the be-all end-all; you need the dedicated books for that. I can, however, guarantee that if you apply the information in this chapter, your system can run faster and smoother than before. (Keep that Bondo away from the monitor.)

Installing Just What You Need

A good case can be made for the proposition that Microsoft wants Windows to be all things to all people. ("Resistance is futile. You will be assimilated.") With every new operating system version, more bells and whistles are added.

The reality is that you don't need all those bells and whistles. You should carefully select what bells and whistles you install on your system. Paring down Windows to just what you need frees up hard drive space and makes your system run faster. In other words, your system becomes less cluttered.

Most people don't actually install their own operating system. It either came installed on your computer or some geek from the IT department took your system away and brought it back with Windows magically installed.

Fortunately, uninstalling Windows Vista components isn't that difficult. Follow these steps:

1. **Choose Start⇨Control Panel.**

   The Control Panel appears on your screen.

2. **Click Programs⇨Turn On or Off Windows Features.**

   The Windows Features dialog box appears, as shown in Figure 13-1.

Figure 13-1:
You can remove a number of Windows' pieces and parts.

3. **Pick and choose what you want removed or installed.**

   Your goal is to remove all those items you no longer need (or never did need) because each thing you remove frees up space on your hard drive. For instance, most people don't need Windows DFS Replication Service or Windows RDC; these are good candidates for removal.

In previous versions of Windows, the dialog box told you how much hard drive space you would save through your paring-down efforts. Not so in Vista. Trust me, though — you can save a bunch of hard drive space just by getting rid of what you no longer need.

4. **For more information about a particular option, hover the mouse pointer over the item in the list.**

   A ToolTip appears. Some ToolTips are helpful, some are clear as mud, all of them are terse. If you need more information, check out Google to see what others have been saying about the Windows component in question.

5. **When you're satisfied, click OK.**

   Windows goes through the steps necessary to remove (or install) the options you've chosen. This process could take a while; be patient.

6. **Close the Control Panel.**

You probably don't need the Windows installation CDs if you're removing features. You'll probably need them, however, if you try to install features. Either way, it's a good idea to have the CDs close by.

Perhaps it's the pragmatic ogre coming out in me, but if you're using your computer in a business environment, you really don't need to have games installed. After all, games aren't considered business for most companies. You can free up more than 10MB of disk space just by uninstalling the Microsoft-installed games.

Setting Performance Options

Talk about performance options, and most guys think about supercharging their car. Microsoft, single-handedly, is trying to change that perception. When Microsoft uses the phrase, it wants you to think about making your computer run faster. Windows even has a configuration area where you can set performance options for your system. It's pretty hard to track down, unless you know where to look. I'm gonna show you where to look.

To display the Performance Options dialog box, click Start, right-click Computer, choose Properties, and then click Performance. If your system is configured to have a Computer icon on the desktop, you could right-click that icon, if you prefer. Either way, the Performance Information and Tools portion of the Control Panel appears, as shown in Figure 13-2.

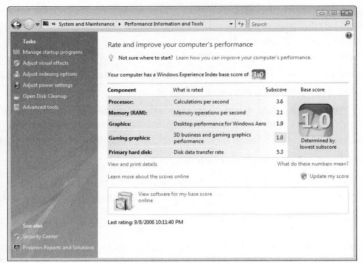

Figure 13-2:
Windows
lets you
know
where your
performance
is suffering.

Note the area at the top of the dialog box, where the light bulb icon appears. If Windows detected anything that it thought was hindering your system performance, it would note it here, along with a helpful link you could use to track down some suggestions.

In addition, there are other options available from the performance center that you could peruse. I say "could" rather than "should" because not all of the options are terribly helpful. In fact, some of them have very little to do with performance and much more to do with superficial appearances of Windows.

If you really want to know where the guts of the Windows Vista performance are located, you need to make a detour away from the performance center. Strange as that may sound, if you make this slight detour, you'll be much happier with the results.

Start by closing the performance center. You should still see the System area of the Control Panel on your screen. (If you don't, click Start, right-click Computer, and then choose Properties.) Click the Advanced System Settings link. In a short while, Windows displays the System Properties dialog box, with the Advanced tab selected. Click the Settings button in the Performance area, and you're treated to the destination of the detour: the Performance Options dialog box, shown in Figure 13-3.

Figure 13-3:
Modify
the visual
effects
used by
Windows.

There are three tabs in the Performance Options dialog box: Visual Effects, Advanced, and Data Execution Prevention. Only the first two of these tabs are germane to your performance purposes right now, and those tabs are discussed in the following sections.

Understanding visual effects

I'll bet you never gave much thought to the visual effects used in Windows Vista. Most people don't; the effects are very subtle. Just little things, such as shadows in key places or screen objects that slide smoothly or fade into obscurity when they're no longer needed.

Visual effects, such as these and so many others, can rob a system of its performance. If you have a fast system with power to spare, you may be able to spare a few processor cycles without any ill effect. On older or minimal systems, systems with slow graphics cards, or those with limited memory, visual effects do nothing except slow a system.

To control what visual effects you want Windows to use, do your work on the Visual Effects tab of the Performance Options dialog box (refer to Figure 13-3). Do so by selecting one of these radio buttons:

- **Let Windows Choose What's Best for My Computer:** On most systems, this option is selected by default. Not surprisingly, some people rile at having Uncle Bill decide anything for them. If you'd rather dictate what Windows does, select one of the other radio buttons.

- **Adjust for Best Appearance:** This option selects *all* the visual effects.

- **Adjust for Best Performance:** This option turns off all visual effects. This should tell you something about what they do to your system performance, right?

- **Custom:** To turn individual effects on and off at your will, select this option. You can then use the check boxes in the list to pick which effects you can't live without.

Advanced performance options

The less noticeable performance options are accessible by clicking the Advanced tab, shown in Figure 13-4.

Figure 13-4:
Change a couple of settings, and you can match system performance to your needs.

You can change only two things on the Advanced tab:

- ✔ **Processor scheduling:** For most desktop systems, you should leave the default, Programs, selected. Select Background Services only if your computer runs some critical programs as system services. (You can find more information about system services in the section "Modifying the startup process," later in this chapter.)

- ✔ **Virtual memory:** This setting indicates how Windows uses hard drive space for system purposes. A *paging file* is a chunk of hard drive space Windows uses for swapping programs in and out of RAM.

If you want to change the paging file settings, click the Change button. For most people, the system defaults for the paging file should be fine. You can modify paging file settings with the goal of better performance, but you should do so only after you understand the ramifications of making a change. You can find out more about paging files in Chapter 17, but explaining the detailed ins and outs of paging files is beyond the scope of this book; refer to a good Windows technical reference guide for the detailed information necessary.

Using the Microsoft System Configuration Utility

When I was a kid, I joined a secret club. (Well, it was only a secret from all those unwise enough to not eat my brand of breakfast cereal.) I got an official membership card, discovered the official handshake, and got this really cool secret decoder ring. Sometimes, I feel like there must be a secret club for Windows users, but they forgot to give me the really cool secret decoder ring. If I just had that ring, I could figure out why Windows is doing what it's doing.

If you've ever belonged to a kid's secret club, you'll understand my glee when I found out about the Microsoft System Configuration (msconfig) utility. It may not be a really cool secret decoder ring that reveals all of Windows' secrets, but it's a really cool almost-secret program that reveals what's going on whenever you start Windows.

The msconfig utility streamlines what happens when you start Windows. According to Microsoft sources, msconfig "automates the routine troubleshooting steps that Microsoft Technical Support engineers use when they diagnose issues" with Windows' configuration. (Sounds idyllic, doesn't it?)

The reality is quite simple: msconfig allows you to modify how your system starts. When Windows starts, it loads all sorts of things, from a variety of places. If your system is sluggish or you're having problems starting at all, it could be because of conflicts between different programs that run when your system starts. You correct such a condition by uncluttering the startup files. Using the msconfig utility, you can see a list of what Windows loads and individually select which of those items should load.

By its very nature, the msconfig utility exemplifies geekiness. If you're not afraid of delving into your system's innards, you may actually enjoy using msconfig. If you don't have a technical streak, you may want to steer clear of it.

To start msconfig, choose Start⇨All Programs⇨Accessories⇨Run. In the Open text box, type msconfig.exe and click OK. The program is executed, and very shortly, you see the System Configuration dialog box, shown in Figure 13-5.

Figure 13-5:
The
Microsoft
System
Configuration
utility sports
a very
simple
interface.

Notice the lack of menu bar for the program; everything is handled through a series of tabs. These tabs represent different aspects of how Windows starts on your system. Besides the General tab (shown in Figure 13-5), you could see a variety of others:

✔ **Boot:** This tab shows the contents of the boot.ini file. This file indicates exactly how your system should boot. On most systems, the file is pretty mundane, but it becomes critical if you have multiple operating systems or different versions of Windows on the same system.

✔ **Services:** This tab lists all the services that Windows can start. (Windows services are discussed in the section "Shut Down Unused Services," a bit later in this chapter.)

✔ **Startup:** This tab lists all the programs automatically started whenever you begin Windows.

✔ **Tools:** A collection of tools that you — or anyone with an IT degree — can use to slice, dice, and otherwise configure Windows. (Most of the tools are beyond the scope of this book.)

Additional tabs may be present, depending on your system's configuration. For instance, you may see tabs that contain environment or international settings.

Modifying the startup process

The General tab of the System Configuration dialog box (refer to Figure 13-5) allows you to specify, in the most general way, how your system starts. Three options are available on the tab:

✔ **Normal Startup:** With this default selected, Windows goes blithely on its way, loading all the programs, drivers, and services it was instructed to load.

✔ **Diagnostic Startup:** This option is, in some respects, similar to starting your computer in safe mode. When you choose this radio button, Windows only loads the most basic of its many potential services and drivers.

Normally, you choose Diagnostic Startup only so you can get rid of all the potential problem areas in one move. If your system starts problem-free with Diagnostic Startup selected, you would then move onto Selective Startup to narrow the problem even further.

✔ **Selective Startup:** This option enables you to make choices regarding which startup files are processed. If you deselect one of the check boxes under this option, the corresponding startup file is skipped when Windows starts.

If you're experiencing startup problems, follow these steps:

1. **Choose Start⇨All Programs⇨Accessories⇨Run, type** msconfig.exe **in the Open dialog box, and click OK.**

   The System Configuration dialog box appears.

2. **Select the Selective Startup radio button, deselect all the check boxes under that option, and then click OK.**

3. **Restart Windows.**

   You should have no problem.

4. **Go back to msconfig, select the first check box (Load System Services), and click OK.**

5. **Restart Windows again to see if your problems crop up now.**

   If your problems crop up, you know the problem is in the system services loaded by Windows. If they don't crop up, you know there's no problem in this area.

6. **Repeat the process until you've selected all the check boxes, one at a time, restarting Windows after each.**

   Through this iterative process, you can determine which startup file is causing problems. You won't yet know which command in the file is causing problems, but you'll know where to look closer.

Modifying startup files

Windows uses a bunch of startup files. You can see these files through msconfig, where you can also modify their effect on the startup process. (See the preceding section.) Figure 13-6 shows a typical tab for msconfig, this one the Boot tab. Notice that the controls on the tab allow you to modify the way in which Windows Vista is booted.

Figure 13-6: You can modify the manner in which Windows Vista is booted.

If you're having problems booting to Windows, you can use the controls in the dialog box to modify what happens during the boot process. Selectively modifying the process allows you to track down — sometimes through the process of elimination — where your problem is in the booting process.

Modifying what's started

Perhaps the most informative tab in msconfig is Startup, shown in Figure 13-7. This tab lists programs that automatically run every time you start Windows. Most of these programs end up as icons in the taskbar's Notification area (see Chapter 12), but some run and leave no outward sign that they're active in memory.

Figure 13-7:
The Startup tab lists all the programs that auto-matically run when Windows starts.

Each startup item has a check box next to it; you can turn off the program next time you start Windows by deselecting the check box next to that program. The really helpful thing about the Startup tab is the Location column. Studying this column can disclose where the actual command to run a program is located.

For instance, if the Location column for a startup item shows a path to a Startup folder, you can easily track down where it's located. To see the folder, right-click the Start button, choose Open (or Open All Users), double-click Programs, and then double-click Startup. The shortcut or program should be in that folder.

Finding programs in the Startup folders isn't particularly difficult; I show you how to do that in Chapter 3. Tracking down programs that run because of Windows Registry entries is more difficult. The msconfig Startup tab makes this identification easier because the Location column can indicate a Registry key that contains the program's startup command.

If you want to remove a startup command from the Registry, doing so isn't for the faint of heart — the Registry can be quite daunting. Refer to Chapter 20 for the necessary information on working with the Registry.

Using msconfig's Startup tab, you can select which programs should be started when you begin Windows and which shouldn't. Deselect the check box for any programs you don't want started and then reboot. If problems crop up, you can also go back to msconfig, select the check box, and restart.

Working with the Latest Drivers

Drivers rule! Device drivers do, anyway. Without device drivers, devices are little more than expensive works of art — nice to look at but not terribly productive. *Device drivers* provide an interface between the operating system and a piece of hardware. Information moving from Windows to the device (or vice versa) travels through the driver, so it's critical to make sure that the drivers work properly.

Unfortunately, drivers often clutter systems unnecessarily. Installation programs often take the shotgun approach to compatibility: Install every possible driver for the device, even if only one of them is ultimately used. The extra drivers take up space and make your system more complex than it needs to be.

The following sections discuss how you can make sure you have the latest (and safest) drivers and how you can remove drivers, if necessary.

Checking a driver's signature

For Windows to function properly, all the pieces and parts that make it up must work together flawlessly. (Trust me; Windows has thousands of parts.) If a problem crops up with one little part, the operating system becomes unstable and can behave erratically — or not at all.

Historically, device drivers are a weak spot in the thousands of pieces that make up Windows. Microsoft has no control over many device drivers, relying upon third parties to create the drivers necessary to support their hardware and software. Some developers do a good job; others don't.

To help mitigate the problem, Windows created something called the Windows Hardware Quality Lab. This lab tests different hardware designed to work with Windows. If the hardware (and its attendant drivers) passes the battery of tests, the driver is granted a digital signature. This signature is essentially a mark of quality assurance, signifying that the driver has passed the tests and can be relied upon.

This doesn't mean that unsigned drivers won't work; it just means that those drivers don't have Microsoft's stamp of approval. Windows even has a tool that allows you to see whether the various drivers in your system are signed.

To run the File Signature Verification utility, follow these steps:

1. **Choose Start⇨All Programs⇨Accessories⇨Run, enter** sigverif.exe **in the Open box, and click OK.**

   The welcome screen for the utility, shown in Figure 13-8, appears.

Figure 13-8:
Getting ready to check file signatures.

2. **To use the program in the simplest way, just click Start.**

   The program can take quite a while to run through its tests; it checks a large number of folders and directories. When the scan is completed, you'll either see a dialog box letting you know that all your drivers were verified successfully or listing those drivers that didn't pass the signature test.

   If you're presented with a list of unsigned drivers, figuring out what they do can be frustrating. After all, how are you supposed to know what acpdf207.dll does or whether it's necessary to have mdiui.dll on your system?

3. **Do a Google search for each unsigned driver's name.**

   Chances are good that you'll find results that indicate more information about the file. You can then decide whether to keep or remove it.

4. **To see a full report of all the drivers checked, click the Advanced button (refer to Figure 13-8), display the Logging tab, and click View Log.**

   The log file can be mind-numbingly long, but you get a real sense of geek pride when you successfully wade through it.

5. **When you finish using the File Signature Verification utility, click the Close button to exit the program.**

Checking for updated device drivers

If you find unsigned drivers (see the preceding section) or experience problems with a signed driver, you may want to look for updates. Similar to other software programs, drivers are updated periodically to fix problems in older versions. You can update drivers in two ways:

- ✔ **Update Windows.** Its *service packs* (major updates to the operating system files) routinely update system drivers. Dealing with Windows updates is covered in Chapter 15.

- ✔ **Check the hardware manufacturer's Web site if a third party developed the driver.** For instance, if you have an Epson printer, go to the support section (generally where you find driver updates) of the Epson Web site, download the appropriate driver, and then install it.

When downloading drivers from third parties, make sure you get the driver version designed for Windows Vista. If more than one driver is available for Windows Vista, check the descriptions to figure out which one is best for you. (For instance, one driver may work best if you have a particular service pack installed.) If you download and install drivers intended for other operating systems, you run the risk of making your system unstable.

Removing device drivers

Like rabbits on overdrive, device drivers tend to multiply quickly. Every new piece of hardware you install adds one or more drivers. Many pieces of software add drivers. These drivers normally end up in the Windows folder (or one of its subfolders) and stay there way too long. Even if you remove the hardware or software, one or more drivers will probably remain behind.

If you have nothing better to do one afternoon, spend some time identifying and removing unneeded drivers. (You might also want to remove unsigned drivers if you know you can get a later, signed version.) The most common file extension for drivers is .DLL, but drivers can have other extensions, as well.

Start by using the File Signature Verification utility, which I describe in the earlier section "Checking a driver's signature," and looking at the full log file it creates. Look at the unsigned files — often drivers you no longer need. You can do a search on Google to determine what the driver does and then make an executive decision to delete it.

Be careful removing drivers — if you delete a critical one by mistake, you may make your system unstable. Instead of deleting it, move the driver to a temporary folder and then restart your system. If you find the driver was necessary, you can move it back to its original location.

Going on a .DLL Diet

The most common file extension for drivers is .DLL. That doesn't mean, however, that all .DLL files are device drivers. To the contrary, many .DLLs are used for other purposes. *Dynamic link library,* for what DLL stands, is a type of file format that allows common code snippets to be shared between the operating system and multiple programs. The original idea of .DLL files was to reduce the overall resources necessary for the code, just by sharing.

Such economy was necessary in the early days of Windows because hard drives weren't as large and memory wasn't as plentiful. As hard drives became larger, memory more plentiful, and Windows bigger, .DLLs also became a bigger problem. My Windows Vista system, with only a portion of my production software loaded on it, has more than 7,700 .DLL files.

Just think about that for a moment — more than 7,700 .DLL files that need to be tracked and swapped in and out of memory. Tracking and swapping aren't the biggest problems, however. The big problem is keeping all the .DLLs updated. If I update one program, it wants to update the .DLLs that it uses. If other programs use some of those .DLLs, the updated .DLLs may "break" the other programs, which aren't expecting a change.

The result is a greater chance for system instability — different programs, over time, become more prone to crashing and malfunction simply because of updating .DLL files. This condition even has a name: .DLL hell. Microsoft has worked hard over the last couple of versions to minimize or eliminate .DLL hell. Windows Vista is much more stable than its predecessors, in large part because of the way it handles .DLL files.

This is great for you, the user. (Increased stability is always better.) It doesn't solve the fact that having 7,700+ .DLL files on a system is common.

The solution lies in recognizing that not all of those files are necessary. The files accumulate over time — new programs (and their .DLLs) are installed; the .DLLs remain when the programs are removed. Orphan .DLL files aren't individually a problem, but collectively, they contribute to an astounding amount of clutter. This clutter makes the operating system work harder and eats up more disk space than should be eaten.

The task devolves to the user (that's you) figuring out which .DLLs can be removed from a system and then doing so. Obviously, sifting through 7,700+ .DLLs to figure out which ones should be deleted isn't something you want to do manually. That's why programs exist to handle it for you.

I haven't seen a good standalone .DLL-winnowing program. Instead, the feature is typically built into a larger software package. You often find the feature in the following types of packages:

✔ **Registry cleaners:** These types of programs search through the Windows Registry, looking for ways to tidy it up. In so doing, they often make a list of deletable .DLL files. (Registry cleaning software is described in more detail in Chapter 20.)

✔ **Uninstallers:** Programs that specialize in uninstalling software have been available for a couple of years. These programs many times do a much better job of removing program remnants — including .DLL files — than the built-in uninstallers provided with the software.

✔ **Disk cleaners:** These utilities were developed specifically to look for unused files (including .DLL files) that can be removed from a system.

Any number of programs could be suggested to perform these tasks. You should figure out which one you think would benefit you most (I tend to like Registry cleaners) and then search for one that makes sense for you. You can often find good shareware versions on the Internet. Just make sure you look for good reviews (and possible awards) on any program you consider using.

Shut Down Unused Services

Even when you think no programs are running in Windows, some probably are. Some run in the background, without you ever knowing it, doing work required to support other programs or to accomplish assigned system tasks.

When Windows is installed, it comes with a whole raft of services that can be started on demand. The problem is other programs can start the services without your knowing it. If those other programs are malicious (such as spyware, discussed in Chapter 10), then those services can be used toward ends you would never approve of.

Because services can be started without your knowledge, they represent a vulnerability. To get rid of this vulnerability, you need to identify the services you never use or need, and configure them so that they can't be run. You can accomplish this task in a couple of ways, which I discuss in the following sections.

If you're familiar with UNIX or Linux systems, the equivalent to Windows services are *daemons.* Both do exactly the same thing — run in the system background.

It's interesting that Microsoft recognized automatic services as a Windows vulnerability, as well. For this reason, Windows Vista is much more verbose when it comes to starting services. If a program wants to start a service, you're asked if it's okay to do so. When you see a dialog box asking you if Windows can start a service, give it due consideration. Did you take an action that requires the service? Did you explicitly ask for the service to start? If so, then you can give permission for the service to run. If not, then it's probably best to pass on starting the service.

Services in the Computer Manager

The Computer Manager is a very powerful administrative tool, but few people know about it. It allows you to manage a passel of things, such as disk drives, devices, and (fortunately for you) services. To start the Computer Manager and see which services are installed, follow these steps:

1. **Click the Start button.**

   Windows displays the Start menu.

2. **Right-click the Computer option and choose Manage.**

   If your system is configured to have a Computer icon on the desktop, you could right-click that icon. Either way, Windows opens the Computer Management window. The window shows a hierarchical display of tools and features on the left of the screen.

3. **If Services and Applications has a right-pointing arrow (in the hierarchy), click it.**

   The tree is expanded, and you see a number of items under Services and Applications.

4. **Click the Services option in the hierarchy.**

   A long list of services appears at the right side of the screen, as shown in Figure 13-9. Pay particular attention to the Status and Startup Type columns. The Status column indicates if a service is currently running. Each running service is noted as Started in the Status column.

Figure 13-9:
Windows
includes
quite a few
available
services.

The Startup Type column can contain one of three values:

- **Automatic:** The service is started whenever Windows is started.

- **Manual:** The service is started manually, explicitly by you, or by another program that needs the service.

- **Disabled:** The service can't be started.

Most of the listed services are optional, but don't start disabling services willy-nilly. Examine the description of a service or even do a Google search on the service name. Seeing a service's full description often helps you decide whether you want to disable it.

5. **Widen the Description column, if desired, or click the Extended tab at the bottom of the services list.**

   The display changes to show the full description of the selected service at the left. See Figure 13-10.

Figure 13-10:
Displaying
the
extended
version of
the services
list can be
helpful.

6. **If you don't want a service to be started, double-click its name.**

   The service's Properties dialog box appears.

7. **On the General tab, you can change the Startup Type to Automatic, Manual, or Disabled.**

8. **Click OK after making your choices and then close the Computer Management window.**

If you use the Disable Startup Type for a service, then it can't be run. If another service depends on the disabled service, then the other service may fail. You can see which other services depend on the one you're changing by clicking the Dependencies tab in the service's Properties dialog box.

Services in msconfig

Earlier sections of this chapter cover how to use the Microsoft System Configuration (msconfig) utility to track down problems and remove clutter from your system. You can also use the utility to identify services that you may want to shut down.

Click Start➪All Programs➪Accessories➪Run and enter **msconfig.exe** in the Open text box. When you click OK, the program window appears. The Services tab, shown in Figure 13-11, reveals the same services listed in the Computer Management window (refer to Figure 13-9), with an additional column: Date Disabled. If you choose to disable a service, Windows keeps track of the date when this action took place.

Figure 13-11:
The msconfig Services tab lists all the services in your system.

Remember that msconfig doesn't allow you to start and stop services. You can disable services only so they don't run when the system is next started. For this reason, you may want to open both the msconfig utility and the Computer Management window at the same time. That way, you can review services in both windows, at the same time, and make educated decisions about which to disable.

Putting System Protection to Work

"Set the Wayback Machine, Sherman." With this simple command, Mr. Peabody would get ready to travel through time with his boy, Sherman. They would take improbable jaunts through history, explaining the events and saving the day, all in an animated cartoon of under five minutes.

Who knew, when *Peabody's Improbable History* debuted in 1959, that more than 40 years later, Windows would include its own Wayback Machine, appropriately (and geekily) named System Restore. Well, this was the name of the feature in Windows XP. Recognizing that it may have been too geeky, Microsoft changed the name to System Protection in Windows Vista. (You gotta love those kinder, gentler names they're using nowadays.)

You can use System Protection to turn back the clock and restore your system's condition to a simpler, happier time. The feature is enabled, by default, on Windows Vista. The utility periodically takes snapshots of the condition of each drive and stores that snapshot in case it's later needed.

To understand how you might need System Protection, consider the scenario where your system is running fine when you install a new piece of hardware and three new programs that use that hardware. About a week later, you discover that one of your older and less-used programs is giving you fits, even though it worked fine before. In addition, Windows now crashes once in a while (which has a tendency to elicit a catechism of four-letter words).

System Protection shines here, allowing you to turn back the dial (always critical on the Wayback Machine) to a point in time before the hardware and software were installed. Presto! Your system operates without the problems introduced by who-knows-what-part of the new hardware and software.

Configuring System Protection

System Protection is turned on by default on your system. The feature requires at least 300MB of space on your system drive (the one where Windows Vista is installed), and it will automatically allocate additional disk space, as necessary.

To see how System Protection is configured on your system, click Start, right-click Computer, choose Properties, and click Advanced System Settings. Windows displays the System Properties dialog box, on which you should choose the System Protection tab, shown in Figure 13-12.

Figure 13-12: System Protection is configured for each drive in a system.

Note the status area near the center of the dialog box. Each disk drive in your system is listed, along with a check box to the left of the drive name. This check box controls whether System Protection is enabled for the drive. If you clear all the check boxes (including the one for the system drive), System Protection is turned off completely.

Setting a restore point

System Protection functions based on the concept of restore points. A *restore point* is a snapshot of a system's state at a given point in time and is stored automatically by System Protection on a regular basis. In addition, Windows sets a restore point whenever you perform a Windows update or install an unsigned device driver. In addition, some third-party utility programs set restore points before changing your system.

You can manually set a restore point whenever you feel the need, such as before installing new hardware or software, or before editing the Registry. Windows allows you to store multiple restore points for each drive. The operating system will allocate whatever space it needs for the restore points you save.

Follow these steps to manually set a restore point:

1. **Choose Start, right-click Computer, choose Properties, and click Advanced System Settings.**

   The System Properties dialog box appears, and you should make sure the System Protection tab is displayed, as shown in Figure 13-12.

2. **Click the Create button, near the bottom of the dialog box.**

   You're prompted to enter a description for the restore point.

3. **Enter a description for the restore point and click Create.**

   In a few moments, you're notified that the restore point is created. Pretty easy, huh?

Reverting to history

If System Protection allows you to save a restore point, it makes sense that it also allows you to restore your system by using one of the stored restore points. Just follow these steps:

1. **Start System Restore by choosing Start⇨All Programs⇨Accessories⇨ System Tools⇨System Restore.**

   The System Restore window appears, as shown in Figure 13-13.

Figure 13-13: Running System Restore is easy.

2. **If you want to restore to the most recent restore point, select the Recommended Restore option.**

3. **If you want to restore to an earlier restore point, select the Choose a Different Restore Point and click Next.**

   A list of available restore points is displayed, and you can select which one you want to use.

4. **Click Next to start the restoration process.**

5. **When prompted, confirm that you want to do a restore.**

   After you confirm, System Protection sets another restore point before actually doing the restore you want. It sets this restore point so that you can undo the restore you're about to do, if need be. How cool is that?

After a reboot, your system behaves exactly as it did when the selected restore point was set.

Chapter 14

Speeding Up the File System

- -

In This Chapter

▶ Making sense of file systems

▶ Converting from one file system to another

▶ Removing disk fragmentation

▶ Checking a disk for errors

- -

In geekspeak, a *file system* is the organizational method that the operating system uses to store information on a disk drive. Read that sentence again; it's not as intimidating as it probably sounds. If your eyes still glaze over a bit when you think about file systems, back up a moment and think about something a bit more mundane. Walk into your kitchen, breathe deep, and take a look around. You probably have a refrigerator, some cupboards, and some counter space. All of these areas can be used to store stuff.

In our kitchen, we store the glasses in the cupboard to the right of the sink, where they're handy. We store pots and pans in a lower cabinet, near the stove. We stack our plates in another cupboard, and our bowls right next to them. One cupboard (which I'm afraid to open) contains a wide assortment of plastic storage tubs and an even wider assortment of lids that don't match. One of the drawers is dedicated to silverware, and another to dishtowels. A holder on the countertop is full of miscellaneous wooden spoons and spatulas.

Our kitchen isn't unique; we store things in there because we use them to prepare food and do other tasks in the kitchen (such as exotic chemistry experiments and impromptu smoke-alarm tests). The idea is that, over the years, we've devised a way to store things that makes it easy for us to later retrieve those things.

Similarly, your operating system needs to organize a hard drive so it can easily store and retrieve things. This is the whole basis of a file system — it defines how the operating system stores and retrieves those things.

Just as you need to periodically examine your kitchen to determine if things can be organized better, this chapter helps you look at your file system to look for better ways to organize.

Which File System to Use?

Windows Vista supports two primary file systems, which go by two typically geeky acronyms: FAT and NTFS. Judging by the acronyms alone, you might think that NTFS is better than FAT. After all, it has more letters (it must be 33 percent better), and it doesn't have the mnemonic baggage that *fat* does.

Although some people may consider the case closed after such an astute analysis, other, more solid reasons are available for using one file system versus the other. The following sections introduce the two file systems, and then you can discover some guidelines for making your choice.

The FAT file system

FAT is an acronym for *file allocation table*. This file system has been around, in one form or another, since the introduction of DOS in 1981. Because it has a long, long history, FAT is supported by all versions of Windows, including Windows Vista.

Two variants exist: FAT (or FAT 16) and FAT 32. FAT 32 was introduced with Windows 95 (SR2) and is still supported in Windows Vista. The difference between the two versions of FAT is in how they allocate space for internally tracking files and the size of the hard drive partitions they can access.

FAT 16 can access drive partitions up to 2GB and can store only up to 512 entries in the root directory. (This has to do with the file system's internal structure and how it tracks files.) FAT 32 can access drive partitions up to 32GB in size and has no limit on the number of files that can be stored in the root directory. (The root directory is discussed more in Chapter 7.)

Windows Vista can format drives to both the FAT and FAT 32 standards, and it will readily read drives already formatted with either standard. (This is particularly useful if you need to format relatively small storage devices, such as floppy disks or thumb drives.)

The NTFS file system

NTFS is an acronym for *new-technology file system*. The file system was introduced with Windows NT. (The NT in Windows NT stands for *new technology*, so NTFS is the file system for Windows NT.)

When the engineers at Microsoft looked at the FAT file system used in DOS systems, they wanted to change how information was stored on a hard drive. In fact, they had to change it to meet some of the demands placed on the file system by Windows NT systems.

Windows NT systems were designed to be used in a networked environment — something never intended for FAT systems. (A *networked environment* is one in which multiple computers are connected in some sort of network.) Wider information accessibility meant greater concern for security and a potentially greater number of people accessing the data. FAT systems just weren't robust enough for such an environment.

The NTFS file system has grown over the years since Windows NT was introduced. NTFS can now access drive partitions up to 2TB in size. That's two terabytes, or 62.5 times larger than the largest partition accessible by FAT 32. Considering that the largest hard drive I can find on the shelf at my local computer store is 1TB, NTFS can handle the load just fine.

Making your choice

The default file system for hard drives in a Windows Vista system is always NTFS. In most situations, NTFS will work just fine for you, and you should accept this default when formatting. Some other nuggets are worth considering:

✔ If your system must be accessed by multiple operating systems (for instance, you have a dual-boot capability on your system), you should use a FAT 32 operating system.

✔ If your hard drive partition is very small (256MB or less), FAT 32 is a fast and efficient choice.

✔ If the hard drive partition is small and you want its data to be accessible if you boot to a floppy, use FAT 32.

✔ If you need to store very large files on your system (such as big databases or multimedia files), you should use FAT 32 or NTFS.

✔ If you need increased file security or you share your data with others over a network, use NTFS.

You can't use a FAT drive as your Vista system drive; it must be an NTFS drive.

Changing File Systems

Most Windows Vista systems that begin as Windows Vista systems (they've never had an older version of Windows on them) are formatted using the NTFS file system. If your system was upgraded a couple of times over the years and finally matured to a Windows Vista system, it may use the FAT or FAT 32 file system.

If your system uses a FAT file system and you don't have a specific need for it, you could benefit by converting to NTFS. The benefit is realized through better disk performance and better data security.

It's a good idea (actually, an excellent idea) to back up your data before you do any file system conversion.

Seeing what file system you use

Most people don't give their file system a second thought. With all this talk of file systems, you may suddenly be wondering what file system you have. To figure this out, follow these steps:

1. **Click the Start button.**

   Windows displays the Start menu.

2. **Right-click Computer and choose Manage.**

   If your system is configured to have a Computer icon on the desktop, you could right-click it. Either way, Windows opens the Computer Management window. The window shows a hierarchical display of tools and features on the left of the screen.

3. **If a right-pointing arrow is next to Storage (in the hierarchy), click it.**

   The tree is expanded, and you see Disk Management under the Storage item.

4. **Click the Disk Management option in the hierarchy.**

   A list of your disk drives appears at the right side of the Computer Management window, as mine are in Figure 14-1. At the top-right, you see a list of all your system's drives. The File System column indicates the file system used for the drive. (Different drives can use different file systems.)

Figure 14-1:
Take a look at your file system in the Computer Management window.

A wealth of information is found in the Computer Management window. If you scroll left and right, you can see each logical drive's capacity, along with how much of that space is available. The Status column indicates if something is wrong with a drive, allowing you to figure out if you need to take some remedial action.

Converting to NTFS

To convert an existing FAT drive to the NTFS file system, you use a program called (appropriately enough) `convert.exe`. You run this program from the command prompt. As an example, the following steps show you how to convert your D: drive to NTFS:

1. **Open a command prompt window by choosing Start⇨All Programs⇨ Accessories⇨Command Prompt.**

2. **In the command prompt window, type** convert d: /fs:ntfs**.**

   If you want to convert a different drive, replace d: with the drive letter desired, followed by a colon.

That's it: two steps. Conversion can take a while, so you may want to take a break, go watch a show, or go home for the evening. When the conversion is done, you should reboot your system.

Converting to FAT

Converting from NTFS to FAT is more difficult than vice versa. Windows doesn't include a utility that converts for you. Instead, you need to back up the data from the drive, reformat the drive, and restore the data. Chapter 7 contains information on how to back up your system. The idea is to make sure that you have a good, reliable backup that you can later use to restore you system.

With the backup in hand, you're ready to reformat the drive by following these steps:

1. **Open the Disk Management tool in the Computer Management window.**

   Follow the steps provided in the preceding section. You want your screen to look similar to Figure 14-1.

2. **Right-click the drive you want to format and choose Format from the context menu.**

   Windows displays the Format dialog box, shown in Figure 14-2.

Figure 14-2:
Getting
ready to
format a
drive.

Format D:	
Volume label:	Data
File system:	NTFS
Allocation unit size:	Default

☐ Perform a quick format
☐ Enable file and folder compression

OK   Cancel

3. **Using the File System drop-down list, choose the file system you want used for the drive.**

   The size of the drive you're formatting dictates the File System drop-down list choices. Only those file systems that can handle the drive you're formatting are listed.

4. **Click OK.**

Windows won't allow you to format a system drive (the one on which Windows is installed). If you want to format a system drive, you must run the Windows Setup program and format the drive from there.

Reformatting a drive erases — permanently — all the data on the drive. Don't reformat a drive unless you've backed up the data you want to keep.

When your reformatting task is complete, you should then restore the information from your backup to your newly formatted drive. The process you follow to restore the backup depends, in large part, on the way in which you created the backup. (As Chapter 7 discusses, there are different ways you can create backups of your data.) Refer to the documentation for your backup software in order to find out how to restore the data, or if you created a backup by simply copying files to a different media, copy those files back to the new drive.

Defragmenting Your Drive

How a file system stores information on a disk drive is interesting. First, it divides the available disk space into bins that can each contain data. Each bin is the same size as every other bin. The file system then goes about storing data in those bins. Each bin is allocated a single file; you can never store more than one file in a bin.

If a file requires more storage space than is available in a single bin, the file system grabs a group of storage bins — as many as necessary — to properly store the file. For instance, if the file requires 12 bins, then the file system allocates 12 bins to that file. As more files are stored, they're placed into bins after the large file.

Later, the large file may be deleted or decreased in size. Either way, it no longer requires the 12 original bins. The file system, recognizing the file is smaller, uses only the number of bins necessary and frees the other bins for use by other files.

After a while, files can become *fragmented,* meaning that they're stored in bins all over the drive. The files are considered fragmented because the bins in which they're stored aren't contiguous (right next to each other).

Fragmented files decrease the performance of Windows. The operating system can keep track of the files; that's not a problem. The problem is that when a file is fragmented, it can't be read from the disk all at once. Instead, the disk drive's read head must move all over the place to gather the file from its different bins.

Recognizing that fragmentation can slow down system performance, Microsoft included a tool with Windows called a *defragmenter,* which basically reads through each file and moves the file to contiguous bins on the drive. After defragmentation is completed, data can be read from the hard drive faster than it was before.

Third-party solutions

Many disk utility programs include disk defragmenters. For instance, both Norton SystemWorks and System Mechanic Professional include defragmenting utilities. (These examples are only two of dozens of such programs.)

Nothing is magical or inherently better about these programs — they work great. Third-party solutions may use different algorithms than the Windows defragmenter does, so they may run at a different speed. They end up with the same result: a defragmented drive.

If you're more comfortable with the user interface in a third-party product, feel free to use its defragmenter. If you don't have a third-party defragmenting utility, don't feel that you need to go out and get one; the one provided with Windows works just fine.

The very nature of defragmenting is very time consuming. You have thousands of files on your hard drive, each of which must be read, analyzed, and possibly moved around on the drive. Because of this, you should only run the defragmenter when other programs aren't running and when you have time to leave the computer. A good time is at the end of the day, when you're ready to quit working on the computer. You can let the defragmenter do its work while you're off doing other things.

To defragment a drive, follow these steps:

1. **Click Start⇨Computer.**

   If you have a Computer icon on your desktop, you can double-click it. Windows displays the Computer window.

2. **Right-click the drive you want to defragment and choose Properties from the context menu.**

   Windows displays the drive's Properties dialog box. Make sure the Tools tab is selected.

3. **Click Defragment Now.**

   You see the Disk Defragmenter window, shown in Figure 14-3.

4. **If you want Windows Vista to run Disk Defragmenter automatically, make sure Run Automatically is selected and then click Modify Schedule.**

   This option makes sense only if you never turn off your computer. Many people leave their computer on all the time, so you can set up Windows to automatically do the defragmenting deed based on whatever schedule you desire.

Figure 14-3:
You can
easily
defragment
drives in
Windows.

5. **To go ahead and defragment your drive right away, click Defragment Now.**

   Windows starts the defragmentation process, which can take a while. You can do other work while defragmenting is occurring, but I've generally found it's best to just turn off the monitor and go do something else for a while. This lets the computer focus its attention on the task at hand, and it stops "restarts" that may be caused by using a program that saves new fragmented files to the drive.

If you don't set defragmentation to be done automatically, you should analyze your drives periodically; perhaps once every other week or once a month. A great time to defragment is after you delete a bunch of files, uninstall software, or install a large software package.

Checking for Errors

Unfortunately, disk drives have been known to develop errors. Perhaps the operating system had a hiccup when it wrote a file to disk or a file wasn't deleted correctly. Any number of errors could develop over time.

For this reason, it's a good idea to check your hard drive for errors periodically. Windows provides two ways to check your system for errors: disk tools and chkdsk. The following sections discuss how you can perform the necessary checks.

Using Windows' disk tools

Okay, I admit it: I'm a closet Trekkie. I don't dress in costume and go to *Star Trek* conventions, but I love to watch the shows. (All except the *Enterprise* series — I never quite got into that one.) After a while, you get used to the characters and have a feel for how things work on the ship.

For instance, every time something went wrong with the computers in *Star Trek: The Next Generation,* Jordi LaForge (the ship's engineer) would always say, "We're running a level-five diagnostic to figure out the error." I never heard them talk about levels one through four; everything was a level-five diagnostic.

Computers don't come up with errors just in the fantasy world of *Star Trek.* Errors can develop on your hard drive. You can run your own equivalent of a level-five diagnostic by using Windows' disk tools to check, analyze, and fix any errors that crop up.

To start an analysis, follow these steps:

1. **Click Start⇨Computer.**

   If you have a Computer icon on your desktop, you can double-click it. Windows displays the Computer window.

2. **Right-click the drive you want to check for errors and choose Properties from the context menu.**

   Windows displays the drive's Properties dialog box. Make sure the Tools tab is selected.

3. **Click Check Now.**

   You see the Check Disk dialog box, shown in Figure 14-4.

Figure 14-4:
Get ready to
check a disk
for errors.

4. **Select either of the check boxes, as desired.**

   Clicking Scan for and Attempt Recovery of Bad Sectors provides the most comprehensive check. If you choose this option, you don't need to choose the one above it; the option automatically fixes all located errors.

5. **Click Start.**

When checking the disk, the program makes sure that the internal operating system links are uncorrupted and then works through all the files on the disk. If the program finds any minor errors, it fixes them. If it discovers anything more serious, and you opted to allow those errors to be fixed, then it works on those, as well.

Checking a hard drive for errors can only be done on a drive that isn't being used. If you're using the drive (or if Windows is using the drive), a full check can't be completed. In that case, the program asks if it can finish the check the next time you start Windows. If you answer affirmatively, then the next time you reboot your system, you won't be able to use Windows until the check is complete. (The check-upon-restart feature automatically uses the chkdsk utility described in the following section.)

Using chkdsk

Those old enough to remember DOS days may remember a utility called chkdsk. (Of course, those old enough to remember DOS may be suffering from memory loss, so they may *not* remember chkdsk.) Short for *check disk,* chkdsk is a command-line utility that checks the operating system and disk drive for any errors and optionally fixes them. (A *command-line utility* is one that you run, oddly enough, from a command line. You'll understand this better in just a moment.)

The chkdsk utility is available in Windows Vista, but only to users who have administrative rights for the system. It doesn't offer anything different than the tool covered in the preceding section, but some people like using a command-line utility. To use it, follow these steps:

1. **Open a command prompt window by choosing Start⇨All Programs⇨ Accessories⇨Command Prompt.**

2. **Enter the proper commands to switch to the drive you want to check.**

   For instance, if you want to check drive E:, then type **E:** and press the Enter key. The drive you specify is made the current drive.

3. **Type** chkdsk **and press Enter.**

   Using chkdsk without any parameters runs the program in read-only mode. This means that it doesn't fix anything; it only reports what it finds. If you want chkdsk to fix errors, use the **chkdsk /f** command instead.

The chkdsk program goes through three checks before reporting its findings. It:

1. Checks the file system to make sure that all the file links are valid.

2. Checks the system indexes for errors.

3. Checks (on NTFS drives) security descriptors to make sure that file security is intact.

You can't run chkdsk in fix mode on a disk that's in use. (An in-use drive is one that has files open.) If you try, the program informs you that the disk is in use and gives you the opportunity to "dismount the volume." If you instruct chkdsk to do this, all the open files on the drive are closed and the drive is made inaccessible. This action could result in data loss. You should choose to dismount only if you're really sure you won't lose critical data.

If the drive is in use and you choose not to dismount the volume, chkdsk offers to perform the check the next time you start Windows. If you choose this option, the check is completed the next time you reboot.

To Compress or Not?

A few years ago, the most expensive part of most computer systems was the hard drive. As a result, people tended to have relatively small hard drives in their computers; they just couldn't afford anything more expensive.

Small hard drives meant there wasn't much room to store information. (I remember routinely running out of hard-drive space on my system.) One solution to the not-enough-space syndrome was to use some sort of disk compression program. Third-party utilities started cropping up, promising to compress the information on your hard drive.

Eventually, Microsoft made compression a feature of Windows itself. Not only could you compress individual files, but you could also compress entire folders and drives. The downside, of course, is that the compression process slows down your system, overall. As information goes through the compression/decompression algorithms, information going to and from the hard drive can bottleneck.

Windows Vista still has the compression feature available in it. Just because the feature is available doesn't mean you should use it, however. The historical catalyst for compression was the expense of large hard drives. Most computer systems now have large hard drives (40GB or more), and hard drives are very, very inexpensive by historical standards.

Bottom line: If you want your system to run faster, don't use disk compression.

Chapter 15

Managing Windows Updates

· ·

In This Chapter

▶ Picking the best way to get updates

▶ Determining which updates to install

· ·

Windows Vista is an amazing operating system. It consists of millions of lines of programming code, all geared toward controlling your computer the way you want.

Along with millions of lines of programming code comes the opportunity for millions of computer bugs. Windows doesn't have millions of bugs (thank goodness), due to good programmers and extensive testing before the operating system was released to the public.

Even so, rest assured that Windows Vista *does* have bugs — there's no way around it. Windows updates come into play here. As remaining bugs are identified and corrected, the more serious bugs are stamped out with updates. As updates accumulate, they're collected into service packs, which provide a wholesale update to Windows.

Unfortunately, some people in the world are committed to breaking Windows or abusing your system. Such attempts typically happen over the Internet. Microsoft tries to stay on top of things, issuing patches designed to make your system more secure in an inherently insecure world. (And aren't you glad that Windows Vista is much more secure than any previous version of Windows?)

To deal with fixed bugs and patched holes, Microsoft normally releases several Windows updates every month. To safely and efficiently deliver updates to millions of Windows users, it developed an update system that's every bit as amazing as Windows itself.

This chapter examines the different ways you can update your Windows system. You can also find out which updates to install and how to remove files left behind in the update process.

The Windows world differentiates between an update and an upgrade. An *update* is a Windows Vista revision. It generally includes new and improved versions of the programs and drivers you already have. An *upgrade* occurs when you actually change your operating system version. For instance, going from Windows XP to Windows Vista is an upgrade.

Getting Updates the Way You Want

Updating Windows couldn't be much easier. For the last couple of versions, updates can be downloaded from the Internet and installed directly on your machine.

Updates are available either manually or automatically. The following sections provide the information you need to understand both options.

Manual updates

Windows Vista is, by default, configured to do automatic updates of itself. For most people, this default setting is fine; it means less work on their part. Others (perhaps you?) mistrust any "automatic" setting in Windows, particularly when it means the automatic download and installation of pieces and parts of the operating system.

If you're of this persuasion, or if your computer was previously used by someone of this persuasion, then you'll need to check for Windows updates manually. It used to be that such updates involved inserting a disk into a drive or a CD into a tray. Not anymore; you can check for updates over the Internet with a minimal amount of fuss.

Here's a good idea: Close any files and shut down any programs you're using before updating. Under very rare circumstances, you can lose data during the update. Even more possibly, the update won't complete because some component that needs updating is being used by the open program.

To manually update Windows, follow these steps:

1. **Make sure you're connected to the Internet.**

2. **Choose Start➪All Programs➪Windows Update.**

   Windows displays the Windows Update window, shown in Figure 15-1. If there are any updates available, you're informed in the window.

Figure 15-1:
Checking
for updates
is an easy
task.

3. **Click Check for Updates.**

   Windows connects to the computers back in Redmond and compares the state of your version of Windows to what's available in the way of updates. If there are any updates available, you'll see an indication of that fact.

4. **If updates are available, click Install Updates.**

   Windows prepares to install the update and then actually performs the installation. (You may be prompted to restart your system as part of the update.)

5. **If your system didn't need to be restarted, close the Windows Update window.**

Automatic updates

Because updates can be delivered via the Internet, Microsoft added a really cool feature that automatically notifies you of any updates. Called, amazingly enough, Automatic Updates, the service can download the updates and install them automatically.

To control the Automatic Updates service, follow these steps:

1. **Choose Start➪All Programs➪Windows Update.**

   Windows displays the Windows Update window. (Refer to Figure 15-1.)

2. **Click the Change Settings link.**

   The Change Settings window is displayed, as shown in Figure 15-2.

Figure 15-2:
Control how
automatic
updates
occur.

3. Choose one of the four options available in the window.

Your options include the following:

- **Install Updates Automatically.** The first radio button tells Windows to automatically download the updates and install them without notice. With this option, you can schedule updates. (If your computer is off when an update is scheduled, the update is done the next time you turn on your system.)

- **Download Updates but Let Me Choose Whether to Install Them.** The second radio button causes Windows to download all updates and store them on disk. After they're downloaded, you're notified that updates are ready. Any updates you decline at that point are deleted from your disk.

- **Check for Updates but Let Me Choose Whether to Download and Install Them.** The third radio button results in you being notified when updates are available, at which point you have the option to accept or decline the update. If you accept, the update is downloaded, and you're notified when it's ready to install. (You have another chance to decline it after it is downloaded and ready to install.)

- **Never Check for Updates.** The fourth radio button results in automatic updating being turned off completely. You can manually check for updates, as described in the preceding section.

4. Click the OK button and then close the Change Settings dialog box.

You can change how updates are done or turn automatic updating off completely.

Don't fall for it!

I just got an e-mail today that has the subject "Use this patch immediately!" It showed as being from Microsoft, and the message said

> Dear friend, use this Internet Explorer patch now!
> There are dangerous virus in the Internet now!
> More than 400.000 already infected!

Yeah, right.

I get several of these messages each week,

using poor English to scare me into running the "update" attached to the message. The problem is, Microsoft never, ever, ever sends its updates via e-mail (and they usually proofread their messages better). This e-mail carries a virus, and if I run the "patch," I'll have the virus.

If you get similar messages claiming to be from Microsoft, delete them right away. They won't hurt you unless you're silly enough to run the program attached to the message.

When you turn on the automatic update feature, Windows handles future updates. You should still do a manual update to check for any previous updates that you need to consider.

Picking an update method

Manual or automatic? Automatic or manual? I remember figuring out how to drive a manual. It was a 1964 Ford Mustang. We were driving through Pennsylvania. I was fine after I got going and nobody slowed down in front of me on the freeway. Coming to a stop was interesting, however, as I would invariably forget to downshift. (My friend was *sooooo* understanding.)

Believe it or not, the decision to use manual or automatic updating is similar to my figuring out how to drive a manual transmission car. If I forgot to push in the clutch or downshift at the right time, the car didn't work the way it should. (But it did make some very interesting sounds.) Same with Windows updates — if you turn off automatic updating and forget to update, you run the risk of your system not working the way it should.

You already know that some updates are critical — you run a security risk if you don't use them. Viruses and all sorts of bad stuff would love to find a home on your system. If you don't have the proper updates in place, you run a greater risk of providing a home to bad stuff.

Big Brother is watching . . .

. . . and his name is Bill. But don't worry — he only wants the best for you!

Some people bristle when they hear that Microsoft sucks information from their systems. Yet, both the manual and automatic update systems do exactly that. It's unavoidable that the systems know a little bit about you, just so they can tell you what updates you need.

Microsoft assures users that it doesn't gather any information that would allow you to be individually identifiable, such as your e-mail address, name, or similar data. Although you can be identified based on the product ID and key (assuming you registered your copy of Windows Vista), the product information isn't maintained beyond the end of the update session. Microsoft

retrieves it during the update just to make sure that the version of Windows being updated is a valid, licensed version.

The company uses the information collected to determine what to offer to you in the way of updates. It also aggregates the information it receives, which allows it to determine collective information about its user base.

If you're concerned about Big Brother Bill watching you, you can contact Microsoft for CD updates at 800-360-7561. (There's no indication of how long Microsoft will continue this method of updating.) Of course, when you update this way, Microsoft still needs to get your name and address so they can send you the CD. (Wave hi to the cameras!)

For me, the easiest way to do the updates is to make them automatic. My personality insists that I like to be notified about updates instead of just having them happen, so I set my update option accordingly in the Change Settings window, shown in Figure 15-2. I may even ignore the update notification for a few days at a time — but at least I know the updates are there and I can run them at any time. Take a hard look at your personality and decide which way you want to go — manual or automatic. Pick the one that means your system is the most up-to-date and works best for you.

The automatic update features are great if you have a high-speed Internet connection. If you have a dial-up connection, you probably don't want to use automatic update. You should instead configure your system for manual updates and make checking part of your weekly regimen.

Which Updates Do You Really Need?

If you install a new version of Windows Vista, you may visit the Windows update site and find a good number of updates that you can download. Of course, doing a lot of updates all at once can take a lot of time — you may wonder if you really need to do them.

The answer is an unqualified maybe. Some updates are critical, meaning you really need to do them. They include updates to the core operating system or updates that fix identified security problems.

You can easily tell which updates fall into which category. If you're doing a manual update and scan for updates, there's a link available under the Install Updates button that says View Available Updates. Clicking the link shows what updates are available, along with an estimation on Microsoft's part of how important those updates are. You'll find categorizations such as these:

- **Important:** These updates are the most pressing. You should update everything in this category. If you don't, you risk leaving your system vulnerable to security problems that Microsoft discovered and corrected.

- **Recommended:** These updates are less pressing. They consist of changes to the operating system files that make up Windows Vista. For instance, an obscure operational error may have come to light.

- **Optional:** These updates are nice to make, but definitely not at the top of the list. They include updates to various hardware drivers, including drivers for hardware you might not even have.

As you review the proposed changes in the second and third categories, you may notice that some updates may be for programs you have installed but never use. If you know you don't need the update, don't worry about installing it.

If you have limited time, you may want to put off updating until you have a chunk of time. A good time to update is at the end of the day, when nothing else is going on. You can visit the Windows Updates site, find out what you need, and download the top one or two critical updates. Work your way through them all, as time allows, and soon your system is updated.

Chapter 16

Getting a New System

In This Chapter

▶ Knowing when a new system is necessary

▶ Determining the type of system to get

▶ Reinstalling your software

▶ Moving data from the old system

I remember walking into my teenage son's room one day and being shocked that it was trashed. Literally trashed — junk-food wrappers everywhere, a few magazines, clothing piles (reeking of eau-de-locker), books, and some DVDs. To top things off, the dog was making himself right at home, having torn up some of the clothes and dragged in his play toys. The dog looked at me (with a semi-menacing-yet-innocent smirk), and I clearly remember being able to figure out that my son was somewhere under the pile of stuff on the bed.

That was it — the last straw — the dog was smirking and my son was being swallowed by his own detritus. Something had to be done! The most satisfying solution was to lock up the room and sell the whole thing. (The room, that is.) I'm sure we could get a new room, with an upgraded son and dog that would work better and smirk less.

You've probably felt the same way about your computer system once in a while: You take a look around, notice how cluttered everything is, and decide it's better to just shut it down and start all over with a new system. (From personal experience, I can tell you that it's much easier to get a new computer than to get a new room, son, and dog.)

This chapter focuses on the ins and outs of getting a new system. (In referring to a *system,* I'm speaking of new hardware here. I figure that you don't really need new software at this point.) I spend very little time actually picking out a new system; most of the information concerns confidently reaching the decision for a new system and making the transition as easy as possible.

If you're satisfied with your current system's speed and capacity but you're just tired of the clutter, you may be better off starting from scratch with your current system. Chapter 21 covers how to start over with the system you have.

When Is a New System Justified?

You can find many ways to justify a new computer system. (Even more ways abound to rationalize one.) Unless you have money to burn, however, you probably don't want to abandon reason and rush out to buy another computer system. No — you need to make sure that getting a new system is the best course of action for you.

If you're thinking about getting a new computer at work, check with your IT department to see if the company has requirements that need to be met for new systems. In addition, you'll undoubtedly have paperwork to fill out. The paperwork, more than likely, includes information on how to justify a computer purchase.

My experience indicates that all the reasons for a new system boil down to only a few primary reasons:

- **A new version of your software requires a new system.** If it's time to upgrade to a new version of some critical software or a new operating system (such as Windows Vista), the new software may require a larger hard drive, more memory, or a faster processor. Check with the software publisher to verify the new version's system requirements.

- **What you need to do has changed.** You may have taken on a new job or project that requires you to work with more or with different types of data. If your old system is no longer suitable for your new job requirements, a new system is in order.

- **External changes require a change.** Changes in your company's computing structure may require that you get a new computer. For instance, your company may install a new network that requires increased horsepower that your current system can't deliver.

- **Hardware has failed or become obsolete.** You may have a major computer component that dies, mandating that you get a new system. In addition, you may seek to upgrade your current system and find that the component cost is just as much as a newer system would be.

- **Clutter has ruined your system.** Clutter can absolutely ruin your system. I'm not talking about unused data files lying about; I'm talking about the type of clutter that comes from spyware, viruses, and other damaging software. If you can't clean it off, you may need to start over from scratch. (See Chapter 10 for info on how to purge all this bad stuff from your system.)

Remember that a computer is nothing but a tool; it helps you accomplish tasks you wouldn't be able to otherwise perform. If getting a different tool (a newer computer) helps you accomplish your work faster and easier, then justifying a new system is relatively easy to do.

Getting a new computer system only makes your computing life uncluttered for a short time. Clutter happens through poor computing habits. If you're not ready to change your habits, your new system is doomed to be just as cluttered as your old. Getting a new system is a great time to make changes in your habits, however — just remember to think through how you use your system on a daily basis.

What Should You Get?

Deciding what type of new system to get depends, in large part, on your budget. If money isn't a concern, reach for the sky! In fact, just walk into your neighborhood computer store and tell the on-commission sales rep that you want the top-of-the-line system. No doubt you'll get something to satisfy your every computational need and keep you happy for at least the next two years.

For most people, such an approach to a new system is unrealistic because money *is* an issue. (It's always an issue.) Before you decide what type of system you want to get, realistically figure out how much you can comfortably afford for your computer. That gives you a starting point.

You should count on your computer system to be usable for about two or three years only. After that time, your software needs change. As new versions of the software (and Windows) come out, they always require larger and faster systems. In a few years, when you want to upgrade your operating system or your software, you may need a whole new system.

The following sections don't provide a definitive shopping guide for computer systems; computer magazines and books devoted to the topic tackle that best. Instead, you can find some guidance here on the general types of systems to look into.

High-end systems

The most expensive systems on the market are always the high-end systems. These systems are defined by the most powerful processors, gobs of the fastest memory, super-fast USB and FireWire connectors, the fastest DVD and CD-ROM drives, and the like. Everything in a high-end system is the newest, fastest, and most powerful. (I can just hear Tim Allen's testosterone pumping as he grunts a primal "Arrrhh, arrrhh, arrrhh.")

The fact of the matter is, most people don't need high-end systems. (A lot of people *want* them, but they don't *need* them.) Typically, high-end systems are appropriate for people using software that requires a lot of resources. For instance, if you use your system for video editing, architectural modeling, generating animations, or crunching large databases, you need a high-end system. Most state-of-the-art game players can benefit from high-end systems, as well.

High-end system purchasers always pay a premium for their systems because equipment on the bleeding edge of technology always costs more. Fully configured high-end systems often cost in excess of $2,000, not including the monitor. (You'll undoubtedly want that to be high-end, as well.)

Before deciding to plunk down a lot of your hard-earned bucks, make sure that you really need the horsepower you're trying to harness.

Mid-range systems

The vast majority of computer users are satisfied with a mid-range system. If you're writing letters to Aunt Martha (or your boss, who happens to be Aunt Martha), juggling the books, browsing the Web, or tracking your pinochle club membership roster, then a mid-range system is just what you need.

Age is the primary thing that sets a mid-range system apart from a high-end system. The components in a mid-range system typically aren't leading edge; they've been on the market for a while and no longer command the premium price they once did.

In addition, mid-range systems normally aren't maxed out on memory or hard drive space. In fact, if you need a mid-range system, memory and hard drive space is something to which you should pay particular attention. Get at least 1GB of memory and at least an 80GB hard drive; otherwise, you'll find Windows Vista to be very sluggish. (Memory and hard drives are discussed more in Chapter 17.)

For your mid-range system, you should expect to pay anywhere from $1,100 to $1,500. The primary difference in price depends on whose name is on the box and how much memory and drive space you get.

If you have high-speed Internet access at the location you plan to use the new computer, make sure the system includes an Ethernet network card. (Network cards allow you to connect to a network, such as the Internet.) Most mid-range and high-end systems are shipped with Ethernet support built in, but check anyway. High-speed Internet access requires that you have a network card installed.

Roll your own

It used to be that only dyed-in-the-wool geeks built their own computer systems. DITW geeks still do, but they aren't the only ones. Most urban areas (and some rural areas) have computer stores that build systems for you. All you do is pick the components you want; they put them together and make them work for a small fee. If you prefer, you can take the components home and put them together yourself.

Building your own system is a great way to ensure that you get exactly the type of system

you want. You can even talk to the geeks on the payroll (at the store) to get the latest word on which components are better and from which to stay away. You can often save money by building your own system when compared to the large commercial computer outlets.

For more information on building your own systems, check out *Building a PC For Dummies*, 4th Edition, by Mark Chambers (published by Wiley).

Low-end systems

Most systems priced below $1,000 are low end. Systems at this price are sold by discount retailers and many mail-order outlets. If your computing needs are very limited — perhaps you need to write letters or check e-mail only — you may be able to get by with a low-end system.

Don't expect high-powered performance from a low-end system. If a system doesn't cost much money, normally it's because the manufacturer left out some things. Two things normally left out: RAM and hard drive space. True, you get some memory (a minimum amount) and a hard drive (a small one), but skimping on these two items can seriously affect a system's performance.

Low-end systems also normally skimp on the video card in the computer. Many software packages today require extremely capable video cards. For instance, some computer games (not necessarily those that require high-end systems) won't even work on low-end systems because of the video cards used.

Portable systems

Seasoned road warriors know that their non-stop mobile life makes a portable computer necessary. In fact, you might want to consider getting rid of your desktop and working solely with a portable if you often hit the road.

If you decide to use a laptop computer as your main system, be prepared to spend a bit more. Actually, you can spend a lot more when compared to a comparable desktop, but that's the price of reliability and style.

To figure out what type of laptop you should get, figure out whether you need a high-, mid-, or low-end system, as described in the preceding sections. After you have your system needs pegged, look for a portable computer that provides those capabilities.

 Consider getting a docking station for your portable, as well. The docking station stays on your desktop, with your monitor, mouse, and full-size keyboard attached to it. When you're not out battling on the road, you slide your system into the docking station and instantly convert it into something more comfortable to use on a desktop.

Preparing for the New System

You've decided: You're going to get a new system. You've done your homework and figured out exactly what system you want and how you can do it. Now you need to get ready for its arrival.

Assuming you're replacing your current system, you can do some things to make the transition go much smoother. The following sections detail things you can do.

Collecting pieces and parts

As you use your computer over time, you may tend to collect what I call "pieces and parts." For instance, I have a small drawer full of installation discs and several files full of manuals. These items become very important when you get a new system.

To prepare for replacing an old system, you need the following:

- **Program inventory:** Chapter 3 provides detailed information on assembling a program inventory. You need one not only because it lets you document what's on your current system, but also because it allows you to see what you need to install on your new one.

- **Printer installation discs:** Many printers ship with discs that contain operating system drivers and monitoring software. If you plan on the new system using the printer your current system uses, you need these discs so you can use the printer. (If you can't locate the printer driver discs, or you know the discs don't contain drivers for Windows Vista, you can probably download the driver files from the printer manufacturer's Web site and create your own disc.)

✔ **Software installation discs:** Whenever I tackle a replacement system, I pull out the aforementioned small drawer and start comparing the discs to what I have on my program inventory. If you're performing an upgrade, make sure to collect the *original* software discs, too. Otherwise, you won't be able to upgrade. See the sidebar, "Avoid this problem!"

In addition to the installation discs, most software needs some sort of installation key or program code to work properly. As you assemble the different software discs, make sure you have the necessary codes to reinstall the software from scratch. The code may be in the software's documentation, on the CD's jewel case, or on a copy of a registration e-mail. Regardless, these pieces and parts are every bit as important as the discs.

Collecting information

To get your new computer system functioning just the way you like, collect some information about the way your current system is configured. Specifically, pay attention to how software is configured and how the network is set up.

Avoid this problem!

The last time I did an installation, I ran into a problem that you can avoid. I had a software program that was an upgrade to an earlier copy I originally had on my system. I dutifully pulled out the installation discs and the installation key, and I had them ready when the new system was up and running. I couldn't install the software, however, because it was an upgrade; an older version of the software wasn't on the new system.

The solution seems easy enough — just grab the discs for the older software version, right? (Most upgrade installations allow you to insert the old discs to make sure you qualify for the upgrade.) Problem was, I had thrown away the original discs in the last big office purge I did, about six months before.

The bottom line was that I wasn't able to install the upgrade. You can avoid the problem if you collect the original discs of any truly upgraded software.

Why can't I just swap out the guts?

In geekspeak, *swapping out the guts* means moving the hard drive from one system to another system. The hard drive, after all, has the operating system, programs, and data that you used on your old system. Moving the hard drive from one system to the other could save quite a bit of time — or not!

An interesting thing happens when you install Windows. The operating system takes stock of its surroundings and writes information about your system into its Registry (and a couple of other places). This includes information about your processor, memory, and peripherals.

Change out your peripherals, no problem. Change the amount of memory, no problem. Change the processor? Big problem. I had a Windows 2000 system that worked great, and I moved the hard drive to an upgraded system that had a much faster processor.

Bam! The system wouldn't boot. It wouldn't even alert me to a problem with the new system;

it looked dead. At least, it looked dead until I put the hard drive back in the old system; then it worked fine.

The only way to fix the problem was to wipe the hard drive, reinstall the operating system, and start fresh. My short, planned-at-two-hour upgrade ended up taking two days. Really big hassle.

Windows Vista is a little smarter — but only a little. If you have Windows Vista on the hard drive, you can move the drive to a new system, but you still must do a system reinstall. Your data and programs remain intact, but stick Vista on the system so it recognizes the new processor.

Of course, the ironic part of this whole scenario (moving the hard drive) is that if you were able to do it successfully, you'd also be moving all the clutter from your old system to your new.

Life sometimes isn't fair.

Software configuration settings

After a piece of software is on a system (such as your current system), you configure it to work properly with other software and to reflect how you want it to perform. If you want the software on your new system to function as it does on your current system, note how you configured the software.

Determining whether the software allows you to export its configuration settings — and then exporting them — is the best way to accurately save the configuration settings. You can store those settings on a diskette to import them onto the new system after the software is installed.

If your software doesn't allow you to export configuration settings, write down your settings for re-creation on the new system. Simply display each configuration dialog box and write down what you see. Make sure you go through all your installed software and either export settings or write them down, as appropriate.

Network settings

If your computer belongs to a network, it uses a collection of settings that specify how communication is to occur over that network. To see what network settings you currently use, follow these steps if your old system uses Windows XP:

1. **Choose Start⇨Control Panel⇨Network Connections.**

   A window shows your different network connections.

2. **Double-click the connection used for your network.**

   You should see a Status dialog box; at the bottom is a Properties button.

3. **Click the Properties button.**

   You see the connection's Properties dialog box, shown in Figure 16-1.

Figure 16-1:
View
network
connection
properties.

The Properties dialog box shows different clients, services, and protocols used by this particular network connection. Quite a few could be listed in the center of the dialog box.

You're interested in the Internet Protocol (TCP/IP) option.

4. **Select the Internet Protocol (TCP/IP) option and click the Properties button.**

   You see a Properties dialog box for the protocol, as shown in Figure 16-2.

   The numbers in this Properties dialog box are very important; they allow your computer to connect to your local area network (LAN), the Internet, or both.

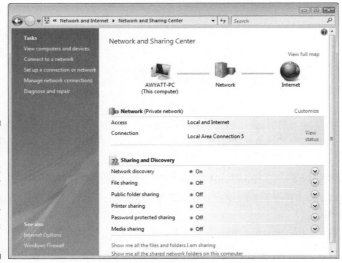

Figure 16-2:
Settings for
a network
connection.

If the old system already has Windows Vista installed on it, you can locate the
important network settings by following these steps:

1. Choose Start⇨Control Panel⇨View Network Status and Tasks.

Windows displays the Network Center, which shows your various
network connections (see Figure 16-3).

Figure 16-3:
The
Network
Center
shows the
way your
network is
set up.

2. **Click the View Status link to the right of your network connection.**

   The Status dialog box for the network springs into view. This dialog box contains some interesting information but not the settings you need to record.

3. **Click the Details button.**

   The Network Connection Details dialog box appears, as shown in Figure 16-4.

Figure 16-4: Details about a network connection are easy to display.

The information in the Network Connection Details dialog box is helpful because it shows you whether the connection is using IPv4 or IPv6 (or both) protocols. If there's information beside either (or both) of these settings, note it temporarily.

4. **Click the Close button.**

   The Status dialog box should still be visible.

5. **Click the Properties button.**

   You see the connection's Properties dialog box, which is very similar to the one shown for Windows XP in Figure 16-1. The dialog box shows different clients, services, and protocols used by the network connection.

6. **Select the Internet Protocol version that corresponds to the protocols being used in the system and then click Properties.**

   This is why you displayed the Network Connection Details dialog box in Step 3. Pick the Internet Protocol Version 4 or Internet Protocol Version 6 option, as appropriate, and then click Properties. You see a Properties dialog box for the protocol, similar to what's shown in Figure 16-2.

The numbers in this Properties dialog box are very important; they represent the configuration of this particular network connection, and you should write them down completely.

Some networks (and some Internet connections) may require that your computer be configured so that both IP and DNS addresses are obtained automatically. If your computer is set up that way, your configuration task on the new system is very easy. If not, write down the information in the dialog box exactly as shown.

Reinstalling Programs

Whenever I set up a new computer system, the most time-consuming part of the process is installing software programs. I normally have to block out half a day or more to get everything installed.

Before reinstalling actual software, you should do these things:

- ✔ Make sure that the operating system is functioning properly.
- ✔ Ensure that all the peripherals (including the printer) have the proper drivers installed and can be used.
- ✔ Set up your Internet connection and make sure it's functioning.

To make installing software smoother, refer to the items you gathered prior to setting up the new system. (See the section "Preparing for the New System," earlier in this chapter.) Pay particular attention to the software inventory; use it as a checklist of programs to install. As you finish each one, check it off the list.

As you install software on the new system, focus on one program at a time. Make sure you fully install each one, start it up, and configure it before moving on to the next one. You may even want to put away any discs and manuals for each software program as you finish it up.

Transferring Data

The last step in setting up a new system is to transfer data from your old system. You probably accumulated quite a bit of data on the old system, and you probably want at least some of it on the new system.

The key in successfully transferring data is to transfer only the data you need — nothing more and nothing less. I recommend archiving the data you don't need onto a CD-ROM drive or other long-term storage medium. (See Chapter 7 for more about archiving.)

If you're unsure whether you need certain data, place it on archive CDs, separate from those you use to archive the data you're certain you don't need. Clearly mark the CDs as "don't know" data and put them near your desk. Over time, you may transfer some data from those CDs, but the rest of the data can eventually be moved into your long-term archive files.

If your system is connected to a network and you can simultaneously connect both the old and new system, then data transfer can be very, very easy. All you need to do is share drives on either the old or new system, and then copy information from one system to the other or do so via shared drives. Just drag and drop — very easy.

If you can't get both systems set up on a network, the next easiest solution is to transfer via CD-ROM. (This transfer process assumes you have a CD-ROM burner on the old system.) Just copy the information to CD, plop the CD into the new system, and copy from the CD.

When you copy information from a CD-ROM to a hard drive, Windows sometimes leaves the read-only file attribute set on any of the files transferred. After you copy a file from the CD-ROM to the hard drive, right-click the file and choose Properties. Make sure the Read-Only flag is deselected in the Properties dialog box.

If the old system doesn't have a CD-ROM burner, look for the largest-capacity medium that works on both systems. This may mean transferring data via Zip drive or even (heaven forbid!) floppy drive — provided the new system even has either of these. The lower the medium's capacity, the more *copying cycles* (copy on to the media then copy off of the media) you need to complete.

If you can get your hands on an external hard drive that connects via USB or FireWire, use it to transfer data. Copy data from the old system to the hard drive and then plug the hard drive into the new system and copy from it to the new system. The whole process is quick and painless.

Part V
Advanced Cleaning for the Truly Brave

The 5th Wave   By Rich Tennant

"Well, the first level of Windows Vista security seems good—I can't get the shrink-wrapping off."

In this part . . .

This part focuses on implementing deep-cleaning strategies:

- ✔ Determine whether you need more memory or a larger hard drive
- ✔ Secure your system
- ✔ Clean up in a networked environment
- ✔ Work with the Registry
- ✔ Fix a corrupted Windows XP installation

Chapter 17

Memory and Storage

In This Chapter

▶ Understanding memory usage

▶ Determining if you need more storage space

▶ Picking an internal or external drive

▶ Looking at alternative storage devices

When I'm asked what a room needs most, I always reply that two things a room can't have too many of are electrical outlets and phone jacks. When asked the same question about computers, I always indicate two things you can't have too much of are memory and storage space.

We live in a time when both memory and disk space are cheap, cheap, cheap. You can get a gig of RAM these days for what you used to shell out for 64MB in the not-so-distant past. In addition, you can get hard drives for next to nothing. My first hard drive, for my original IBM PC, cost $3,000 and stored a whopping 30MB of data. You can get almost 3TB (that's *tera*bytes) for that same cost today — and store 100,000 times as much data!

This chapter focuses on those two essentials of any computer systems: memory and storage. Both are inexpensive, so you can easily get all the memory and storage space you need. In the following sections, you discover how to determine the amount of RAM you need and whether you really need an additional hard drive.

How Windows Uses Memory

Being susceptible to the ills of time just like any other human, I love a bumper sticker I once saw. It said, "Of all the things I've lost, I miss my mind the most." As I get older, I notice that my memory isn't as sharp as it once was. What a pain. I figure it's because my mind, over the years, has become cluttered with too many unessential things. I'm working on a way to get rid of those unessential items. The plan involves a marine battery and a set of jumper cables. Unfortunately, I can't seem to find anyone willing to help me test the plan.

Windows, too, relies on memory. For the most part, Windows doesn't forget things. Windows relies on two types of memory — physical and virtual. *Physical memory* is determined by the actual RAM installed in your system. In most systems, RAM is specified in multiples of 32 megabytes (MB). The majority of systems running Windows Vista have at least 1GB of memory, and some may have much more.

Virtual memory is maintained by Windows in a special area on the hard drive known as a *swap file* or a *pagefile*. (It's a sad commentary on geekdom that the words *page* and *file* have been used together so often that they're now considered a single word: pagefile.) This special file is treated as an extension of your physical RAM. If a program or its data won't fit in the available physical RAM, they're stored in the pagefile.

The pagefile is also referred to as a swap file because the information in the file is "swapped" in and out of physical RAM, as the need arises. For instance, say that Excel is open on your system. You haven't opened a workbook in a while, so Windows shuffles the memory used by Excel to the pagefile. When you click the Excel task on the taskbar, Windows quickly stores another program's memory into the pagefile and loads the Excel memory image from the pagefile into physical RAM.

This may sound confusing, but it allows you to work with quite a few more programs than you otherwise could; the technology is neat. The downside to virtual memory is that relying on too much of it reduces performance. Face it — even the fastest hard drive is slower than the slowest RAM. If Windows spends a lot of time swapping information to and from the pagefile, it can't be doing things it should be doing.

Determining Whether You Need More Memory

The single biggest thing you can do to increase the performance of a Windows Vista system is to add memory. Most systems have less memory than they should. Fortunately, memory prices are not terribly high right now. If you can determine how much additional memory you need, then you should do the upgrade.

Windows provides a relatively simple way to determine how much more memory you should add. The only problem is that you have to understand a foreign language (geekspeak) to know what's going on! (I'll do a little translation as you go along; you'll see what I mean.) Just follow these steps:

1. **Turn on your system and use it for a while: Load some of the programs you normally use, work with some good-sized files, and print a few reports.**

   The idea is to put a normal load on your system that reflects the way you use your computer.

2. **After using the system for a while, right-click any blank area of the taskbar and choose Task Manager.**

3. **When the Windows Task Manager window appears, choose the Performance tab, shown in Figure 17-1.**

Figure 17-1: Windows monitors how memory is used.

The Performance tab has a ton of information; some of it may even be meaningful to some geek, somewhere. Most normal people look at this tab and see terms such as *Cached* and *Kernel Memory,* their eyes glaze over, and they quietly shut the dialog box. You aren't going to do that, however. You need to pay attention only to a few of the figures shown. With my gentle guidance, you can extract those figures without your eyes glazing too much.

4. **Look at the Total figure in the Physical Memory area.**

   This figure indicates the amount of physical RAM currently installed, in megabytes.

5. **Look at the System area.**

> This area tells how your memory is being used by all the pieces, parts, and partisans of Windows. The Page File item is particularly helpful because it tells you both how much of your swap file is being used and what the max size is for your swap file.
>
> If the amount of your pagefile being used is getting pretty close to the maximum size of your pagefile, then you don't have enough memory in your computer. (Simple, huh?) The idea is to add RAM until the pagefile being used is quite a bit lower than the maximum for the file.

After you know that you need more memory, trot down to your local computer store and let them know. Better yet, take your computer box with you (you don't need the cables, keyboard, mouse, or monitor) so their on-staff tech-type person can see exactly the type of memory you need. Memory is cheap these days, so have them add enough memory so that you have 1.5 to 2.0 GB. They'll be able to let you know if your motherboard (the heart of your computer) can handle even more memory and how much that could cost.

With the additional memory installed, you should notice an immediate performance improvement in your system.

Will Another Hard Drive Help?

I've developed a theory that the entire self-storage industry was built on the basis of poor individual habits. In my town, every block or two, you can see self-storage facilities, with row after neat row of little garages, waiting to be filled with who knows what.

Two generations ago, people raised families of eight or more children in houses of about 800 square feet. Today, people with one or two children can't fit all their stuff into a 2,700 square-foot house with an attached three-car garage. So, rather than cull out some stuff, they go rent a storage shed so they can collect even more.

This pack-rat mentality spills over to computer use. People collect gigabytes of data and fear deleting any of it because they may, at some unknown future time, need it. Because you can't go rent a storage shed for the data, they do the next best thing and think about adding a hard drive.

If you're tempted to get another hard drive, you need to know — right up front — that more hard drive space won't solve any clutter problems. All it does is provide more space to spread out the clutter.

This being said, you can benefit from a new hard drive for a couple of reasons, as described in the following sections.

Hard drive prices continue to be low — very low. I purchased an 80GB Samsung drive a couple of days ago for the regular price of only $59.98. Right next to that was space for the 300GB Samsung drives, available on sale for only $79.99. (I would have bought the 300GB drive, but they were all sold out.) If you shop around, you can get some amazing prices on huge hard drives.

Faster speed

New hard drives are faster than old hard drives; it's a fact of life. The newer drives have rotational speeds of 7,200 and even 10,000RPM — almost twice as fast as the drives available a couple of years ago. In general, a drive transfers information faster if it can spin faster.

If you're dealing with data-intensive applications (video editing and large database crunching), faster disk drives are a huge boon. Installing one in your system and copying your data to the drive can result in better overall performance.

Move your pagefile

Assuming that the newer hard drive is faster than your old hard drive, better performance is yours if you move your pagefile to the newer hard drive. (The pagefile is discussed in the section "How Windows Uses Memory," earlier in this chapter.) You can move the pagefile to the faster drive by following these steps:

1. **Click Start, right-click My Computer, choose Properties, then click Advanced System Settings.**

   If your system is configured to have a My Computer icon on the desktop, you could right-click it. Either way, Windows opens the System Properties dialog box. Make sure the Advanced tab is selected, as shown in Figure 17-2.

2. **In the Performance area of the dialog box, click Settings.**

   Windows displays the Performance Options dialog box.

Figure 17-2:
Your
pagefile
setting is
accessed
through the
Advanced
settings.

3. **On the Advanced tab, click the Change button in the Virtual Memory section of the dialog box.**

   Windows displays the Virtual Memory dialog box, shown in Figure 17-3. The settings in the dialog box control the location of your pagefile. At the top of the dialog box, you see your system drives and how much space each drive allocates to the pagefile. You should see both your old drive and your newer, faster drive listed in the dialog box, although the information may be "grayed out," so it's difficult to see.

Figure 17-3:
The Virtual
Memory
dialog box
controls the
location
and size of
pagefiles.

4. **Clear the Automatically Manage Paging File Size for All Drives check box.**

   This check box is selected by default on most Vista systems. You'll need to clear the setting so you can set the location of the pagefile manually.

5. **From the list of drives, select the fast drive.**

6. **In the center of the dialog box, select Custom Size and set the Initial Size equal to the Minimum Allowed setting from the bottom of the dialog box.**

7. **Set the Maximum Size just a bit larger than the Recommended setting at the bottom of the dialog box.**

   If you don't feel comfortable setting your pagefile's size, select the System Managed Size radio button. This setting allows Windows to decide the best size.

8. **When everything is set the way you want it, click Set.**

   The settings you specified should show up in the top portion of the dialog box.

9. **Select the old drive (probably C:) from the list at the top.**

   This drive has your current pagefile. The current drive settings should show up in the middle of the dialog box.

10. **Select the No Paging File radio button and click Set.**

    You should always have a pagefile somewhere on some drive. Thus, you need to set the new pagefile location and size before removing the old pagefile. Failure to do so could cause Windows to be unstable and perhaps unusable.

11. **Close the Virtual Memory dialog box.**

    Windows lets you know that you need to restart your system. (Moving the pagefile is one of the few things that requires a system restart in Windows Vista.)

12. **Click OK.**

    Your system restarts.

Assuming your system routinely swaps a fair amount of memory out to the hard drive's pagefile, you should notice an improvement in your system's performance after completing the preceding steps.

Choosing Between Internal or External Hard Drives

Most newer computer systems are equipped with high-speed connections, such as USB 2.0 and FireWire. These connections are important when you're using peripherals, such as video cameras and printers. (Some video cameras can be plugged directly into a FireWire port so you can transfer video directly to your hard drive.)

An interesting side effect to faster connections is the emergence of external hard drives as a viable option. In the old days (by *old*, I mean shortly after the IBM PC emerged), hard drives were large and couldn't fit into the computer case. Many hard drives were external, out of necessity.

Then drives started getting compact, and storing them inside the computer case became the norm. With the advent of FireWire and USB 2.0, drives are crawling back out of the computer case. External drives can be found on any computer retailer's shelves. The price for an external drive ranges typically from $80 to $300, depending on its capacity.

The interest in external drives is driven by two primary reasons: easy backups and easy data transfer.

Easy backups

As the amount of data on a typical PC gets larger, the ease of doing backups — even on CDs — gets harder. CDs can handle just over 600MB of data, but most hard drives are now at 80GB or more. That's a lot of CDs to use for backup!

DVDs are the answer for some people, but they're not widespread due to confusion about what encoding algorithm should be used to write data on the disc. In addition, it takes quite a bit of time to store all that data and then verify it.

An easier and faster solution is to use an external hard drive. Plug it in — normally via a USB or FireWire cable — and Windows recognizes it as just another hard drive. You can copy your files to the hard drive, unplug it, and store it in a safe place. The process is much faster than using either CD or DVD solutions.

Recognizing that external hard drives are being used for backups, a number of hard drive manufacturers (led by Maxtor) have come out with external drives geared toward doing those backups. The drives have a capacity of anywhere from 160GB to 500GB. (That's a *lot* of data.) Depending on the manufacturer, the drive enclosure may even include a button that can be programmed to do the backup for you. Plug in the drive, push the button, and the backup automatically occurs. Pretty cool!

Easy data transfer

Suppose that you work part time at an office and the rest of the time at a client's location — or even at home. If you work on the same projects in both places, synchronizing data between locations quickly becomes a big chore.

The solution is an external drive. If you store your data on the external drive, you can take it with you and plug it into all the systems. When you do, the data is immediately available and ready to use.

If you decide to move your system pagefile to a different drive (using information supplied in the section "Move your pagefile," earlier in this chapter), make sure you don't move it to a removable drive. If you try to start Windows without the removable drive accessible, Windows can't create the necessary pagefile.

Alternative Storage Solutions

When considering additional storage space, many people think only of hard drives. You aren't limited to hard drives. Consider a few of these other devices:

- **CD-ROM drives:** Commonplace on most systems these days, CD-ROM drives make a great archival medium and are wonderful for transferring data from system to system. The thing that makes CDs so attractive is that you can get blank CD-R discs for about 25 cents each. That price is cheaper than what you pay for floppy disks and much cheaper than what you pay for blank DVDs.

- **DVD-ROM drives:** Though currently less common than CD drives, DVD-ROM drives are becoming more common as the need to store large amounts of data becomes critical. In fact, I was shopping for graphics packages the other day, and one was available on either eight CDs or a single DVD. The hassle of swapping CDs when browsing images made the idea of purchasing a DVD drive very enticing.

- ✔ **Zip drives:** These drives have been around for quite a while but are becoming less common in new systems. Zip disks are very handy for short-term archives or for transferring moderate amounts of data from one system to another. Data capacity ranges from 100MB to 250MB (for the common system used today) to 750MB for the newest drives. The biggest drawback to the Zip drives is the price of the disks they use. The 250MB disks are approximately $10 each, and the 750MB disks are about $13.50 each.

- ✔ **Flash drive:** This must be the coolest device on the market these days. This storage device is nothing but a bank of static RAM connected to a USB plug. You plug it into a USB port, and it looks just like another drive. As of this writing, flash-drive capacities commonly range from 64MB to 2GB, so they're not huge. What makes them cool, however, is their small size. You can find drives not much bigger than a quarter, and most are about the size of your thumb. Because flash drives have no mechanical parts, they're very fast, as well.

These devices are good for a variety of purposes. Think through how you could use each of them to help reduce the clutter on your existing system.

Chapter 18

Becoming Security Conscious

• •

In This Chapter

▶ Improving the system's local security

▶ Securing a system from Internet attack

▶ Increasing security by utilizing a firewall

• •

Security is one of those things you seldom think about, until you realize that you really should have been thinking about it all along. That point of realization typically comes right after someone breaks into your machine, steals the data, or makes your system unusable. The ironic part of security is that after the realization occurs, it's too late to counteract the problem that caused the realization.

Whoa! I don't mean to get philosophical, but with so much "realizing" going on, you should realize that you can save yourself a lot of grief if you become more security conscious today.

Computer security is its own specialty within the larger field of computer technology. This chapter doesn't provide all the security answers you need, but it does provide a good general introduction to the topic. You can discover some of the simplest things to make your system more secure.

Realize that if you make your system more secure, you also decrease the potential for clutter on your system. If someone breaks into your system — either locally or remotely across the Internet — it's hard to have confidence in your system again. The fact is, you don't know what programs or data the intruder placed on your system.

Let me give you an example. I had a system that was a server connected to the Internet. I felt fairly confident that the system was secure, but after a few weeks, someone broke into the system. They didn't take over the machine, but they broke in through an FTP server and stored a lot of huge files on my system. These files were illegal digital copies of movies. After I discovered the problem, I was able to delete the files, free up the system space, and shore up my defenses so the problem wouldn't happen again. You can avoid similar problems if you take a little time to increase security.

Battening Down the Hatches

The buzz about security these days is all about the Internet. Everyone's worried about all the nefarious programs that can be delivered right to your system via the Internet. Problem is, the Internet isn't your biggest security problem. The biggest threat you face is to your local machine — security issues would exist even if you unplugged the network cable that leads to the Internet.

This isn't to say that you shouldn't pay attention to Internet-related security; you should. Later in this chapter, you can find out some of the things you can do to increase security. You just need to be aware of this point:

> If you don't make your system secure from non-Internet–related threats, you're missing the most likely source of security problems that you're likely to face.

The following sections examine the biggest security threats to your local machine.

Physical security

Why it's a security threat: Studies have shown that the biggest threat to a business's data is the person who can sit down in front of the computer containing the data. If someone can sit there, think what could be accessed. For most people, unfettered access to a computer means someone can get at all the sensitive data — checking accounts, phone lists, customer transactions, letters, memos, and much more.

What you can do about it: At a most basic level, having a secure system means keeping other people from getting to your system. You can do a few things to improve the physical security of your computer and its data:

- ✔ **Lock doors.** If the area housing your computer has a door on it, make sure the door has a lock and that you use it. A locked door puts a roadblock between your system and someone who may abuse your system.

- ✔ **Turn off systems.** An eternal difference of opinion exists regarding whether systems should be left on or turned off when not in use. One plus to turning them off: doing so makes it harder for people to surreptitiously use your system for short periods.

✔ **Use passwords.** A lot of advice could be (and has been) given concerning selecting a good password. Passwords are a pain for most people, but using a good password can help thwart others' access to your system.

✔ **Reconfigure booting.** Most PCs can be booted to a floppy, a CD-ROM, the hard drive, or the network. Reconfigure your BIOS so that people can't boot your system by using either a floppy or a CD-ROM. If they can do that, they can use programs on the floppy or CD-ROM to bypass security and directly access your hard drive data.

Data loss

Why it's a security threat: You have hundreds, if not thousands, of hours invested in the data on your system. The old adage is true: Time is money. So the time you spend amassing your data represents a huge investment. Losing data is a huge security risk. If you run a small business and lose your data, your business could be severely damaged.

What you can do about it: The more your investment is worth, the more important it is to back up data. Minimize the chances of damage by periodically doing backups.

Data recovery

Why it's a security threat: When you delete information from your hard drive, Windows marks as free the hard drive locations previously occupied by the data. This means the locations are once again available to store information. Notice that Windows only marks the locations as available; it doesn't actually delete data. That's right — the data previously stored on the hard drive is still there, until it's overwritten by new data. With the right tools, the data in these deleted locations can be recovered and viewed.

What you can do about it: The accessibility of previously deleted information poses a security threat if someone starts using your system. To avoid this problem, many disk utilities include programs that completely erase data by overwriting it with new data and then deleting it. For instance, System Mechanic (www.iolo.com) includes a program called Drive Scrubber, and McAfee's Internet Security Suite (www.mcafee.com) includes a tool called Digital Shredder. Either program — or their counterparts from other system utilities — helps ensure the security of deleted data.

If you give your system away or sell it to someone else, they can use software to access your deleted data. Make sure you use a secure deletion program, such as Drive Scrubber or Digital Shredder, to remove all traces of your data before the old system leaves your hands.

Malicious programs

Why it's a security threat: The world is full of malicious programs. An innumerable variety of viruses, Trojan horse programs, and worms await the unsuspecting.

Some people, new to computer security, believe that malicious programs are something introduced with the advent of the Internet. Malicious programs have been around much, much longer.

Before everyone was connected to the Internet, destructive programs typically spread by people sharing infected programs. It wasn't unusual for college campuses or large companies to become infected with viruses because someone loaded a game from a floppy disk to the hard drive. Unbeknownst to the user, the game included a virus that was activated after the copying was complete.

What you can do about it: Even if you disconnect your computer system from the Internet, you can still get a virus if you allow others, including your own children, to use your computer. (I've known some people who have even disconnected their floppy drive because they don't want to chance destructive programs being introduced through that doorway.) I recommend being very selective about who you let use your computer.

You should also make sure that you have an up-to-date virus checker on your system. Such programs routinely check the content of floppy disks to make sure they contain no known viruses. See Chapter 10 for more about virus checkers.

Insecure passwords

Why it's a security threat: Passwords are one of the fundamental means of physically securing your data. Everything these days — from your checking account to your online recipe cache — seems to require a username and password. When you use obvious passwords, you make it easier for dubious folks to guess those passwords and steal your data.

What you can do about it: When selecting a password, don't use anything obvious. Things such as your name, birth date, address, or favorite sports team are all pretty obvious. You need to make sure that your password contains a seemingly random set of letters, interspersed with seemingly random numbers. In addition, passwords should be at least six characters long. (Some systems may require a password of at least eight characters.)

Beware of programs that offer to help you remember your passwords or promise to automatically fill out password information on Web forms for you. Some of these programs are proven spyware or deliver pop-up ads to your system. If you need to keep track of your passwords, do so in a small notebook that you can secure in a locked drawer. Whatever you do, don't write your password down and leave it where others can find it.

Staying Secure on the Internet

Most computer systems in the United States are connected, at one time or another, to the Internet. The Internet presents an irresistible urge, fueled by the siren song of vast amounts of information, easy communication, and far-flung resources.

Unfortunately, the Internet also presents a security risk. When you connect to the Internet, you open a unique doorway to your system. The doorway allows you to leave your computer to wander around cyberspace, but it also allows fellow travelers to enter your computer — unless you take security seriously.

The following sections discuss some of the more common Internet-related security issues.

Using Internet zones

Internet Explorer allows you to assign different Web sites to what it calls *Internet zones.* These zones are nothing more than a way for you to categorize Web sites. Different zones have different security settings applied to them. (The different security levels for the Internet Explorer zones are described in Chapter 11's cookie discussion.)

Microsoft established four security zones in Internet Explorer:

- **Local Intranet:** For addresses either on your local computer or on your local network. The default security level for this zone is Medium.

- **Trusted Sites:** Contains sites you designate as trustworthy. The default security level for this zone is Low.

- ✔ **Restricted Sites:** Contains sites you don't trust. The default security level for this zone is High.

- ✔ **Internet:** Contains all sites that you haven't assigned to a zone. The default security level for this zone is Medium.

In my experience, most people don't use zones, even though doing so can make your system more secure. The idea behind them is that you can designate which sites you trust and which you don't. Those trustworthy sites automatically have a lower security level, which means they can store and read cookies. Those sites you don't trust aren't given this level of access.

All Web sites belong to the Internet zone unless you assign them to one of the other zones. To assign a Web site to a specific zone, open Internet Explorer and follow these steps:

1. **Choose Tools➪Internet Options.**

   Internet Explorer displays the Internet Options dialog box. Ensure that the Security tab is chosen, as shown in Figure 18-1.

Figure 18-1:
Security zones are controlled on the Security tab.

2. **Click one of the security zones.**

   The four security zones are at the top of the page. Click the one to which you want to assign the site.

3. **Click Sites.**

   Internet Explorer displays a list of sites assigned to the zone, as shown in Figure 18-2.

   If you're working in the Local Intranet zone, click the Advanced button to see the desired dialog box.

Figure 18-2:
Modify the addresses assigned to a zone.

4. **Enter the Web site's address in the Add This Web Site to the Zone text box; click Add.**

   The specified URL appears in the Web Sites list. You can remove a site from the list by selecting it and clicking Remove.

5. **Click Close.**

   Your zone changes are saved. You can close all the other open dialog boxes.

If you want Internet Explorer to verify that the server for each Web site in this zone is secure before connecting to any Web sites in this zone, select the Require Server Verification (https:) for All Sites in This Zone check box. The check box is shown in Figure 18-2.

Whenever you visit a site via Internet Explorer, its security designation is shown on the status bar. If you haven't assigned the site to a particular zone, the designation shows a small globe and the word *Internet,* meaning the site belongs to the Internet zone.

A quick way to display the Security tab shown in Figure 18-1 is to double-click the zone notation on the Internet Explorer status bar.

Harnessing SSL

One way to make transferring data safer is to encrypt it. Entire books discuss the ins and outs of data encryption. Of the many encryption methods available, perhaps the most common is SSL.

SSL is an acronym for secure sockets layer. This seemingly unassuming phrase actually hides a tremendous amount of complexity. SSL capability is built into most Web browsers, including Internet Explorer.

SSL is handled transparently for most people, meaning that you may not even be aware it's in effect. For instance, if you visit a Web site to order a product, you may be unaware that the ordering page uses SSL to encrypt the information you enter.

You can tell if SSL is in effect through two indicators:

- ✔ **Look at the URL that accesses the site.** Most sites begin with the `http://` protocol designator. A secure site using SSL begins with `https://` instead. (Notice the addition of the *s.*)

- ✔ **Look at your browser for a small security icon.** In Internet Explorer, a secure page has a small padlock that appears at the right side of the address bar, near the top of the program window.

Be careful when dealing with sites requesting sensitive data. If the site doesn't use an SSL, your data isn't transferred to the site in a private manner. This means that your data is less secure than you may be comfortable with.

Closing down security problems

With the widespread acceptance of high-speed Internet connections, a new problem is spreading. High-speed connections such as DSL or cable modems are always on, meaning they provide a continuous Internet connection. If you leave your system turned on, your computer is constantly and continuously connected to the Internet.

In case you didn't realize it, the Internet is a two-way superhighway. You can reach out from your computer to access resources around the Internet, and people all over the world can reach out and access your computer. What!? Most people don't realize that others can access their computers. The fact of the matter is they can — and with minimal trouble. In fact, if security precautions aren't in place, Windows Vista can allow others to easily access your entire system.

Fortunately, Windows Vista is more secure when it comes to the Internet than its predecessors, including Windows XP. (This, in itself, is perhaps the best reason to upgrade to Windows Vista.) If Windows were a house, you might consider it a fairly impressive house. It locks the front door, but experienced troublemakers know there are more ways to get into a house than just through the front door.

Windows Vista, as it comes installed, leaves the windows and doors to the house all closed; this is a good thing. But someone (well, actually, some software) may have opened windows or doors to your system without your knowledge. The solution is to do a security checkup and see what weaknesses you can fix. A good place to start is with the ShieldsUP! utility from Gibson Research. This free check takes only a few minutes but provides many ways to secure your system.

To use ShieldsUP!, visit Gibson Research at `http://grc.com/default.htm`. Scroll down the page just a bit and click the ShieldsUP! link. You see the first page of the ShieldsUP! Check, as shown in Figure 18-3. Click the Proceed button and work your way through the checkup to discover where your vulnerabilities are and how to fix them.

Figure 18-3: Check your system for Internet vulnerabilities.

Adding Firewalls

When constructing an apartment building, a contractor often includes a firewall between apartments. This firewall is specially reinforced and retards the spread of a fire, should one start in an apartment. Similarly, firewalls exist at the front of most cars, between the passenger compartment and the engine space. The purpose of such firewalls is to provide protection for people on one side of the firewall from what may be happening on the other side. It's the same with computers. In the context of the computing world, a *firewall* is a security device that limits the effect outside people have on people inside.

Firewalls come in all shapes, sizes, and capacities. Large networks often have specialized computers that do nothing but act as a firewall. Smaller networks often have smaller, less expensive versions, and individual computers connected to the Internet can have individual software firewalls installed.

The following sections describe the firewall built into Windows Vista, the most popular individual software firewall, and dedicated hardware firewalls.

The Windows firewall

Windows Vista includes a firewall built into the operating system. This firewall, technically named Windows Firewall (how do they come up with these names?), lets you limit what information is communicated to and from the Internet. This firewall is ideal for those computers connected directly to the Internet through either a dial-up or full-time high-speed connection.

Windows Vista, by default, has Windows Firewall turned on. You control the firewall by choosing Start⇨Control Panel⇨Security⇨Windows Firewall. Shortly, you see the Windows Firewall dialog box, in which you should click the Change Settings link. Doing so displays the Windows Firewall Settings dialog box, shown in Figure 18-4.

You can turn off the Windows Firewall, but that's not really a good idea unless you're sure you have some other firewall in place. Another time that you can safely turn off Windows Firewall is if you completely disconnect your computer from the Internet; in this case, there's no need for the service it normally offers.

If you have a favorite program that's having problems operating over the Internet, it could be because the ports being used by the program are blocked by Windows Firewall. If you suspect such a case, contact the technical support department for your software, and they'll probably have you make some changes on the Exceptions tab of the Windows Firewall dialog box. This is the tab where you can customize how the firewall blocks (or allows) connections with your system.

Unsuccessful attempts to get through the firewall are logged in a file. You can review the log file, stored at `c:\windows\pfirewall.log`, anytime you need to know what's happening with your Internet connection.

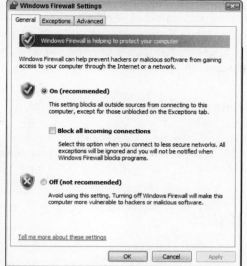

Figure 18-4:
Windows
Firewall can
be turned
on, off, or
customized
completely.

The Windows Firewall is designed primarily as a personal system for your individual computer. If your computer is part of a network that already has a firewall in place, you don't need to use Windows Firewall; disable it. Check with your network administrator for more details.

ZoneAlarm

Several personal firewall programs are available, but none has garnered the market share that ZoneAlarm has. ZoneAlarm is published by Zone Labs (www. zonelabs.com); the company makes both a free and commercial version.

ZoneAlarm essentially does the same thing that the Windows Firewall does — it blocks people and programs on the Internet from getting into your computer.

Because both programs serve the same purpose, it's reasonable to ask why anyone would need ZoneAlarm when they can use Windows Firewall. Both approaches offer benefits:

- If you like visual notification of break-in attempts, use ZoneAlarm. It provides a pop-up screen every time one of these events occurs, but this feature can be turned off.

- If you want protection but don't want interruptions, use Windows Firewall. It purposely does its work silently, writing any firewall transgressions to a log file.

✔ If you want protection "closer" to the operating system, use Windows Firewall. It functions as an actual part of Windows Vista, at a lower level than ZoneAlarm can.

✔ If you want protection beyond what a firewall normally provides (e-mail quarantine, pop-up blocker, cookie monitoring, and the like), purchase ZoneAlarm Pro ($39.95).

You don't need to use both Windows Firewall and ZoneAlarm; you need only one firewall. If you decide to use ZoneAlarm, make sure you turn off Windows Firewall. Although there's no real danger in using both at the same time, doing so provides no benefit. (It's like putting two garage doors on the same garage — one in front of the other. It doesn't hurt, but it makes no sense.)

Hardware firewalls

If you're responsible for a network — for even as few as five systems — you should consider getting a *hardware-based firewall.* These firewalls are more expensive than software-based firewalls, but they provide a better level of protection than you can get with products such as ICF or ZoneAlarm.

Literally scores of hardware firewall products are available, and finding the right one can be time consuming. When I needed to find a good hardware firewall for my network, I did a lot of searching and settled on products made by SonicWALL (www.sonicwall.com). SonicWALL offers a wide range of products, suitable for all types of needs, ranging in price from about $700 to several thousands of dollars.

Sometimes, firewall capabilities are integrated into other hardware devices, such as routers or proxy servers. Check with your hardware vendor to see exactly what its products provide in the way of protection.

Hardware firewalls are normally placed between your network router and the entry point for your Internet connection. For instance, if you're using a DSL line, you plug the DSL line from the wall into the hardware firewall, and then connect a plug from the firewall to your network's hub or switch (the network device to which each of your computers connects). In that way, nothing that the firewall should catch ever gets on your network — which reduces the data load on your network.

Managing a hardware firewall can be a bit more challenging than managing a software firewall, but it's not overly difficult. With SonicWALL, for instance, the firewall can be managed over the Internet. (To make it secure, management can be configured so it can only be performed from machines using specific IP addresses.) I can manage the firewall by using forms presented on my Web browser, which is very convenient. Devices from other vendors may require using a serial port or some secure protocol.

If you use a hardware firewall, the systems connected to your network don't need to use their own software firewalls. This means that firewall management is done at a single point and that the network's clients have one less piece of software to master.

Chapter 19

Cleaning House in a Networked Environment

In This Chapter

▶ Purging old user accounts

▶ Moving data to shared or network drives

▶ Improving shared printer use

▶ Eliminating shared drives

▶ Removing your system from the network

*W*hen my children were growing up, our home was often the center of the neighborhood. It wasn't unusual for our children's friends to come calling at all hours of the day or night. Some of the kids would even walk right in the door without knocking. We would only hear "Hi, Mr. Wyatt!" as the child dashed through the kitchen on the way to the family room, the living room, or a bedroom.

With the continual parade of people through our home, we got used to finding the oddest things lying about. One day we'd find a shirt that didn't belong to us, another day a pair of smelly socks. A couple of times, I even found pairs of pants that I knew belonged to neighborhood children, and I often wondered how they got home without them.

If you have a computer connected to a network, it's possible that other network users could traipse through your system at all hours of the day or night. Just like the neighborhood kids, they may leave things behind, adding to the general clutter and making your cleaning job even more challenging.

This chapter focuses on some things you can do to help decrease the clutter on your networked system.

Getting Rid of Old User Accounts

User accounts on both your local machine (the computer you're using) and the network are analogous to passports — they allow access to various areas of the network or various resources on your system.

By careful user accounts management, you can make sure that your system and the network as a whole remain less cluttered and run smoother. The actions you can take with user accounts depend on the type of network you're a part of: client-server or peer-to-peer. (See the nearby sidebar for an explanation of these network types.) In addition, you may have different user accounts set up on your local computer.

Deleting network user accounts

On most networks, a user (such as yourself) needs an account to access network resources. This account, along with the permissions that define what your account can do on the network, is normally set up by your network administrator.

Managing different network user accounts can be a large part of an administrator's job, depending on the network size. The user accounts set up by the administrator may also affect your system and how it's utilized by others on the network.

If you belong to a client-server network and believe that other network users are abusing your system, talk to your network administrator about either changing the user's permissions or deleting the user account entirely. Little can be done to modify the account, unless (of course) you're the administrator.

Deleting local system user accounts

Windows is a *multi-user system,* which means that multiple people can use the same computer. This lets you set up accounts for different coworkers or family members.

Each user can add programs and create unshared files. If a user no longer needs an account on your system, his programs and files take up hard drive space that you may want to reclaim. To reclaim that space, remove the user's account by following these steps:

1. **Restart your system and log in as system administrator.**

   Windows Vista created an administrator account for your system when it was set up. Because only the administrator can delete users, you need to use that account. (If your personal account was set up with administrator's rights, then you can delete users when logged in under your own account. The easiest way to see if you can do this, however, is to try. If you can't delete users, you need to log in as the administrator.)

2. **Choose Start⇨Control Panel⇨Add or Remove User Accounts.**

   The Add or Remove User Accounts link is located under the much bigger link called User Accounts and Family Safety. (It's physically there; you don't need to click User Accounts and Family Safety to see it.) Windows displays the Manage Accounts window, which contains a list of all the user accounts and some tasks you can perform. See Figure 19-1.

3. **Click the user account you want to delete.**

   Windows displays a list of tasks you can perform in relation to the account.

4. **Click Delete the Account.**

   Windows asks whether you want to keep the files associated with the account.

5. **Click Delete Files.**

   Windows deletes the files. Deleting can take a while, depending on how many files were created using the account.

6. **Click Delete Account.**

   Windows finishes deleting the specified account.

Figure 19-1:
Performing administrative tasks on user accounts.

Client-server and peer-to-peer

In the grand scheme of things, two general classifications of networking exist:

✔ **Client-server:** These networks rely on centralized resources, using things such as file servers and print servers. A *client* (your computer) connects to the file server to access shared files or to a print server to create printed output. In addition, client-server networks rely on a centralized repository of security information that dictates how clients can utilize the network's resources.

✔ **Peer-to-peer:** In a peer-to-peer arrangement, no centralized resource management or centralized security repository is used. Instead, the network is composed of *peers* — systems with equal authority to utilize the network. Each system on the network has the ability to make resources available to others and to

define how others can use those resources. Others can use those resources in accordance with the wishes of the system doing the sharing.

Clutter happens on individual computers, and it happens on networks. If you're using a client-server network, most of the clutter happens on file servers. That type of clutter generally needs to be managed and removed by network administrators.

If you're using a peer-to-peer arrangement, the clutter is spread across the network on whatever machine opened its doors for others. If you share resources, your system could have clutter related to your generosity. You need to monitor the situation carefully to make sure your system doesn't become a victim of the inevitable clutter that results from your largesse.

When the specified account is deleted, you can see the Manage Accounts window again. You can continue to delete accounts, if desired, or you can close the window when you're finished with your tasks.

Restart your computer after completing these steps. You don't want to stay logged in as administrator and inadvertently change other settings.

Moving Frequently Accessed Data

My home has areas accessible to different people in the family. If I want something to be accessible to everyone, I can place it in the middle of the living room or on a kitchen counter. If I want something to be more private, I can place it in my bedroom closet or in a closed-off area of my home office.

Your computer is the same way — you probably have data that you use for your programs. Other users don't need to access that data. Conversely, some of your data may have wide appeal.

If you have data that others need, perform the digital equivalent of moving it from the bedroom closet to the middle of the living room. You do that by either setting up a shared folder on your system or moving the data to a shared drive accessible through your network. Moving the data to a network drive can help free up space on your local hard drive, which is a good thing.

Don't keep a private copy of data that others can change. Doing so, you run into data synchronization problems. If a coworker changes the public copy of the data file, that change isn't reflected in your private copy. Likewise, if you change the private copy, it doesn't show up in the public copy. Before long, a lot of discrepancies exist between the two file versions. Solve the problem by making sure only a single copy of the data file exists. Marking a document as private or public and syncing data are concepts outside the scope of this book. If you're unfamiliar with these concepts but want to know more, check out *Networking For Dummies,* 7th Edition, by Doug Lowe, or *Home Networking For Dummies,* 3rd Edition, by Kathy Ivens (both published by Wiley).

Removing Shared Printers

You may have a connected printer that others want to access. On a network, you can give others access to the printer; they can then print to their heart's content. Your printer becomes a focal point, and you get to see more of your coworkers than you may want to.

If you find that being a print station isn't for you, you can do a couple of things to help alleviate the situation. The following sections discuss how you can limit when people print and how to remove the shared printer completely.

Limiting shared printer hours

My most productive time of the day is early in the morning. After I'm wide awake, I find myself able to churn through work needing my attention before the cares of the day start to eat away at my focus. If I can limit phone and e-mail interruptions, I can get quite a bit done during those hours.

If you're like me, you may want to limit interruptions during the morning hours. For instance, you might not want people to print documents to your printer before 10:30 a.m. Fortunately, Windows makes limiting the printer availability easy; just follow these steps:

1. **Choose Start➪Control Panel➪Printer.**

   Windows displays the Printers window, which includes a list of all the printers defined on your system.

2. **Right-click the printer you want to change and choose Properties from the context menu.**

   Windows displays the printer's Properties dialog box. Make sure the Advanced tab is chosen, as shown in Figure 19-2.

Figure 19-2:
Specify the hours when a printer is available.

3. **Click the Available From radio button.**

   The controls for beginning and ending time become accessible.

4. **Specify the beginning and ending times.**

   Pick a time range in which you want the printer available. You can specify only a single range, with a starting and ending time.

5. **Click OK.**

When specifying the hours your printer is available, pick something that balances your needs with those of others. For instance, if you don't want people to use the printer before 10:30 a.m., you could set the beginning time to 10:30 a.m. and the ending time to 5:00 a.m. The printer would then be unavailable between 5:00 a.m. and 10:30 a.m.

Setting availability hours for your printer doesn't mean that others can't print to it around the clock. If someone prints outside the specified hours, the job is held in the print queue until the printer becomes available. Thus, if your printer is popular, you could see a whole rash of print jobs come through right after the starting time occurs. (Sort of like the rush after the opening bell of the stock exchange.)

Turning off shared printing

If you want to rescind your kind offer of allowing others to use your printer, turn off sharing altogether. Doing so is easy; follow these steps:

1. **Choose Start➪Control Panel➪Printers.**

   The Printers window pops into view, handily listing the printers defined on your system.

2. **Right-click the printer you want to change and choose Sharing from the context menu.**

   Windows displays the Properties dialog box for the printer, with the Sharing tab displayed (see Figure 19-3). Notice that the controls in the dialog box aren't available for changing.

3. **Click the Change Sharing Options button.**

   The controls in the dialog box aren't magically accessible.

4. **Select the Do Not Share this Printer radio button.**

5. **Click OK.**

The printer is immediately unavailable to others on your network. If people try to print to your printer, they see an error message.

You can help others on your network by letting them know when you change the printer's shared status. When you remove sharing, others can remove the printer definition on their systems. Doing so allows Windows to remove the printer drivers previously installed. The result is that unnecessary clutter is removed from their systems, as well.

Figure 19-3:
Windows
allows you
to specify
how a
printer is
shared.

Removing Shared Folders

Windows allows you to share data with other people on your network. It doesn't allow you to share individual files but entire directories. In other words, you aren't sharing documents, but the containers (folders) in which the documents are stored.

When you share folders on your system, people can read data from the folder and sometimes store information in the folder. Allowing others to access data on your system can slow down your system; allowing others to place data on your system can encourage clutter. You can reduce clutter (and perhaps increase system performance) by unsharing the previously shared folder. Just follow these steps:

1. **Display the folder window containing the folder you no longer want to share.**

   You can use My Computer or Windows Explorer to display the folder. The icon for the intended folder should be shown with a couple of people's heads in front of it. (Don't snicker at me; I didn't create the new shared icon. In fact, I prefer the old outstretched hand used in Windows XP.)

2. **Right-click the folder icon and choose Share from the context menu.**

   Windows displays the File Sharing dialog box, shown in Figure 19-4. You have two options in the dialog box. The first allows you to change who can access the folder and the other allows you to stop sharing all together. (Can you figure out which one you should use?)

Folders versus drives

Old timers like me often refer to shared folders as *shared drives* because we used to map shared folders — on someone else's computer — to drive letters on our systems. Windows doesn't require drive mapping anymore, so making shared folders synonymous with shared drives is somewhat anachronistic. That, of course, doesn't stop us from sitting in our rocking chairs on the porch of the Old Windows Users Retirement Home and discussing the "good old days." (Don't worry, Junior — you'll catch up with us old timers soon enough.)

3. **Click the Stop Sharing option.**

   Windows does its magic, and shortly you see a message that you've stopped sharing the folder. The data in the folder (and, in fact, the folder itself) is now inaccessible to others. If someone is actively using data in the folder, you may see a dialog box warning you that someone else is using your data. If you want to cut off the user's access to your data, click OK.

4. **Click Done.**

   You can now go back to work as you normally would.

Figure 19-4:
You have control over how others share your data.

Cutting off another user while she has a file open on your system can result in a corrupted data file. If possible, get the other person to exit the application (thereby closing the data file) before cutting off access.

Cutting Your System Off the Network

Just because Windows allows you to share your local resources (files and printers) on a network doesn't mean you have to share them. If you want to keep your resources to yourself, you can disable sharing all together by following these steps:

1. **Choose Start⇨Control Panel⇨View Network Status and Tasks.**

   You see the Network Center, which includes icons representing the different connections defined on your system, as shown in Figure 19-5.

Figure 19-5: Windows shows exactly how your resources are shared.

2. **In the Sharing and Discovery area, click a down-arrow next to a resource you want to change.**

   Each down-arrow expands the options available, and you can choose to turn them off. If you want to turn off access to your resources completely, make sure all the options show as "Off."

3. **Close the dialog box.**

After you disable resources, nobody can utilize any of them on your system. For instance, if you disable file sharing and printer sharing, nobody can utilize those particular resources on your system. Cutting off others won't stop you from using resources on their systems, if they're sharing.

If you turn off Network Discovery, that means that people won't even be able to see your system when they go browsing around your network.

If you don't foresee a time when you'll ever share system resources with others, you may want to uninstall the sharing component from your network. In the Network Center (what you see after Step 1 in the preceding steps), choose View Status⇨Properties. This displays the Properties dialog box for your connection to your network, which includes all the components for interacting with that network. Select the File and Printer Sharing for Microsoft Networks component and click Uninstall. The component is removed entirely from the operating system. If you later change your mind, you can reinstall the component by clicking Install and choosing File and Printer Sharing for Microsoft Networks from the Services area.

Chapter 20

Jumping Into the Registry

. . . .

In This Chapter

▶ Understanding the Registry

▶ Making Registry changes

▶ Cleaning the Registry with special software

▶ Fixing the Registry in case of problems

. . . .

*I*f Windows were a sentient being, the Registry would be its central nervous system. The Registry is related to and used by virtually every program on your system and by the operating system itself. Windows checks the Registry to see how programs should be installed, accessed, used, and uninstalled. It checks to see if a program (or a user) is allowed to access different areas of the computer.

From when your system starts to when you turn it off, the Registry is being used. In fact, much of the Windows start-up time is spent reading and checking the Registry, and virtually all of the Windows shut-down time is spent writing information to the Registry.

Even still, Windows does a pretty good job of masking the Registry's ever-present, pervasive nature. Most users go through the motions of customizing Windows and their software without the slightest hint that they're making changes to the Registry.

This chapter focuses on the Registry, giving you the info you need to make sure it's in tip-top shape. Just like your hard drive, your Registry can become cluttered with outdated information. Understanding what the Registry is, how to change it, and how to clean it can help you keep your system at its peak performance.

You can rest assured that you can live your life satisfactorily and with much joy without ever dealing with the Registry. If you don't want to know about the Registry, then skip this chapter. You can find quite a bit of technical information covered here — not as much as you might find in some geek-centered book, but definitely more than your normal book for novices.

Groking the Registry Behemoth

When I was a teen, I loved the sci-fi book *Stranger in a Strange Land* by Robert Heinlein. I wasn't alone; during the latter half of the 1960s, the book was adopted by many as a counterculture bible, of sorts. It tells the tale of a human, abducted by Martians in his infancy and raised on Mars. While a young adult, he returns to Earth. The book provides insight into his reactions to Earth's various cultures and the cultures' reactions to an earthling from Mars.

One of the terms introduced in the book is *grok,* a Martian verb meaning to totally and fully understand something, well beyond any earthly understanding. The verb made headway into the underground lexicon, and you can still hear it used at times today — such as in this section's title.

Looking at and trying to understand the Registry is, for many, an exercise in frustration. With a little background, the frustration can be alleviated, and you can surpass worldly understanding of what the Registry does. (After all, the Microsofties that Uncle Bill hired to develop the Registry may be human, but they were definitely raised on Mars.)

The Registry is nothing more than a hierarchical database maintained by Windows as a repository of configuration information. All the settings stored in the Registry are used by not only the operating system, but all the installed programs. The Registry consists of four distinct parts:

- ✔ **Trees:** The major Registry divisions
- ✔ **Hives:** Major divisions of the Registry trees
- ✔ **Keys:** Groups of related settings within a hive
- ✔ **Values:** The data stored within a key

As you make changes to system settings — for instance, in the Control Panel or in various Properties dialog boxes — the new changes are stored in the Registry. Information is stored in the form of values, which are placed in keys that are determined by the nature of the placing program. Thus, if you use the Control Panel to change display settings, your information is stored in either the keys that control the desktop's appearance or the keys that control your video hardware.

Seeing the trees in the Registry forest

The Registry consists of five major trees. These *trees* comprise all aspects of the operating system:

- **HKEY_CLASSES_ROOT:** Information related to the file types and actions that can be performed on files, including shortcuts. Also includes information on file associations.

- **HKEY_CURRENT_USER:** Specific profile settings for the user currently logged on to the system.

- **HKEY_LOCAL_MACHINE:** Machine-related specifics, such as installed hardware, swap-file settings, startup settings, and so on.

- **HKEY_USERS:** User-specific settings for all user profiles defined for the system.

- **HKEY_CURRENT_CONFIG:** Configuration information about the current hardware settings, such as notebooks that plug into a docking station.

The Registry has five trees, but this can be deceiving. Windows uses pointers for several keys. For instance, HKEY_CLASSES_ROOT is nothing but a pointer to the HKEY_LOCAL_MACHINE\SOFTWARE\CLASSES subkey. Likewise, HKEY_CURRENT_USER is a pointer to a subkey within HKEY_USERS. Thus, of the five trees, only three (HKEY_LOCAL_MACHINE, HKEY_CURRENT_CONFIG, and HKEY_USERS) actually represent information stored on disk.

Buzzing through the Registry hives

The first major division under each tree is known as a hive; hives were named as such because of their resemblance to beehives. Your Registry information is stored here on disk. According to Microsoft information, a *hive* is a discrete body of keys, subkeys, and values rooted at the top of the Registry hierarchy.

For instance, the HKEY_LOCAL_MACHINE tree contains the following hives:

- COMPONENTS
- HARDWARE
- SAM
- Schema
- SECURITY
- SOFTWARE
- SYSTEM

Hives are the part of the Registry either stored on disk or constructed in memory. Of the seven hives here, only the second (HARDWARE) and fourth (Schema) are constructed in memory when your system is first started. The other five hives utilize two separate files each.

The first file is the Registry file, which uses the same name as the hive. The second file is a log file, which uses the same name as the hive, with a filename extension LOG. Most of the hive files are stored in the `c:\windows\system32\config` folder but don't need to be there.

Table 20-1 shows the different hives used in the Registry, along with the files that store those hives. (If no file is listed for a hive, then the hive is created in memory every time you use Windows.)

Table 20-1	Registry Hives		
Tree	*Hive*	*Registry File*	*Log File*
HKEY_LOCAL_MACHINE	COMPONENTS	Components	Components.log
HKEY_LOCAL_MACHINE	HARDWARE		
HKEY_LOCAL_MACHINE	SAM	Sam	Sam.log
HKEY_LOCAL_MACHINE	Schema		
HKEY_LOCAL_MACHINE	SECURITY	Security	Security.log
HKEY_LOCAL_MACHINE	SOFTWARE	Software	Software.log
HKEY_LOCAL_MACHINE	SYSTEM	System	System.log
HKEY_CURRENT_CONFIG	SOFTWARE		
HKEY_CURRENT_CONFIG	SYSTEM		
HKEY_USERS	.DEFAULT	Default	Default.log
HKEY_USERS	Varies	Varies	Varies

Unlocking Registry keys

Registry hives are divided into *keys,* organizational units for Registry information. Because keys are designed to contain information, they're similar to folders on your hard drive. (This explains why the Registry Editor, presented in the section "Editing the Registry," later in this chapter, displays keys by using a file-folder symbol.)

Registry keys can contain values and subkeys. In turn, the subkeys can contain additional values and subkeys. Just as directory folders can contain files and additional folders, the keys under each hive can contain values and subkeys. This organization is the basis of the Registry's hierarchical structure and means it can be presented in a tree fashion.

Appreciating Registry values

Values contain data that represent configuration settings for Windows or for a program installed on your system. For instance, a value may contain the starting position for a window or the amount of memory in your system.

Data can be of six basic types:

- ✔ **REG_BINARY:** Numeric information of any length.
- ✔ **REG_DWORD:** Numeric information limited to a length of 32 bits.
- ✔ **REG_QWORD:** Numeric information limited to a length of 64 bits.
- ✔ **REG_EXPAND_SZ:** String information of any length and whose length can change over time. Normally, this data type is used for system and program variables.
- ✔ **REG_MULTI_SZ:** A series of string values, each separated by a NULL character. This data type is typically used for information lists, such as those displayed in drop-down lists.
- ✔ **REG_SZ:** A string value, of any length, that doesn't change. The value is static.

In addition, applications can define their own special data types. The exact type maintained for a value is determined by the purpose for which the value is used.

Editing the Registry

The Registry is a very dynamic place, with changes happening all the time. Because it contains all your system's settings and configuration information, that makes sense. In some cases, the Registry is updated automatically by Windows itself. The following list highlights the ways the Registry changes:

- ✔ **Automatically:** For instance, you may add a hardware device that Windows automatically detects. In such a case, the drivers are loaded automatically and settings are changed. The information about these drivers, the device, and any settings is stored automatically in the Registry.

  The Registry can also be changed by some action you take. For instance, you may use an applet in the Control Panel, in which case, the Registry stores the change. Other changes are introduced by programs you use and settings you make in them.

✔ **Manually:** Windows allows you to manually change the Registry. Although manual changes are tougher than changes made by using the Control Panel (or other tools), the effect is the same because system settings control how Windows functions.

The tool that manually changes the Registry is the Registry Editor. This program isn't available from any of the regular Windows menus (probably due to the potentially adverse consequences of misuse). Instead, start the program from the Start menu's Run option. Follow these steps:

1. **Choose Start➪All Programs➪Accessories➪Run.**

   Windows displays the Run dialog box.

2. **In the Open field, type** regedit, **and click OK.**

   Regedit, short for Registry Editor, is the name of the Registry Editor program.

   Shortly, you see the Registry Editor, shown in Figure 20-1.

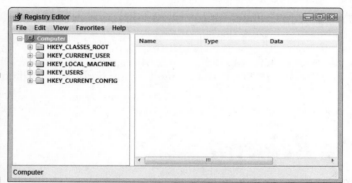

Figure 20-1:
The Registry Editor uses a hierarchical interface.

The Registry Editor window has two parts. The left part displays the different trees, hives, and keys, and the right part displays anything within the element selected in the left portion of the window.

The Registry Editor's hierarchical interface is very similar to interfaces used in other programs, such as Windows Explorer. If you're already familiar with the interface, you should have no problem getting around in the Registry Editor.

Differences in Registry Editors

In reading other books (or information on the Internet), you may have read that two Registry Editors are available in Windows: regedit and regedt32. In older versions of Windows (at least two versions ago), quite a bit of difference existed between these two programs. Regedit was the 16-bit Registry Editor, and regedt32 was its 32-bit counterpart. In Windows Vista, there's no difference between regedit and regedt32. In fact, if you run regedt32, Windows turns right around and runs regedit for you.

If you manually make changes in the Registry, you do so at your own risk. Whenever you make changes in the Windows configuration, those changes are stored in the Registry. Windows includes many safeguards to protect you from making changes that don't make sense or that may harm your system. When you manually edit the Registry, no such safeguards exist. Make sure you know what you're changing before you make the change.

Backing up the Registry

The Registry Editor allows you to export the Registry to a text file and later import the text file back into the Registry. This capability provides the means for backing up the Registry.

Before you make any changes to the Registry, you should back it up. Doing so helps you in case of a catastrophic error — such as deleting an entire hive. (I've done that. It's not a pretty picture.)

To export the Registry, follow these steps:

1. **In the Registry Editor, choose the key that you want to export.**

   If you want to export the entire Registry, don't worry about this step. For a reminder of how to open the Registry, refer to the preceding steps.

2. **Choose File⇨Export.**

   The Registry Editor displays the Export Registry File dialog box, shown in Figure 20-2.

Figure 20-2:
Exporting
the Registry.

3. **Use the dialog box controls to locate and select the drive and folder you want used for the exported Registry.**

   Unless you're exporting a small key, don't try to save to a floppy disk. (Do you even have a floppy drive on your system?) You can save to a more capacious medium, such as a thumb drive or an external hard drive.

4. **In the File Name text box, enter a name for the export file.**

5. **In the Export Range area, select what you want to save.**

   The default is Selected Branch, meaning the key you select in Step 1. If you want to save the entire Registry, select the All radio button.

6. **Click Save.**

When you later decide to import the Registry file, you can do so by choosing File➪Import. You see a dialog box that allows you to select a file. The file you specify is imported to the current Registry. If the import file contains keys or values that already exist in the Registry, the existing keys and values are overwritten with the new information. Conversely, if the Registry has any items with names that don't exist in the import file, these items remain in the new, modified Registry.

Finding information

Men are always accused of being reluctant to ask for directions. When my wife and I go out driving, she knows better than to ask if I need to ask how to get somewhere. After driving around for a while (and seeing the same scenery a couple of times), she may ask if I'm lost. Invariably, I'll say, "No, I'm not. I've been lost before, and this doesn't look anything like it."

Such an attitude may have no huge marital consequences in real life, but it can have huge consequences if you decide to go romping through the Registry without knowing where you're going. Its sheer size and amount of information make it mandatory to know what you want to edit before you begin poking around.

It's not unusual to browse through the Control Panel, find a new capability, have it catch your imagination, and then make some changes based on your discovery. Not so with the Registry. Though you can snoop through the Registry, the chance of intuitively finding something to change is remote. Thus, you must know what you want to do before you start your editing trek.

Many times, you can determine what you should edit by reviewing an application's documentation or talking to a program's technicians. Unfortunately, no comprehensive guide exists to possible Registry entries, and anyone who claims to have a comprehensive guide is yanking your chain.

When you do want to find information in the Registry, the biggest help is the Registry Editor's search command:

1. **With the Registry Editor open, press Ctrl+F or choose Edit⇨Find.**

   The Find dialog box opens, as shown in Figure 20-3.

Figure 20-3:
Searching through the Registry.

2. **In the Find What field, enter what you want to find.**

3. **At the bottom of the dialog box, specify where the Registry Editor should look for the information: Keys, Values, or Data.**

4. Click the Find Next button.

The Registry Editor attempts to find the string you entered. If a match is found, it's highlighted in one of the Registry Editor windows, depending on where the information was found.

For instance, if the match was found in a key name, the information is displayed in the left portion of the Registry Editor. Conversely, if the match was found in a value, the information is displayed in the right portion.

Editing values

After you locate a value that you want to change (see the preceding section), carefully examine it in the context of what you understand about the Registry structure; then make an educated guess regarding whether it's the value that you want. The problem, however, is that when you're poking about on your own, you're never really sure unless you try things. Thus, in many respects, working with the Registry Editor is a high-stakes trial-and-error proposition unless you're given a detailed reference or specific guidance.

To edit a value, follow these steps:

1. Open the Registry Editor by choosing Start⇨All Programs⇨ Accessories⇨Run, typing regedit **in the Open field, and clicking OK.**

Most editing tasks take place in the values shown in the right portion of the Registry Editor window. Refer to Figure 20-1.

2. Either double-click the value name or highlight the value and press Enter.

A dialog box prompts you to change the value's contents. The exact dialog box depends on the value's data type. For instance, if you're changing a value that contains binary data, you see a dialog box similar to the one shown in Figure 20-4.

3. Make your changes and click OK.

The Registry value is changed.

Even though your changes are saved immediately, many times those changes don't take effect until you restart your system. Whenever you're done editing the Registry, it's always a good idea to restart your system.

Figure 20-4:
Use the
Registry
Editor to
change
values.

Adding keys or values

The Registry Editor allows you to add new values or new keys to the Registry. Why would you want to add keys or values? Quite honestly, it doesn't do you much good to add either item unless you know that an application or Windows can use it.

To add a key, select the existing hive or key under which the new key should appear. Select the hive or key on the left side of the Registry Editor window; then choose Edit⇨New⇨Key. The new key is added, and you can change its name as desired.

If you want to add a value to an existing key (or to a key you just added), you do so in much the same manner. To add a value, follow these steps:

1. **In the left pane of the Registry Editor (refer to Figure 20-1), navigate to the hive or key where you want the new value stored.**

   Click the plus signs at the left of the hive or keys that lead to the new value's desired location. The Registry tree expands to show the path to the key in which you want the value placed.

2. **Choose Edit⇨New.**

   You see a submenu of items you can create.

3. **Click the choice that represents the type of value you want to create.**

   The new value appears in the hive or key you selected. The value's name is selected, so you can change it as desired.

These steps create the value only; they don't store anything in the value. To store something in the value, edit the newly created value, as described in the preceding section.

Deleting Registry items

Deleting keys or values is quite easy: Select the item that you want to remove and press the Delete key. Windows checks to make sure that you really want to delete the item. If you click the Yes button, the item is immediately — and *permanently* — deleted from the Registry.

The Registry Editor is very obedient about deleting items. You need to make very sure that you want to delete something before you do so. If you delete a critical key or value by mistake, you're simply out of luck. (If you delete the wrong thing, you can cripple your software or disable your entire system.) In such a circumstance, you have only a couple of options available:

- ✔ Manually re-create the deleted keys and values.
- ✔ Reload the Registry keys, if you previously exported them to a text file for safekeeping.
- ✔ Reinstall Windows.

None of these are particularly attractive options. Because, in this case, an ounce of prevention really is worth a pound of cure, take extra care when working with the Registry.

Cleaning up software references

The Registry can easily become cluttered with pieces and parts of old programs no longer on your system. In your never-ending quest to clean your system, you may want to remove all references to a program from your Registry. Doing so is theoretically easy, albeit time consuming:

1. **If you know the name of the program, search the Registry (using the Registry Editor's Find command) for all occurrences of the program name.**

   Make sure you start your search from the beginning of the Registry.

2. **Delete every value or key that contains the name.**

3. **Search for any program nicknames.**

   For instance, Word is often referred to as WinWord, and some Registry values reference this term *(winword)*.

If you do your search-and-destroy mission after you uninstall the unwanted software, you may be surprised at how many references still remain.

Using Registry Cleaning Software

Programs in addition to Windows use the Registry. Virtually every single program you install on your system uses it. (Some programs are small enough that they don't affect the Registry.) Some programs write only a few things into the Registry; others write a lot.

As new information gets stuffed in, the Registry's size increases to accommodate the changes. Windows stores the Registry on disk (in the hives, discussed in the section "Buzzing through the Registry hives," earlier in this chapter) and in memory, so both disk space and memory are required to manage the Registry.

If your Registry grows too large, your system performance can suffer. The larger the Registry, the more resources Windows requires just to manage the sheer file size and the entry numbers.

Unfortunately, removing software isn't the answer to a bloated Registry. When you uninstall a program, that program is supposed to remove its entries from the Registry. Some programs do this completely, but most leave some orphan entries. The result is unused "stuff" in the Registry, cluttering up the other, more important information there.

Even if the Registry entries are deleted, Windows doesn't shrink the size of the hives stored on disk — they remain large. Windows Vista does a better job of managing the Registry than did previous versions, but large Registry files still place an unnecessary burden on Windows.

The solution to a cluttered Registry is to use software to go through and suggest things you may want to clean up. In general, three types of programs can be used on the Registry: analyzers, cleaners, and compactors.

Registry analyzers

A *Registry analyzer* does just what its name suggests: It analyzes the Registry, looking for and finding unused keys, invalid characters in keys, broken keys, and other common problems. Different programs analyze the Registry in different ways, but most of them do these things. Not all Registry analyzers fix the errors they find, but most provide information that explains how you can fix them. The focus in analyzers is on the analysis, not the repair.

Dozens of Registry analyzers are available. If you do an Internet search, you can find freeware, shareware, and commercial versions. Here are just two:

- **Registry Drill at** www.easydesksoftware.com/regdrill.htm: I particularly like this one. It's won many awards and does in-depth analyses that other programs seem to skip.

- **Registry Analyst from YavSoft at** http://yavsoft.com/registry: This analyzer is easy to use and very inexpensive.

Registry cleaners

Software billed as a *Registry cleaner* includes analysis (as discussed in the preceding section) but also provides a more automatic approach to fixing errors in the Registry. Although the analyzers are intended for folks who feel at home in the Registry, the cleaners do things without user intervention. Of the many Registry cleaners available, I recommend a couple:

- **The Registry cleaner included with System Mechanic at** www.iolo. com: This cleaner is my favorite. It runs easily and takes only a few clicks to fix most problems. The speed with which you can streamline a Registry is very impressive.

- **Registry Mechanic from PC-Tools Software at** www.pctools. com/registry-mechanic: Another good option, this software is almost as easy to use as System Mechanic and even catches some Registry errors that other tools don't.

Registry compactors

The Registry doesn't shrink, even when Registry entries for uninstalled software are removed. To fix this situation, a class of software called *Registry compactors* was developed. This software essentially reads the Registry and rewrites a new, smaller version of all the hives.

A good choice for compacting is RegCompact.NET, an open source program at www.experimentalscene.com/download.php. No cost; great reviews (that combination is hard to beat).

Because of the way the Registry is handled in Windows Vista, compaction doesn't offer as much benefit as it did in earlier versions of Windows. You can find programs that compact the Registry in Windows, but don't feel that it's mandatory to get a Registry compacter for your system.

Restoring the Registry

By this point, you should be very aware that everything in Windows revolves around the Registry. The Registry is so powerful in its system control that I can't stress strongly enough that you shouldn't make Registry changes without being sure of exactly what you're changing. The Registry Editor provides no undo feature. Changes are essentially written to the Registry immediately.

If the Registry becomes corrupted for some reason, you have Trouble with a capital T. A couple of things can be done, however, to attempt recovery:

✔ **Import the backup copy:** The first thing you should try is importing the backup copy of the Registry that you should have made before making changes. During the import process, the saved version of the Registry overwrites the new, corrupted version, hopefully solving the problem.

✔ **Restart the system:** If you don't have a copy to import, restart your system. Whenever you restart your system, you can press F8 to display the Windows startup options. With the startup options displayed, you can press F8 a second time to display the Advanced Startup Options screen. (This isn't a dialog box because Windows hasn't yet started. It's a text menu displayed by the Windows startup functions.)

Last Known Good Configuration is one option. Every time Windows starts, it copies the last-used Registry to a backup copy of the Registry. If you choose Last Known Good Configuration — which you should do if you've corrupted the Registry — then the backup copy of the Registry isn't made. Instead, the backup copy starts the system. You may lose all of the Registry changes that you made since your last startup, but that can be a good thing if your Registry is corrupted.

After you start Windows, you should do a few additional tasks:

✔ If you have a copy of the Registry that you recently exported to a text file, start the Registry Editor and import the copy. This overwrites the current Registry settings and restores your system to its latest condition.

✔ If you installed programs during your last Windows session, you must reinstall them. Even though the program files are on disk, the configuration information that was written to the Registry was lost when you tossed out the last version of the Registry.

✔ If you deleted programs during your last Windows session, you must delete them again. This may sound strange because the programs are no longer on your hard drive. Because you restored an earlier version of the Registry, however, Windows thinks that the programs are installed. Deleting them again updates the Registry.

✔ If you made changes in your desktop configuration during your last session, make the changes again.

Chapter 21

Wiping the Slate Clean

In This Chapter

▶ Repairing your Windows installation

▶ Running your system vendor's restore disc

▶ Starting fresh by wiping out your system

Cleaning your system is an ongoing task. Systems either get dirty on a daily basis or they get clean on a daily basis. If a system suffers from months or years of neglect, you need to balance the time required for a thorough cleaning with the time necessary to simply wipe the slate clean and start all over. In some cases, the clear choice is starting over.

This chapter presents the three main ways to start over with your current system: doing a reinstall, doing a system restore, and wiping out everything. None of these tasks should be undertaken lightly by anyone. Starting over destroys data (hopefully data you've backed up), disrupts work for a day or two, and generally is a huge pain.

Doing a Windows Reinstall

If clutter on your system has caused Windows to malfunction in any way, or if you deleted some system files when trying to clean up, then you may want to reinstall Windows. The Setup program for Windows includes the ability to reinstall operating system files without hurting any of the data on your hard drives.

Technically, when I say *reinstalling* Windows Vista in this context, I mean *repairing* your system. This process is different from (and much faster than) reinstalling Windows Vista from scratch — a process I describe in the "Wiping Out Your System" section, later in this chapter.

For Windows to fix itself, you need to get the original Windows Vista installation disc provided by Microsoft.

With your computer turned off and the Windows Vista DVD in the drive, follow these steps:

1. **Turn on the PC.**

   The computer should go through its normal startup machinations. A prompt saying Press Any Key to Boot from CD or DVD appears.

2. **Press a key — you want to boot from the DVD.**

   Most PCs manufactured in the past five or six years allow you to boot from CD-ROM or DVD. If you never see a prompt about booting from either of these, you may need to modify your system BIOS so that it tries to boot from the CD or DVD before booting from other sources, such as the hard drive.

   For information on how to access your system BIOS, refer to the manual that came with your computer. The process is different on different systems. It normally involves pressing a key when first booting, such as F1, Esc, or Del.

   During the boot process, information is loaded from the DVD and your system is inspected. Eventually, you see an Install Windows screen where you can select a language in which to do your install.

3. **Click Next.**

   The language and regional settings options were probably defaulted to the correct settings for you; that is why I didn't explain what you should select. Besides, you can probably figure this one out on your own.

   You'll see a new screen that, front and center, has an Install Now option. A Repair Your Computer option appears at the bottom of the screen.

4. **Click the Repair Your Computer option.**

   Windows displays the System Recovery Options dialog box. In it is a list of the operating systems found on your computer.

5. **With the copy of Windows Vista selected in the dialog box, click Next to indicate you want to repair that copy of Windows.**

   You are presented with a list of tools you can use to repair your system. There are a bunch of tools available, and you can certainly play around with them at your leisure. For the purposes of reinstalling Windows, however, you'll want to use the Startup Repair tool. It checks your system to make sure that you have good copies of Windows files necessary for successful use of the operating system.

6. **Click Startup Repair.**

   The Startup Repair tool looks at your system, determines what to copy from the DVD, and then copies it. Eventually, you see a screen indicating that the process is complete.

7. **Click Finish.**

   You're magically whisked back to the recovery tools screen, the same one you were at in Step 5.

   You're done for now. Gently yank the Windows Vista DVD out of the drive so that you can get ready to restart your system.

8. **Click Restart.**

   Windows should now start up, fresh and ready to please.

Repairing Windows as described here involves copying operating system files from disc to your system. This means you need to visit Microsoft's update site for Windows so you can download the latest updates for your system.

Using an OEM System Restore Disc

OEM is a computer-industry acronym for *original equipment manufacturer*. Just think of the OEM as the company that put your computer together and shipped it to you.

When I purchased a system from Gateway, I eagerly awaited its arrival. When the delivery guy dropped it off, I ripped open the box, took out the gleaming new system, and set it up in a place of honor in my office. It was so cool! Then, I started rooting around in the box and the wrappings to see if I had missed anything. (I go through the same process after opening Christmas presents — you never know what you may be throwing away.)

One of the things I had missed was a little packet of CDs, all in a handy, petite binder. One of the CDs had the title System Restore Disc. It wasn't until about a year later that I would fully understand how helpful this disc could be.

You see, my system got seriously messed up due to an unfortunate set of events, compounded by too much caffeine and not enough sleep. At the end of the mess, it became obvious that I would need to start over with the system.

The really cool thing is that all I needed to do was plop the System Restore Disc into the CD-ROM drive and reboot the computer. Windows didn't boot, but the CD did. In no time, I saw a menu that provided me with a set of options ranging from a partial reinstall to a full-bore remake of my entire system.

After a few simple choices, the programs on the CD went to work, and I went to lunch. When I got back, the system was completely restored to the pristine condition it existed in on the day I unpacked it from the shipping box — it couldn't have been much simpler!

Gateway isn't alone in providing a System Restore Disc; I use it as an example only because I have firsthand experience with its version of system recovery. Other vendors, such as Dell, also include such discs.

Hopefully you kept the discs that came with your system. If you decide to restore your system, make sure to use the disc that came with your system. If you try to use a disc from a different system (even one from the same manufacturer), the results may not be pretty because of hardware and the drivers that work with that hardware. System restoration discs install drivers based on the hardware that was with the system when it shipped to you. That means that the disc is tied closely to the system it's for. If you use a different disc, you run the risk of installing drivers intended for a system different from yours.

When you're done doing a system restore, you still aren't done. Remember that your system now looks exactly like it did when you first unboxed it. To make the system better reflect the way you work, you need to do a few more things:

- ✔ **Configure the system.** Change your system configuration, as necessary, to match your preferences and requirements. Pay special attention to things such as display settings and Internet configuration.

- ✔ **Update Windows.** Connect to the Windows update site to download updates to Windows. Remember — your system is fresh-from-the-box, without the critical updates released since the CD was created.

- ✔ **Remove the chaff.** Many systems come with preinstalled software that's helpful when trying to make a buying decision. Get rid of these programs; uninstall them as discussed in Chapter 5.

- ✔ **Reinstall programs.** Install the programs you really need and configure them for your working style.

Wiping Out Your System

It used to be that I kept a bootable diskette lying around that contained everything I needed to wipe out a system and start over from scratch. Of course, that was back in the days when the operating system files could fit on a single diskette and they actually shipped systems with floppy drives.

Those days are long gone, but wiping out your system and starting all over again in this day and age is easier than you may think. All you need is your original Windows Vista DVD and a system that can boot from the disc.

Reinstalling the Windows Vista operating system from scratch takes a lot of time. It's not unusual to spend a full day installing the operating system and all the programs you need. It can take even longer, depending on the type of data you need to use. Allow enough time to wipe and reinstall the system correctly.

Preparing for the wipeout

Do a few things before wiping out your current Windows system. Hopefully, your Windows Vista system is usable enough that you can still perform these tasks:

- **Find your product key.** You need the Windows product key to install the operating system. It's a long one, and should be somewhere on the Vista packaging.

- **Create a program inventory.** As discussed in Chapter 3, a program inventory is invaluable when it comes to figuring out what you really want on your system. It's much easier to create the program inventory based on your current system than it will be after wiping out that system.

- **Archive your data.** If you have old data on your system, transfer it to archive media. Chapter 7 covers how to archive your data.

- **Back up your remaining data.** Figure out what data you want to keep from your old system. Transfer it to CDs or other easily accessible media. Remember that you're wiping out everything and need the data in a format you can later access.

- **Print screen shots of configuration dialog boxes.** If you're like most people, you spend a fair amount of time setting up Windows and other programs just the way you want them. Display the dialog boxes where you do configuration changes and print screen shots of them. (Don't forget a screen shot of your Internet configuration settings.) The screen shots are very helpful when you need to configure your newly installed system.

The easiest way to print a screen shot is to display the dialog box, then hold down the Alt key as you press the Print Screen key. The screen shot of the dialog box is now in the Clipboard, and you can paste it into your favorite word processor, such as Microsoft Word. Print the page with the dialog box, and you have your record.

Doing the deed

After performing the preparatory tasks that I outline in the preceding section, follow these steps to wipe out your system:

1. **Shut down your computer and put the Windows Vista DVD in the drive.**

2. **Boot to the DVD.**

   You should see the Setup program running. One of the first screens you see is an Install Windows screen where you can select a language in which to do your install.

3. **Click Next.**

   A new screen appears showing an Install Now option, front and center.

4. **Click the Install Now option to signify that you want to set up Windows Vista.**

   The Setup.exe program huffs, puffs, and checks out your system. Shortly you are prompted for your product key.

5. **Enter your product key and click Next.**

   Setup displays the Windows license agreement.

6. **Accept by clicking I Accept the License Terms and then click Next.**

   You're asked whether you want to do an upgrade or a custom install.

7. **Click the option to perform a Custom install.**

   This allows you to start fresh — which is what you want to do. Setup checks out your hard drive and displays a screen that shows the existing hard drive partitions. Your system might have a single partition, or it might have multiple partitions.

8. **Click the Drive Options (Advanced) link.**

   Setup displays additional options that allow you to make changes to your hard drive structure. The idea here is to wipe out the partitions, re-create them, and then install Windows Vista.

9. **Select the first partition on the hard drive and click Delete.**

10. **When Setup asks you to confirm that you really want to delete the partition, do so.**

   You again see the screen that shows existing partitions.

11. **If other partitions remain, select them and click Delete for each one, in turn.**

   When the partitions are all deleted, the entire hard drive should show as unpartitioned space. Everything on the hard drive has been wiped out, and you're ready to start clean.

12. **Select the unpartitioned space and click New.**

   Setup asks you to specify the size you want for the partition. If you accept the default, Setup uses all the space for a single drive.

   In Chapter 7, I mention that partitioning your system into multiple drives can be beneficial. You can use one for the system, one for programs, and one for your data. Now is the time you could implement such a plan, if desired.

   When you're done partitioning your hard drive, you need to format it.

13. **Select the first partition and click Format.**

   You have to format your partitions before you can copy information — including Windows Vista — to them. Format each of the partitions using the NTFS file system. (See Chapter 14 for a discussion of file systems.)

   After the formatting is complete, you're ready to select a partition as the destination for Windows Vista.

14. **Select the first partition and click Next.**

   Setup starts copying files to the hard drive and then reboots the system. The setup process continues.

15. **Answer additional questions about how you want Windows configured.**

   You can refer to your screen shots of dialog boxes to determine how to answer some questions.

   When you're done answering questions, Windows reboots one more time. You're almost ready to start using the system.

Picking up the pieces

After installing Windows, you still have quite a bit to do before your system is usable:

✔ **Configuring your Internet connection:** If you didn't configure your Internet connection during Setup, now is a great time to do it. Grab the screen shot you made of your connection settings and refer to it while entering the settings.

✔ **Installing Windows updates:** With the Internet connection active, visit the Windows update site to download the latest updates and patches. Perform these updates before you start installing programs on the system.

✔ **Formatting partitioned drives:** If you partitioned your hard drive into multiple drives and didn't format them during Setup, now's a great time to format those other drives. (You need to format each of them except the one where Windows was installed.) To format the other drives, follow these steps:

   1. **Choose Start⇨Computer, right-click the drive you want to format, and choose Format.**

      Windows displays the Format dialog box, shown in Figure 21-1.

   2. **Choose the file system you want to use from the File System drop-down list.**

      In most instances, you should choose the NTFS file system. In some instances, you may want to use a different file system, as discussed in Chapter 14. Leave the Capacity and Allocation Unit Size options set at their default settings.

Figure 21-1:
Format a fresh hard drive.

> **3. In the Volume Label text box, enter a name for the drive.**
>
> **4. Click Start.**
>
> You can do other work while the hard drive is formatting.
>
> ✔ **Installing other programs:** Gather your program installation discs and any program keys necessary to install the software. When all of your hard drives are formatted, install your software programs one at a time. Make sure you start each program and configure it by using the information you gathered before starting to wipe your system.
>
> ✔ **Transferring the data from the temporary storage media back to the hard drive:** Do this last. You may need to modify where the data is stored, based on how you partitioned your hard drive and installed software. After it's copied, make sure you can load the data into your system.

Voilà! You have a brand new system, fresh from the mill.

Part VI

The Part of Tens

"I really think the Home Basic version will work fine for you. Besides, there is no Yurt Basic version of Vista."

In this part . . .

*I*f you're looking for extra tidbits of information, you've come to the right place. In these chapters you find troubleshooting ideas, a multitude of online resources, and cool things about Vista.

Chapter 22

Ten Troubleshooting Ideas

. . . .

When trouble strikes, everyone needs ideas. The ideas in this chapter are designed to provide a starting point for pinpointing the cause of your troubles.

Check Your Startup Files

Loading too many programs at startup can cause system problems. Make sure you load only the programs you really need.

To find out what's running at Startup, check the Startup folders by right-clicking the Start button and choosing either Open or Open All Users. After choosing one, double-click Programs, Startup. Then choose the other and do the same.

For a more in-depth analysis of what's going on when you start Windows, use either msconfig (see Chapter 13) or, for an even more complete analysis, the Autoruns utility, available free from www.sysinternals.com.

Install Windows Updates

Keeping your system updated can help head off and remedy problems. To get your system up to date, choose Start⇨Control Panel⇨System and Maintenance⇨Check for Updates.

To keep your system updated, turn on the automatic updating capability of Windows Vista, as described in Chapter 15.

Run a Spyware Removal Program

Spyware is the bane of many a system, and most people don't even know it. For instance, most people who use a pop-up blocker don't realize they're only treating the symptom, not the problem. The cause of most pop-ups is spyware.

Use a good spyware removal program, such as Spybot Search & Destroy (www.safer-networking.org) or Ad-Aware (www.lavasoftusa.com). I cover removing spyware and other noxious Internet programs in Chapter 10.

Remove Unused Programs

Like dust bunnies under the bed, programs seem to collect and multiply on our systems. If you fail to keep them cleaned out, they eventually clutter your system, and you could run out of disk space or other resources.

As a general rule, you should remove programs that you don't use on a regular basis. If you don't use it once in six months, for instance, you can probably get rid of it. For more about removing old programs, see Chapter 5.

See What Processes Are Running

If you feel your system is becoming sluggish, a lot of programs may be running on your system that you don't know about. The easiest way to see what's running is to use the Task Manager.

Right-click an empty area of the taskbar and choose Task Manager. Use the Applications tab to see what full programs are running and the Processes tab to see what's running behind the scenes.

If you don't know what a process does, search Google for the process name — you can find a ton of information.

Run the Disk Cleanup Utility

Windows includes a free utility that helps clear much of the easy clutter on your system. It doesn't do a deep-cleaning job, but it provides a great starting point. It can get rid of temporary Windows, Internet, and program files; download controls and applets; set up log files; and empty your Recycle Bin.

To run Disk Cleanup, choose Start⇨All Programs⇨Accessories⇨System Tools⇨Disk Cleanup. Chapter 6 contains more detail about this tool.

Defragment Your Disk Drives

The daily grind of adding programs and creating data can, over time, clutter up your hard drive. As files are added, resized, deleted, and overwritten, they become fragmented on the drive. This fragmentation can slow down your overall system performance.

To defragment your disk drive, choose Start⇨Computer, right-click a drive, and choose Properties. On the Tools tab, click Defragment Now. You can find out more information about defragmenting your disk drives in Chapter 14.

Check File Sizes

If you use database or spreadsheet programs, developing monster database files is easy. (I have some almost-15MB data files.)

Big files can lead to big problems for some programs. If you suspect you need smaller data files, look for ways to archive older data and move it off your system. For more about archiving data, check out Chapter 7.

Check the Size of Your Registry

Checking your Registry's size isn't easy, but its size can affect your entire system's performance. If it gets quite large, running Registry-cleaning software can help alleviate some types of problems.

To check the size of your Registry, display the folder containing the Registry hives and add the sizes of the different hive files. If the total seems inordinately high, run a cleaner. Chapter 20 contains information about the Registry and its cleaning software.

Start Your System in Safe Mode

Safe Mode — the idyllic haven of anyone having trouble running Windows. *Safe Mode* is established by starting Windows without loading drivers and other startup programs. In essence, Safe Mode presents a bare-bones Windows system.

While in Safe Mode, you can do what the geeks do: tinker to find out what's causing problems. Change configuration settings, remove drivers, modify the Registry, and so on, until you nail down exactly what the problem is.

Start Safe Mode by pressing F8 early in the boot sequence, before any Windows screens appear. To find more information on Safe Mode, check out *Troubleshooting Your PC For Dummies,* 2nd Edition, by Dan Gookin (published by Wiley).

Chapter 23

Ten Online Resources
to Help You Clean

· ·

*W*hen it comes to cleaning your system, the Internet is full of much more useful information than I could possibly distill to a single chapter. That leaves me with a huge problem: coming up with the ten best online resources for everyone. Part of the problem is that no two people's systems and cleanup needs are the same. Because of this, I tried to make this list of sites as broad as possible. I provided many of the sites I use on a regular basis to help keep my own systems clean.

Sysinternals

www.sysinternals.com

Sysinternals was started by Mark Russinovich and Bryce Cogswell, two consummate system geeks, and recently purchased by Microsoft. Their free tools and utilities are unique and uniquely powerful. I particularly like the Autoruns utility, which shows every program scheduled to run when your system starts — even those listed only in the Registry.

Google

www.google.com

It may seem odd to include a search engine as a cleaning aid, but I find Google very helpful. If I have a question about a file on my hard drive or a process running on my system, all I need to do is type in the file or process name, and I can find information about it. This makes Google a great research tool for tracking down potential problems.

Gibson Research Corporation

www.grc.com

This site includes a number of helpful resources. Perhaps the most helpful online resource is the ShieldsUP! Analysis tool, which is a free security check that analyzes your system's weaknesses (as viewed from the Internet) and tells you how to make your system more secure.

Symantec Security Response

www.symantec.com/security_response

If you want to find out about the latest virus and security issues for PCs, Symantec Security Response is the place to do it. You can search its extensive database, or you can browse through information about various viruses and threats.

SpywareGuide

www.spywareguide.com

A great resource for figuring out the latest spyware scams and how they can affect your system. It includes an online spyware scanning tool to help check your system. This site also features information on different privacy and systems tools that can help you protect your system.

SpywareInfo

www.spywareinfo.com

This site is dedicated not just to education, but to getting spyware removed from your system. It publishes a weekly newsletter that has updates on the latest spyware threats. I find the online forums particularly helpful because you can post questions and get answers from others willing to help you clean your system.

Experts Exchange

www.experts-exchange.com

Have a gnarly question? Why not go directly to where the experts hang out? This site is a great place to pose questions and get reliable answers from people who regularly "work under the hood" of Windows systems.

Spam Arrest

www.spamarrest.com

This challenge/response tool helps block unwanted e-mail from your inbox. Challenge/response works because most spam is generated by computer and sent from unresponsive or fake addresses. All incoming e-mail is challenged and requires unique human response before the mail actually makes it to you.

Urban Legends Reference Pages

www.snopes.com

Did you get the e-mail about the dying child who wanted postcards, the one that told you to delete a file on your computer, or the one about how camel hunting is illegal in Arizona? These and thousands of other urban legends are cataloged at the Urban Legends Reference Pages. If you receive a lot of e-mails containing stories that you consider passing on to others, visit this site first to see if the story's true.

Vista Software Archive

http://www.vista-files.org

Nice site that includes a bunch of programs that work with Vista. Take a look around; the available programs change all the time. You might find something you like that can help you clean or organize your system.

Chapter 24

Ten Cool Things in Vista

*W*indows Vista is all the rage these days — it is coming installed on new machines and is the subject of countless upgrades on existing systems. It is the latest and greatest version of Windows yet. That means that there are a lot of cool things in Vista that can help to make your computing experience better than with earlier versions of Windows. This chapter covers ten of the things I consider cool about Vista. (As you use the operating system, you no doubt will come up with your own "cool list" that may or may not include some of the same items I do.)

Windows Firewall

Granted, Windows XP had a firewall installed, but it wasn't nearly as robust and secure as the one in Vista. The firewall, which is turned on by default, both protects your system from others and others from your system as it puts an end to malicious information sent to or from your computer. For more information about firewalls and, in particular, the Windows Firewall, see Chapter 18.

Sidebar and Gadgets

The Sidebar is the area at the right side of your desktop. It allows you to display gadgets, which are a new type of accessory to your computing. If you aren't careful, the Sidebar can become a place to add to the clutter on your desktop, but it really is pretty cool in that it allows you to quickly access programs (the gadgets) that you may need on a regular basis.

Greater System Protection

Every time you try to do something in Vista that may result in some powerful program running or accessing resources, the operating system asks for your permission. This may seem a bit bothersome at first (particularly because you never saw these dialog boxes in older versions of Windows), but they provide an unparalleled level of protection against something ending up on your system that you may regret.

Parental Controls

Got children who use your computer? If you set them up with their own account, you can — as the wise and semi-omnipotent parent — use the Vista parental controls to determine what they can and cannot do on the system. Just open the Control Panel and click the Set Up Parental Controls for Any User link, click which account you want to control, and then set up what can be done with the account. You can even monitor activity through the account; a real bonus for some parents.

Performance Information

Windows now includes a way to benchmark or measure the performance of your system. This measure is established when Vista is first installed and can be periodically recalculated for your system. Open the Control Panel, click System and Maintenance, and then click the Performance Information and Tools link. The information in the resulting dialog box can be quite helpful in figuring out how to improve the performance of your system.

Network Administration

If you're a network administrator, Windows Vista provides all sorts of improvements over previous versions of Windows. You'll find tools that are both secure and powerful, with greater reach across your network.

Network administration is obviously beyond the scope of this book, but if you are a network admin, you should pay special attention to the new and improved features of Vista. I'm sure you'll agree that the tools can make your life easier as you accomplish an otherwise difficult (and thankless) task.

Virtual Folders

One of the most-touted additions to Vista is the ability to create virtual folders. These are nothing but search results, presented as if they were a folder on your system. This means that they can be dynamic; as the search results change over time, so does the contents of the virtual folder. Of course, if you have historically had trouble organizing traditional folders on your system, virtual folders may add a level of complexity that just compounds the trouble. While cool, virtual folders should not be tackled until you are comfortable in controlling the regular folders on your system. (See Chapter 7 for help in this regard.)

Snipping Tool

One of the tools added to Vista that is often overlooked is the Snipping Tool. This handy, easy-to-use tool allows you to "snip" portions of your desktop and create graphic files from them. Start the tool (Start⇨All Programs⇨Accessories⇨Snipping Tool) and a simple cross-hair cursor allows you to click and drag to define the area you want to snip. You can then make small modifications to what you snipped and save it to a graphic file — quick, easy, and cool.

Tabbed Browsing

What's a new release of Windows without a new release of Internet Explorer? Vista is no exception; it includes a new version of IE that has some pretty cool features. My favorite is the addition of tabbing, which allows you to open different Web pages in individual browser tabs and organize your browsing better. (Other browsers have had tabbing for years; it's about time that IE caught up.)

Phishing Filter

Internet Explorer now includes an integrated "phishing filter," which checks Web sites to assess whether they may be trolling for information about you that you don't want to give. This helps to protect your identity and your financial information, which makes your online experience better than ever.

Index

• *Symbols and Numerics* •

~ (tilde) in file names, 87

• *A* •

accounts on network, deleting, 272–274
ads, pop-up, blocking, 152–155
Agent program, 162
All Programs list, organizing, 179–180
annual cleaning tasks, 32–33
antivirus programs, 145–146
applications. *See* programs
archives
  definition of, 32, 106–107
  for e-mail, 61, 138–142
  storage media for, 107–108
  where to store, 109–110
attachments, regularly deleting, 137–138
audio files. *See* multimedia files
AutoArchive feature, Microsoft Outlook, 139–140
autoresponders, 122
avast! 4 Home Edition, 144–145

• *B* •

backups
  on external hard drive, 254–255
  making, process for, 108–109
  making, schedule for, 30
  making before cleaning, 23
  as protection from data loss, 259
  of Registry, 289–290
  where to store, 109–110
.bak file extension, 87
Bayesian filters, 124
Billminder feature, in Quicken, 58–59

blacklists, 124–125
books. *See* publications
booting. *See also* startup process
  restricting options for, 259
  in safe mode, 313–314
boot.ini file, 194
browser
  blocking pop-ups in, 153–154
  browser hijacker, 151
  Favorites list, cleaning, 32
  Favorites list, organizing, 163–164
browser hijacker, 151
Building a PC For Dummies (Chambers), 235
buying e-mail addresses, 120

• *C* •

cache, Web
  changing size of, 169
  cleaning, 29, 165–167
  definition of, 165
  location of, 167–169
CD-ROM drive, 255
challenge/response (C/R) systems, 125–126
Chambers, Mark (*Building a PC For Dummies*), 235
children, managing computer use by, 65
chkdsk utility, 221–222
cleaning computer system
  benefits of, 15–16, 17, 18–19
  hiring someone else for, cost of, 17
  indications of needing to, 10–15
  order of cleaning tasks to perform, 22–23
  precautions to take during, 23–25
  programs for, on Windows Vista, 25–27
  programs for, reputable, 24
  programs for, third-party, 27–28

cleaning computer system *(continued)*
  by reformatting hard drive, 33
  scheduling, 28–33
  time and effort required for, 16–17
Cleanse program (Zards Software), 75
client-server network, 274
CloneMaster program (SoftByte
    Labs, Inc.), 92–94
CNET web site, 27
COMPONENTS hive, 285–286
compressing hard drive, whether to, 222
computer. *See* hardware
Computer Manager, 203–205
Computer Viruses For Dummies (Gregory), 143
Control Panel
  cleaning, 184–185
  Installed Programs area, deleting
      programs using, 29, 74–75
  installed programs listed on, 43–44
  network settings, 239, 240, 273, 276, 277
  parental controls, 320
  performance options, setting,
      189–191, 320
  uninstalling components of Windows
      Vista, 188–189
  Windows Firewall, 266
  Windows updates, 311
conventions used in this book, 4–5
Cookie Pal software (Kookaburra
    Software), 160
cookies
  blocking, 158–160
  definition of, 157–158
  deleting, 29, 160–162
  how installed, 158
  managing, 160
  saving, 161
.CPL file extension, 185
C/R (challenge/response) systems, 125–126
CWShredder program, 151

• D •

daemons. *See* services
data. *See* files

data keys, in Registry, 24, 286
database
  exporting old data, 61
  file system choice for, 213
  hard drive speed for, 251
  high-end systems for, 234
  large, improving access speed of, 60–62
  Registry as, 23, 284
default folders, whether to use, 104
defragmenting hard drive
  how often to, 31–32
  process for, 218–219
  reasons for, 217
  third-party software for, 218
Deleted Items folder, Microsoft Outlook,
    135–136
desktop
  cleaning, 31
  icons on, adding from Personalize dialog,
      174–175
  icons on, default, 174
  icons on, deleting, 175
  icons on, differentiating from programs,
      175
  icons on, renaming, 175
  icons on, too many, 10–11
  icons on, unknown, 24
  organizing, 173–176
  programs on, determining, 40–42
  screensavers on, 175–176
  shortcuts on, deleting, 80
  shortcuts on, differentiating from
      program icons, 175
  Sidebar on, 319
  themes on, 175–176
device drivers
  definition of, 198
  needed for new hardware transition,
      236–237
  removing, 200–201
  signature of, checking, 198–200
  updating, 32, 200
dictionary attack, 119–120
Digibin program, 162
Digital Shredder (McAfee Internet
    Security Suite), 259

disk cleaning software, 202
Disk Cleanup program
  Recycle Bin emptied by, 94
  using, 88–90
.DLL file (dynamic link library), 201–202
Documents folder, changing, 105–106
Drive Scrubber (System Mechanic), 259
drivers
  definition of, 198
  needed for new hardware transition,
    236–237
  removing, 200–201
  signature of, checking, 198–200
  updating, 32, 200
DVD-ROM drive, 255
dynamic link library (.DLL file),
  201–202

• E •

electronic greeting cards, 121
e-mail
  archiving, 61, 138–142
  attachments to, regularly deleting,
    137–138
  benefits of cleaning for, 18
  checking and responding to less often,
    116–118
  deleting, cutoff points for, 135
  deleting, from Deleted Items folder,
    135–136
  deleting, from junk mail folder, 136–137
  deleting, locations to delete from, 29
  incoming, organizing, 114–115
  incoming, processing with mail rules,
    129–134
  multiple accounts for, 114–116, 122
  organizing, using folders, 128–129
  spam, books about, 121, 143
  spam, causes of, guessing addresses,
    119–120
  spam, causes of, harvesting
    addresses, 118–119
  spam, causes of, purchasing
    addresses, 120
  spam, challenge/response (C/R)
    systems for, 125–126
  spam, definition of, 118
  spam, filters for, 122–125
  spam, reducing, 115–116, 121–122
  spam, regularly deleting junk mail
    folder for, 136–137
eTrust Antivirus, 145
Everett-Church, Ray (*Fighting Spam For
  Dummies*), 121, 143
Excel (Microsoft)
  external links in, 57
  graphics display option in, 58
Experts Exchange web site, 317
external client spam filters, 123
external hard drive, 254–255
external links, in Word or Excel, 57

• F •

false positives in filtering, 125
Fast Save feature, in Word, 57
FAT (file allocation table) file system
  converting from NTFS to, 216–217
  converting to NTFS file system, 215–216
  definition of, 212
  when to use, 213
Favorites list
  cleaning, 32
  organizing, 163–164
Fighting Spam For Dummies (Levine, Levine
  Young, and Everett-Church), 121, 143
file allocation table (FAT) file system
  converting from NTFS to, 216–217
  converting to NTFS file system, 215–216
  definition of, 212
  when to use, 213
file size of zero, 87
file systems
  choosing, 213
  converting to FAT from NTFS, 216–217
  converting to NTFS from FAT, 215–216
  default for Windows Vista, 213
  determining file system being used,
    214–215

file systems *(continued)*
  FAT file system, 212
  NTFS file system, 212–213
  supported by Windows Vista, 104
files
  additional storage for, new hard drive,
    250–255
  additional storage for, other drives,
    255–256
  age of, too old, 13–14
  archiving, 32, 106–108
  backing up, 108–109
  benefits of cleaning for, 18
  deleting, being sure of, 23
  deleting, with Disk Cleanup program,
    88–90
  duplicate, finding and deleting, 91–94
  dynamic link library, 201–202
  large, improving access speed of, 60–62
  losing, protection against, 259
  organizing, among drives and partitions,
    98–99
  organizing, folder structure for, 99–100
  orphan data, finding and deleting, 87–88
  in Program Files folder, 44–45
  project data, archiving, 31
  recovery of deleted files, as security
    threat, 259–260
  in Recycle Bin, emptying, 29
  size of, too large, 313
  temporary files, deleting, 30, 84–87
  transferring to new computer, 242–243
  transferring with external hard drive, 255
filters for spam, 122–125
Find Fast program, 56–57
firewalls
  definition of, 265–266
  hardware firewalls, 268–269
  Windows Firewall, 266–267, 319
  ZoneAlarm firewall (Zone Labs),
    267–268
Flash ads, 155
flash drive
  definition of, 256
  improving file access speed, 61
folders (e-mail), 128–129

folders (file)
  default folders, 104–106
  depth of, 101
  manipulating, with folders list, 102–103
  manipulating, with menus, 101–102
  root directory, cleaning, 30, 103–104
  root directory, limitations on, 104
  shared folders, removing, 278–279
  shared folders, when to use, 274–275
  structuring, for file organization, 99–100
  virtual folders, 100, 321
fragmented files, 217
freeware, 160
F-Secure Antivirus, 145

• *G* •

gadgets, in Sidebar, 319
games
  improving speed and reliability of, 64–66
  installed by Windows, uninstalling, 189
Gibson Research
  ShieldsUP!, 265
  web site, 316
Google
  searching for process names on, 50, 315
  toolbar, as spyware, 153
graphics display option, in Word
    or Excel, 58
Gregory, Peter (*Computer Viruses For
    Dummies*), 143
guessing e-mail addresses, 119–120

• *H* •

hard drive
  adding another hard drive, moving
    pagefile to, 251–253
  adding another hard drive, type of drive
    for, 254–255
  adding another hard drive, whether to,
    250–251
  alternatives to, 255–256
  cleaning, 312
  compressing, whether to, 222

cost of, 251
defragmenting, 31–32, 217–219, 313
errors on, checking for, 219–222
faster, to improve file access speed, 61
multiple, organizing files on, 98–99
partitioned, organizing files on, 98–99
reformatting, cleaning system by, 33
running out of space, warnings for, 91
shared drives, when to use, 274–275
size of, allowing files to accumulate, 84
speed of, 251
transferring to new computer, 238
hardware
  adding, to improve file access speed,
    60–61
  building yourself, 235
  for games, 66
  high-end systems, when needed,
    233–234
  laptops, when needed, 235–236
  lifetime of, 233
  low-end systems, when needed, 235
  mid-range systems, when needed, 234
  new, choosing, 233–236
  new, preparing for, 236–242
  new, reinstalling software on, 242
  new, transferring data to, 242–243
  new, when needed, 34, 232–233
  physical security for, 258–259
hardware drivers
  definition of, 198
  needed for new hardware transition,
    236–237
  removing, 200–201
  signature of, checking, 198–200
  updating, 32, 200
hardware firewalls, 268–269
HARDWARE hive, 285–286
harvesting e-mail addresses, 118–119
hijacker, browser, 151
HijackThis program, 151
hives, in Registry, 285–286
HKEY_CLASSES_ROOT tree, 285
HKEY_CURRENT_CONFIG tree, 285
HKEY_CURRENT_USER tree, 285
HKEY_LOCAL_MACHINE tree, 285

HKEY_USERS tree, 285
Home Networking For Dummies (Ivens), 275
`http://` protocol designator, 264
`https://` protocol designator, 264

• *I* •

icons in Notification area
  determining program for, 41
  removing, 182–184
  too many, 14–15
icons on desktop
  adding from Personalize dialog, 174–175
  default, 174
  deleting, 175
  determining program for, 41
  differentiating from programs, 175
  renaming, 175
  shortcuts, deleting, 80
  shortcuts, differentiating from program
    icons, 175
  too many, 10–11
  unknown, not running, 24
icons used in this book, 5
information. *See* files
insecure passwords, 260–261
Installed Programs area, Control Panel
  accessing, 43
  deleting programs using, 29, 74–75
integrated client spam filters, 123
internal hard drive, 254–255
Internet. *See also* e-mail; spyware; viruses
  benefits of cleaning for, 18
  cookies, blocking, 158–160
  cookies, definition of, 157–158
  cookies, deleting, 29, 160–162
  cookies, how installed, 158
  cookies, managing, 160
  cookies, saving, 161
  Favorites list, cleaning, 32
  Favorites list, organizing, 163–164
  newsgroups, 162–163
  pop-up ads, blocking, 152–155
  security for, firewalls, 265–269
  security for, Internet zones, 261–263

Internet
   security for, SSL, 264
   security for, Windows Vista features for, 264–265
   security zones for, 261–263
   Web cache, changing size of, 169
   Web cache, cleaning, 29, 165–167
   Web cache, definition of, 165
   Web cache, location of, 167–169
Internet Explorer. *See* Web browser
Internet zones, 261–263
ISP-provided spam filters, 123
Ivens, Kathy (*Home Networking For Dummies*), 275

• J •

Journal feature, in Outlook, 58
journal for program inventory, 39–40
junk e-mail, options, Microsoft Outlook, 136–137

• K •

keys, for software, 24
keys, in Registry, 24, 286
kids, managing computer use by, 65
Kookaburra Software, Cookie Pal software, 160

• L •

laid-back approach for program inventory, 39–40
laptops, when needed, 235–236
Lee, Barry (developer of No! Flash program), 155
Levine, John R. (*Fighting Spam For Dummies*), 121, 143
Levine Young, Margaret (*Fighting Spam For Dummies*), 121, 143
Local Intranet, security zone, 261

log files
   deleting, using Disk Cleanup program, 89
   for program installations, 80–81
Lowe, Doug (*Networking For Dummies*), 275

• M •

macros
   in Outlook, 141–142
   speed of, improving, 59
mail rules, 129–134
Mailbox Cleanup tool, Microsoft Outlook, 140–141
Major Geeks web site, 28
malicious programs. *See* viruses
McAfee Internet Security Suite, Digital Shredder, 259
McAfee VirusScan Professional, 145
Meaya Software, Popup Ad Filter, 154
memory
   adding, to improve file access speed, 61
   types of, 248
   whether to add more, 248–250
menu items, deleting, 80
menus, for folder tasks, 101–102
Microsoft Excel
   external links in, 57
   graphics display option in, 58
Microsoft Office, improving speed of, 56–58
Microsoft Outlook
   AutoArchive feature, 139–140
   Deleted Items folder in, 135–136
   junk e-mail, options for, 136–137
   macros in, 141–142
   mail rules in, 129–134
   Mailbox Cleanup tool in, 140–141
   speed of, improving, 58
Microsoft System Configuration utility, 193–198
Microsoft Word
   external links in, 57
   Fast Save feature in, 57
   graphics display option in, 58
monthly cleaning tasks, 30–32

msconfig utility
 modifying system startup using, 193–198
 services, managing, 205–206
multimedia files
 editing programs for, improving speed
  of, 66–67
 storage needs for, 94
My Documents, changing folder for,
  105–106

• *N* •

network
 administration of, features for, 320
 affecting performance of computer, 54–55
 books about, 275
 client-server network, 274
 file system choice for, 213
 peer-to-peer network, 274
 settings for, needed for new hardware
  transition, 239–242
 shared drives, when to use, 274–275
 shared folders, removing, 278–279
 shared folders, when to use, 274–275
 shared printers, availability of, 275–277
 shared printers, turning off, 277–278
 sharing, disabling, 280–281
 user accounts, old, deleting, 272–274
Networking For Dummies (Lowe), 275
NewsBin Pro program, 162
newsgroups, 162–163
new-technology file system. *See* NTFS
No! Flash program, 155
Norton AntiVirus, 145
Notification area
 definition of, 182
 icons in, determining program for, 41
 icons in, removing, 182–184
 icons in, too many, 14–15
NTFS (new-technology file system)
 converting from FAT to, 215–216
 converting to FAT file system, 216–217
 as default, 213
 definition of, 212–213
 when to use, 213

• *O* •

OEM (original equipment manufacturer)
  system restore disc, 301–302
Office (Microsoft), improving speed of, 56–58
Office Startup Assistant, 57
off-site storage for archives and backups,
  109–110
.old file extension, 87
operating system. *See* Windows Vista
original equipment manufacturer (OEM)
  system restore disc, 301–302
orphan data, 87–88
Outlook (Microsoft)
 AutoArchive feature, 139–140
 Deleted Items folder in, 135–136
 junk e-mail, options for, 136–137
 macros in, 141–142
 mail rules in, 129–134
 Mailbox Cleanup tool in, 140–141
 speed of, improving, 58
overhauling computer system, whether to, 33

• *P* •

pagefile
 definition of, 248
 moving to new hard drive, 251–253
 settings for, 193
Panda Software, 145
parental controls, 320
Partition Commander 10 (VCom), 99
partitions
 definition of, 99
 organizing files on, 98–99
passwords
 importance of using, 259
 insecure, 260–261
PC-Tools Software, Registry Mechanic, 296
peer-to-peer network, 274
performance
 information about, provided by Windows,
  320
 network affecting, 54–55
 Windows Vista options for, 189–193

Personalize dialog, adding icons to desktop from, 174–175
phishing filter, 321
photos. *See* multimedia files
physical memory, 248
physical security, 258–259
Popup Ad Filter (Meaya Software), 154
pop-up ads, blocking, 152–155
printers
  shared, availability of, 275–277
  shared, turning off, 277–278
  transitioning to new computer, 236–237
problems, finding and resolving. *See* troubleshooting
processes
  checking, 312
  currently running, determining, 48–50
processor scheduling, 193
Program Files folder
  determining programs in, 44–45
  determining programs to remove from, 70–72
  hidden by Windows security, viewing, 71
programs. *See also specific program names*
  All Programs list, organizing, 179–180
  benefits of cleaning for, 18
  for cleaning, on Windows Vista, 25–27
  for cleaning, reputable, 24
  for cleaning, third-party, 27–28
  configuration settings, transferring to new hardware, 238
  currently running, determining, 48–50, 184
  currently running, in Notification area, 182, 184
  deleting, process for, 24, 29
  deleting, using brute-force method, 75–80
  deleting, using Disk Cleanup program, 89
  deleting, using Installed Programs area, 74–75
  deleting, using third-party tools, 75
  deleting, using uninstall command, 72–73
  deleting Registry entries for, 294
  differentiating from shortcuts, 175
  downloading, whether to, 155–156
  file access speed of, improving, 62
  gadgets, in Sidebar, 319
  games, improving speed and reliability of, 64–66
  incompatible with Windows Vista, running, 62–64
  installation discs, transferring to new hardware, 237
  installed, determining from Control Panel, 43–44
  installed, determining from current processes, 48–50
  installed, determining from desktop, 40–42
  installed, determining from program folders, 44–45
  installed, determining from Start menu, 42–43
  installed, determining from Startup folder, 45–48
  inventory of, creating, 37–40
  inventory of, needed for new hardware transition, 236
  inventory of, updating, 33
  not working or installed correctly, deleting, 80–82
  in Notification area, too many, 14–15
  original discs of, having before cleaning, 24
  preinstalled, whether to remove, 70
  reinstalling on new hardware, 237, 242
  run at startup, 311
  run automatically, determining, 45–48
  running slowly, 13
  on Start menu, too many, 12–13
  unknown, not running, 24
  unused or unneeded, deleting, 29, 312
  unused or unneeded, determining, 51, 70–71
  upgrading, whether to, 55–56
  whiz-bang features of, turning off, 54
publications
  Building a PC For Dummies (Chambers), 235
  Computer Viruses For Dummies (Gregory), 143
  Fighting Spam For Dummies (Levine, Levine Young, and Everett-Church), 121, 143

Home Networking For Dummies (Ivens), 275
Networking For Dummies (Lowe), 275
purchasing e-mail addresses, 120

• *Q* •

Quicken, improving speed of, 58–60

• *R* •

Recycle Bin
  created by other programs, 96
  emptying, 29, 94–96
  resizing, 95
REG_BINARY data type, 287
RegCompact.NET, 296
REG_DWORD data type, 287
REG_EXPAND_SZ data type, 287
Registry
  analyzers, 295–296
  backing up, 289–290
  backing up, before cleaning, 24
  cleaning, after deleting program files, 77–79
  cleaning, .DLL files cleaned during, 202
  cleaning, software for, 295–296
  compacting, 296
  corrupted, 297
  data keys in, 24, 286
  definition of, 23, 283–284
  editing, 287–289, 291–294
  hives in, 285–286
  parts of, 284
  restoring, 297
  size of, checking, 313
  trees in, 284–285
  values in, 287
Registry Analyst (YavSoft), 296
Registry cleaner (System Mechanic), 296
Registry Drill, 296
Registry Editor, 288–289, 291–294
Registry Mechanic (PC-Tools Software), 296
REG_MULTI_SZ data type, 287

REG_QWORD data type, 287
REG_SZ data type, 287
resources. *See* publications; web sites
Restricted Sites, security zone, 262
root directory
  cleaning, 30, 103–104
  limitations on, 104
rules, for incoming e-mail, 129–134
rules-based filters, 124

• *S* •

safe mode, booting in, 313–314
SAM hive, 285–286
Schema hive, 285–286
screensavers on desktop, 175–176
secure sockets layer (SSL), 264
security. *See also* viruses
  checking for vulnerabilities in, 264–265
  data loss, 259
  data recovery, 259–260
  firewalls for, 265–269
  insecure passwords, 260–261
  for Internet, firewalls, 265–269
  for Internet, Internet zones, 261–263
  Internet security zones, 261–263
  for Internet, SSL, 264
  for Internet, Windows Vista features for, 264–265
  parental controls, 320
  phishing filter, 321
  physical security, 258–259
  precautions for, updating, 32–33
  SSL (secure sockets layer), 264
  Windows features for, 320
SECURITY hive, 285–286
security zones, 261–263
server-based filters, 123
services
  definition of, 202–203
  managing in Computer Manager, 203–205
  managing in msconfig utility, 205–206
shared drives
  compared to shared folders, 279
  when to use, 274–275

shared folders
  compared to shared drives, 279
  disabling, 280–281
  removing, 278–279
  when to use, 274–275
shared printers
  availability, 275–277
  disabling, 277–278, 280–281
shareware, 160
Shareware.com web site, 27
sharing, disabling, 280–281
ShieldsUP! (Gibson Research), 265
shortcuts
  deleting, 80
  differentiating from program icons, 175
Sidebar, 319
signature files, for antivirus software, 146
signature of device driver, 198–200
Snipping Tool, 321
SoftByte Labs, Inc., CloneMaster program,
    92–94
software. *See* programs
SOFTWARE hive, 285–286
software keys, 24
SonicWALL firewall, 268–269
spam
  books about, 121, 143
  causes of, guessing addresses, 119–120
  causes of, harvesting addresses, 118–119
  causes of, purchasing addresses, 120
  challenge/response (C/R) systems for,
    125–126
  definition of, 118
  filters for, 122–125
  reducing, 115–116, 121–122
  regularly deleting junk mail folder for,
    136–137
Spam Arrest program, 126, 317
Spybot Search & Destroy program,
    150–152, 155
spyware
  definition of, 146
  deleting, 150–152
  eliminating, 31

Google toolbar as, 153
  how installed, 148–149
  legality of, 149
  resources about, 150
  seriousness of, 149
  symptoms, 147–148
SpywareGuide web site, 150, 316
SpywareInfo web site, 150, 316
SSL (secure sockets layer), 264
Start menu
  All Programs list, organizing, 179–180
  customizing contents of, 177–179
  layout for, specifying, 176–177
  programs on, determining, 42–43
  programs on, too many, 12–13
Startup folder
  checking for troubleshooting purposes, 311
  for specific user, determining programs
    in, 47–48
  for Windows, determining programs in,
    46–47
Startup menu, 47
startup process. *See also* booting
  list of programs run at startup, modifying,
    197–198
  modifying startup files, 196–197
  msconfig utility for, 193–195
  type of startup used, changing, 195–196
storage. *See* archives; backups; hard drive
swap file, 248
Symantec Security Response web site, 316
Sysinternals web site, 28, 315
System Configuration utility (Microsoft),
    193–198
SYSTEM hive, 285–286
System Mechanic
  Drive Scrubber, 259
  Registry cleaner, 296
System Protection
  configuring, 207–208
  definition of, 206–207
  restore points, setting, 208
  reverting to a restore point, 208–209
system tray. *See* Notification area

• T •

tabbed browsing, 321
Task Manager (Windows), 48–50
taskbar
  definition of, 180
  grouping tasks on, 180–182
  icons on, determining program for, 41
  Notification area of, definition of, 182
  Notification area of, icons in, 14–15, 41, 182–184
temporary files
  deleted by Disk Cleanup program, 88–89
  deleting, 30, 84–87
  finding, 85–87
themes on desktop, 175–176
think-tank approach for program inventory, 38–39
tilde (~) in file names, 87
.tmp file extension, 87
tools. *See* programs
trash. *See* Recycle Bin
trees, in Registry, 284–285
troubleshooting
  booting in safe mode, 313–314
  file sizes, checking, 313
  hard drive, cleaning, 312
  hard drive, defragmenting, 313
  processes, checking, 312
  programs, unused, removing, 312
  Registry, size of, checking, 313
  spyware removal program, running, 311–312
  startup programs, checking, 311
  Windows Vista, updating, 311
Trusted Sites, security zone, 261
Tucows web site, 27

• U •

uninstall command for programs, 72–73
uninstaller software, 202
uninstalling components of Windows Vista, 188–189, 281

updates for Windows Vista
  automatic updates, 225–227
  categories of, which to install, 228–229
  choosing method of, 227–228
  definition of, 224
  e-mails claiming to be, 227
  manual updates, 224–225
upgrading programs, whether to, 55–56
Urban Legends Reference Pages, 317
user accounts, old, deleting, 272–274
user interface. *See also* desktop; Start menu; taskbar
  Control Panel, cleaning, 184–185
  Control Panel, Installed Programs area, deleting programs using, 29, 74–75
  Control Panel, installed programs listed on, 43–44
  visual effects in Windows Vista, options for, 191–192

• V •

values, in Registry, 287
VBA macros, improving speed of, 59
VCom, Partition Commander 10, 99
video files. *See* multimedia files
virtual folders, 100, 321
virtual memory
  definition of, 248
  performance settings for, 193
viruses
  attached to e-mails, 227
  blocking, 145–146
  books about, 143
  checking for, 144–145
  definition of, 260
  preventing, 260
Vista
  benefits of cleaning for, 19
  cleaning tools on, 25–27
  file systems supported by, 104
  performance options for, 189–193
  programs incompatible with, running on, 62–64
  reinstalling, 299–301
  restoring, 301–302

Vista *(continued)*
  running slowly, 13
  uninstalling components of, 188–189, 281
  updating, 224–229, 311
  visual effects in, performance affected
    by, 191–192
  wiping out and reinstalling, 303–307
Vista Software Archive, 317
visual effects in Windows Vista, options
  for, 191–192

• W •

Web. *See* Internet
Web browser
  blocking pop-ups in, 153–154
  browser hijacker, 151
  Favorites list, cleaning, 32
  Favorites list, organizing, 163–164
Web cache
  changing size of, 169
  cleaning, 29, 165–167
  definition of, 165
  location of, 167–169
web sites
  antivirus programs, 145
  cleaning software and resources, 315–317
  cookie managing software, 160
  C/R systems, 126
  erasing data, software for, 259
  firewalls, 267–268
  Flash ad blockers, 155
  hijacker removal software, 151
  newsreader programs, 162
  partitioning utilities, 99
  pop-up blockers, 154
  Registry analyzers, 296
  Registry cleaners, 296
  Registry compactors, 296
  security check software, 265
  spyware detection software, 150
  spyware information, 150

  for third-party cleaning tools,
    27–28, 75, 92
  virus checkers, 144
weekly cleaning tasks, 30
whitelists, 124–125
whiz-bang features, turning off, 54
Windows Application Compatibility mode,
  63–64
Windows Firewall, 266–267, 319
Windows Office icon, 57
Windows Task Manager, 48–50
Windows Vista
  benefits of cleaning for, 19
  cleaning tools on, 25–27
  file systems supported by, 104
  performance options for, 189–193
  programs incompatible with, running on,
    62–64
  reinstalling, 299–301
  restoring, 301–302
  running slowly, 13
  uninstalling components of, 188–189, 281
  updating, 224–229, 311
  visual effects in, performance affected by,
    191–192
  wiping out and reinstalling, 303–307
Word (Microsoft)
  external links in, 57
  Fast Save feature in, 57
  graphics display option in, 58
World Wide Web. *See* Internet

• Y •

YavSoft, Registry Analyst, 296
yearly cleaning tasks, 32–33

• Z •

Zards Software, Cleanse program, 75
Zip drive, 256
ZoneAlarm firewall (Zone Labs), 267–268

Notes

Notes

Notes

Notes

BUSINESS, CAREERS & PERSONAL FINANCE

0-7645-9847-3

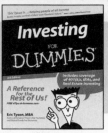

0-7645-2431-3

Also available:
- Business Plans Kit For Dummies
  0-7645-9794-9
- Economics For Dummies
  0-7645-5726-2
- Grant Writing For Dummies
  0-7645-8416-2
- Home Buying For Dummies
  0-7645-5331-3
- Managing For Dummies
  0-7645-1771-6
- Marketing For Dummies
  0-7645-5600-2

- Personal Finance For Dummies
  0-7645-2590-5*
- Resumes For Dummies
  0-7645-5471-9
- Selling For Dummies
  0-7645-5363-1
- Six Sigma For Dummies
  0-7645-6798-5
- Small Business Kit For Dummies
  0-7645-5984-2
- Starting an eBay Business For Dummies
  0-7645-6924-4
- Your Dream Career For Dummies
  0-7645-9795-7

HOME & BUSINESS COMPUTER BASICS

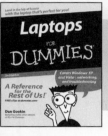

0-470-05432-8

0-471-75421-8

Also available:
- Cleaning Windows Vista For Dummies
  0-471-78293-9
- Excel 2007 For Dummies
  0-470-03737-7
- Mac OS X Tiger For Dummies
  0-7645-7675-5
- MacBook For Dummies
  0-470-04859-X
- Macs For Dummies
  0-470-04849-2
- Office 2007 For Dummies
  0-470-00923-3

- Outlook 2007 For Dummies
  0-470-03830-6
- PCs For Dummies
  0-7645-8958-X
- Salesforce.com For Dummies
  0-470-04893-X
- Upgrading & Fixing Laptops For Dummies
  0-7645-8959-8
- Word 2007 For Dummies
  0-470-03658-3
- Quicken 2007 For Dummies
  0-470-04600-7

FOOD, HOME, GARDEN, HOBBIES, MUSIC & PETS

0-7645-8404-9

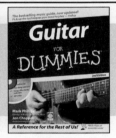

0-7645-9904-6

Also available:
- Candy Making For Dummies
  0-7645-9734-5
- Card Games For Dummies
  0-7645-9910-0
- Crocheting For Dummies
  0-7645-4151-X
- Dog Training For Dummies
  0-7645-8418-9
- Healthy Carb Cookbook For Dummies
  0-7645-8476-6
- Home Maintenance For Dummies
  0-7645-5215-5

- Horses For Dummies
  0-7645-9797-3
- Jewelry Making & Beading For Dummies
  0-7645-2571-9
- Orchids For Dummies
  0-7645-6759-4
- Puppies For Dummies
  0-7645-5255-4
- Rock Guitar For Dummies
  0-7645-5356-9
- Sewing For Dummies
  0-7645-6847-7
- Singing For Dummies
  0-7645-2475-5

INTERNET & DIGITAL MEDIA

0-470-04529-9

0-470-04894-8

Also available:
- Blogging For Dummies
  0-471-77084-1
- Digital Photography For Dummies
  0-7645-9802-3
- Digital Photography All-in-One Desk Reference For Dummies
  0-470-03743-1
- Digital SLR Cameras and Photography For Dummies
  0-7645-9803-1
- eBay Business All-in-One Desk Reference For Dummies
  0-7645-8438-3
- HDTV For Dummies
  0-470-09673-X

- Home Entertainment PCs For Dummies
  0-470-05523-5
- MySpace For Dummies
  0-470-09529-6
- Search Engine Optimization For Dummies
  0-471-97998-8
- Skype For Dummies
  0-470-04891-3
- The Internet For Dummies
  0-7645-8996-2
- Wiring Your Digital Home For Dummies
  0-471-91830-X

* Separate Canadian edition also available
† Separate U.K. edition also available

SPORTS, FITNESS, PARENTING, RELIGION & SPIRITUALITY

0-471-76871-5

0-7645-7841-3

Also available:
- Catholicism For Dummies
  0-7645-5391-7
- Exercise Balls For Dummies
  0-7645-5623-1
- Fitness For Dummies
  0-7645-7851-0
- Football For Dummies
  0-7645-3936-1
- Judaism For Dummies
  0-7645-5299-6
- Potty Training For Dummies
  0-7645-5417-4
- Buddhism For Dummies
  0-7645-5359-3

- Pregnancy For Dummies
  0-7645-4483-7 †
- Ten Minute Tone-Ups For Dummies
  0-7645-7207-5
- NASCAR For Dummies
  0-7645-7681-X
- Religion For Dummies
  0-7645-5264-3
- Soccer For Dummies
  0-7645-5229-5
- Women in the Bible For Dummies
  0-7645-8475-8

TRAVEL

0-7645-7749-2

0-7645-6945-7

Also available:
- Alaska For Dummies
  0-7645-7746-8
- Cruise Vacations For Dummies
  0-7645-6941-4
- England For Dummies
  0-7645-4276-1
- Europe For Dummies
  0-7645-7529-5
- Germany For Dummies
  0-7645-7823-5
- Hawaii For Dummies
  0-7645-7402-7

- Italy For Dummies
  0-7645-7386-1
- Las Vegas For Dummies
  0-7645-7382-9
- London For Dummies
  0-7645-4277-X
- Paris For Dummies
  0-7645-7630-5
- RV Vacations For Dummies
  0-7645-4442-X
- Walt Disney World & Orlando
  For Dummies
  0-7645-9660-8

GRAPHICS, DESIGN & WEB DEVELOPMENT

0-7645-8815-X

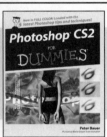

0-7645-9571-7

Also available:
- 3D Game Animation For Dummies
  0-7645-8789-7
- AutoCAD 2006 For Dummies
  0-7645-8925-3
- Building a Web Site For Dummies
  0-7645-7144-3
- Creating Web Pages For Dummies
  0-470-08030-2
- Creating Web Pages All-in-One Desk
  Reference For Dummies
  0-7645-4345-8
- Dreamweaver 8 For Dummies
  0-7645-9649-7

- InDesign CS2 For Dummies
  0-7645-9572-5
- Macromedia Flash 8 For Dummies
  0-7645-9691-8
- Photoshop CS2 and Digital
  Photography For Dummies
  0-7645-9580-6
- Photoshop Elements 4 For Dummies
  0-471-77483-9
- Syndicating Web Sites with RSS Feeds
  For Dummies
  0-7645-8848-6
- Yahoo! SiteBuilder For Dummies
  0-7645-9800-7

NETWORKING, SECURITY, PROGRAMMING & DATABASES

0-7645-7728-X

0-471-74940-0

Also available:
- Access 2007 For Dummies
  0-470-04612-0
- ASP.NET 2 For Dummies
  0-7645-7907-X
- C# 2005 For Dummies
  0-7645-9704-3
- Hacking For Dummies
  0-470-05235-X
- Hacking Wireless Networks
  For Dummies
  0-7645-9730-2
- Java For Dummies
  0-470-08716-1

- Microsoft SQL Server 2005 For Dummies
  0-7645-7755-7
- Networking All-in-One Desk Reference
  For Dummies
  0-7645-9939-9
- Preventing Identity Theft For Dummies
  0-7645-7336-5
- Telecom For Dummies
  0-471-77085-X
- Visual Studio 2005 All-in-One Desk
  Reference For Dummies
  0-7645-9775-2
- XML For Dummies
  0-7645-8845-1

HEALTH & SELF-HELP

0-7645-8450-2

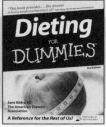

0-7645-4149-8

Also available:

- Bipolar Disorder For Dummies
  0-7645-8451-0
- Chemotherapy and Radiation
  For Dummies
  0-7645-7832-4
- Controlling Cholesterol For Dummies
  0-7645-5440-9
- Diabetes For Dummies
  0-7645-6820-5* †
- Divorce For Dummies
  0-7645-8417-0 †

- Fibromyalgia For Dummies
  0-7645-5441-7
- Low-Calorie Dieting For Dummies
  0-7645-9905-4
- Meditation For Dummies
  0-471-77774-9
- Osteoporosis For Dummies
  0-7645-7621-6
- Overcoming Anxiety For Dummies
  0-7645-5447-6
- Reiki For Dummies
  0-7645-9907-0
- Stress Management For Dummies
  0-7645-5144-2

EDUCATION, HISTORY, REFERENCE & TEST PREPARATION

0-7645-8381-6

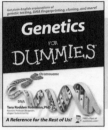

0-7645-9554-7

Also available:

- The ACT For Dummies
  0-7645-9652-7
- Algebra For Dummies
  0-7645-5325-9
- Algebra Workbook For Dummies
  0-7645-8467-7
- Astronomy For Dummies
  0-7645-8465-0
- Calculus For Dummies
  0-7645-2498-4
- Chemistry For Dummies
  0-7645-5430-1
- Forensics For Dummies
  0-7645-5580-4

- Freemasons For Dummies
  0-7645-9796-5
- French For Dummies
  0-7645-5193-0
- Geometry For Dummies
  0-7645-5324-0
- Organic Chemistry I For Dummies
  0-7645-6902-3
- The SAT I For Dummies
  0-7645-7193-1
- Spanish For Dummies
  0-7645-5194-9
- Statistics For Dummies
  0-7645-5423-9

Get smart @ dummies.com®

- **Find a full list of Dummies titles**
- **Look into loads of FREE on-site articles**
- **Sign up for FREE eTips e-mailed to you weekly**
- **See what other products carry the Dummies name**
- **Shop directly from the Dummies bookstore**
- **Enter to win new prizes every month!**

Separate Canadian edition also available
Separate U.K. edition also available

Available wherever books are sold. For more information or to order direct: U.S. customers visit www.dummies.com or call 1-877-762-2974.
U.K. customers visit www.wileyeurope.com or call 0800 243407. Canadian customers visit www.wiley.ca or call 1-800-567-4797.